HHS IN THE 21ST CENTURY

CHARTING A NEW COURSE FOR A HEALTHIER AMERICA

Committee on Improving the Organization of the U.S. Department of Health and Human Services (HHS) to Advance the Health of Our Population

Leonard D. Schaeffer, Andrea M. Schultz, and Judith A. Salerno, *Editors*

INSTITUTE OF MEDICINE
OF THE NATIONAL ACADEM

THE NATIONAL ACADEMIES PRESS
Washington, D.C.
www.nap.edu

THE NATIONAL ACADEMIES

Advisers to the Nation on Science, Engineering, and Medicine

The **National Academy of Sciences** is a private, nonprofit, self-perpetuating society of distinguished scholars engaged in scientific and engineering research, dedicated to the furtherance of science and technology and to their use for the general welfare. Upon the authority of the charter granted to it by the Congress in 1863, the Academy has a mandate that requires it to advise the federal government on scientific and technical matters. Dr. Ralph J. Cicerone is president of the National Academy of Sciences.

The **National Academy of Engineering** was established in 1964, under the charter of the National Academy of Sciences, as a parallel organization of outstanding engineers. It is autonomous in its administration and in the selection of its members, sharing with the National Academy of Sciences the responsibility for advising the federal government. The National Academy of Engineering also sponsors engineering programs aimed at meeting national needs, encourages education and research, and recognizes the superior achievements of engineers. Dr. Charles M. Vest is president of the National Academy of Engineering.

The **Institute of Medicine** was established in 1970 by the National Academy of Sciences to secure the services of eminent members of appropriate professions in the examination of policy matters pertaining to the health of the public. The Institute acts under the responsibility given to the National Academy of Sciences by its congressional charter to be an adviser to the federal government and, upon its own initiative, to identify issues of medical care, research, and education. Dr. Harvey V. Fineberg is president of the Institute of Medicine.

The **National Research Council** was organized by the National Academy of Sciences in 1916 to associate the broad community of science and technology with the Academy's purposes of furthering knowledge and advising the federal government. Functioning in accordance with general policies determined by the Academy, the Council has become the principal operating agency of both the National Academy of Sciences and the National Academy of Engineering in providing services to the government, the public, and the scientific and engineering communities. The Council is administered jointly by both Academies and the Institute of Medicine. Dr. Ralph J. Cicerone and Dr. Charles M. Vest are chair and vice chair, respectively, of the National Research Council.

www.national-academies.org

COMMITTEE ON IMPROVING THE ORGANIZATION OF THE U.S. DEPARTMENT OF HEALTH AND HUMAN SERVICES (HHS) TO ADVANCE THE HEALTH OF OUR POPULATION

LEONARD D. SCHAEFFER (*Chair*), Judge Robert Maclay Widney Professor, University of Southern California
DAVID W. BEIER, Senior Vice President of Global Government and Corporate Affairs, Amgen
KATHLEEN BUTO, Vice President, Health Policy, Johnson & Johnson
MOLLY JOEL COYE, Founder and CEO, Health Technology Center
ROBERT GRAHAM, Professor of Family Medicine, Robert and Myfanwy Smith Chair, Department of Family Medicine, University of Cincinnati College of Medicine
MARK B. McCLELLAN, Senior Fellow, Economic Studies, Brookings Institution
STANLEY B. PRUSINER, Professor of Neurology, Director, Institute for Neurodegenerative Diseases, University of California, San Francisco
DONNA E. SHALALA, President, University of Miami
STEPHEN M. SHORTELL, Blue Cross of California Distinguished Professor of Health Policy and Management; Professor of Organization Behavior; Dean, School of Public Health, University of California, Berkeley
SUSANNE A. STOIBER, Consultant, Stoiber Health Policy, LLC
LOUIS W. SULLIVAN, President Emeritus, Morehouse School of Medicine
DAVID N. SUNDWALL, Executive Director, Utah Department of Health
GAIL L. WARDEN, President Emeritus, Henry Ford Health System
MYRL WEINBERG, President, National Health Council
CATHERINE E. WOTEKI, Global Director of Scientific Affairs, Mars, Inc.

Study Staff

JUDITH A. SALERNO, Executive Officer
ANDREA M. SCHULTZ, Associate Program Officer
KATHARINE BOTHNER, Research Associate
AMY PACKMAN, Administrative Assistant
JUDITH L. ESTEP, Program Associate

Institute of Medicine Consultants

DARREL J. GRINSTEAD, Hogan and Hartson, LLP
BOB KOCHER, McKinsey and Company
PAUL C. LIGHT, Robert F. Wagner School of Public Service, New York University
NEIL E. WEISFELD, NEW Associates, LLC
VICTORIA D. WEISFELD, NEW Associates, LLC

Independent Report Reviewers

This report has been reviewed in draft form by individuals chosen for their diverse perspectives and technical expertise, in accordance with procedures approved by the National Research Council's Review Committee. The purpose of this independent review is to provide candid and critical comments that will assist the institution in making its published report as sound as possible and to ensure that the report meets institutional standards for objectivity, evidence, and responsiveness to the study charge. The review comments and draft manuscript remain confidential to protect the integrity of the deliberative process. We wish to thank the following individuals for their review of this report:

Alex M. Azar II, Eli Lilly and Company
Jo Ivey Boufford, New York Academy of Medicine
David Brailer, Health Evolution Partners
Robin H. Carle, The Sullivan Alliance, Joint Center for Political and Economic Studies
Jack C. Ebeler, Ebeler Consulting
Arthur L. Kellermann, Department of Emergency Medicine, Emory University School of Medicine
Howard K. Koh, Division of Public Health Practice, Harvard School of Public Health
Judith R. Lave, Pennsylvania Medicaid Policy Center, Graduate School of Public Health, University of Pittsburgh
Lawrence S. Lewin, Executive Consultant
Philip A. Pizzo, Stanford University School of Medicine
Beryl A. Radin, Scholar in Residence, Department of Public Administration and Policy, American University School of Public Affairs

David Satcher, Satcher Health Leadership Institute Initiative, Morehouse College School of Medicine
Michael R. Taylor, School of Public Health and Health Services, The George Washington University

Although the reviewers listed above have provided many constructive comments and suggestions, they were not asked to endorse the conclusions or recommendations nor did they see the final draft of the report before its release. The review of this report was overseen by **Gilbert Omenn,** Center for Computational Medicine and Biology, University of Michigan Medical School, and **Floyd E. Bloom,** Department of Molecular and Integrative Neuroscience, Professor Emeritus, The Scripps Research Institute. Appointed by the National Research Council and Institute of Medicine, they were responsible for making certain that an independent examination of this report was carried out in accordance with institutional procedures and that all review comments were carefully considered. Responsibility for the final content of this report rests entirely with the authoring committee and the institution.

Foreword

"Form follows function" is a principle of architectural design and a truism of biology. It is not, however, an imperative of human organizations, and certainly not of government agencies. Rather, over a period of years, new responsibilities may be layered onto an existing agency, and old responsibilities removed, without a responsive realignment of positions, procedures, and structures. From time to time, it is worth taking a step back from the current way of conducting government business, examine practices in light of contemporary responsibilities, and seek ways to enable government to fulfill its obligations more successfully and efficiently.

Prompted by a letter from Representatives Henry A. Waxman and Tom Davis, respectively the chair and ranking minority member of the House Committee on Oversight and Government Reform, the Institute of Medicine undertook just such an assessment of the Department of Health and Human Services. This large and diverse department profoundly affects the lives of Americans every day. To advise on how the department's work can be improved, the IOM assembled an able and experienced committee, admirably led by its chair, Leonard D. Schaeffer. With an intensive effort, outstanding contributions from a select group of consulting experts, and superb support by staff member Andrea Schultz and IOM Executive Officer Judy Salerno, the committee prepared the following report and recommendations. We offer it in the hope that it will help a new secretary, Congress, and administration to serve the public and advance the health and well-being of the American people.

Harvey V. Fineberg, M.D., Ph.D.
President, Institute of Medicine

Acknowledgments

This report is the result of the contributions of many individuals who provided their expertise and shared their time throughout the study. The committee wishes to acknowledge those whose contributions energized our deliberations and enhanced the quality of our report.

We would first like to thank the National Research Council Presidents' Circle, whose generous funding made this study possible.

Invaluable information was provided by the authors of two commissioned papers, Darrel Grinstead and Paul Light. During our meeting, Bob Kocher provided his expertise and insight. Our deliberations were captured and organized into the text of this report by Neil and Vicki Weisfeld. Throughout, Dana McMurtry provided research assistance to the committee chair.

The committee is greatly appreciative of the study staff for their tireless work. We would like to give special thanks to Judith Salerno for her oversight and guidance and Andrea Schultz for her daily direction and dedication to the study. Thanks also go to Katharine Bothner for her excellent research assistance, Amy Packman and Judy Estep for their administrative support, and Florence Poillon and Mark Goodin for copyediting the final report.

Finally, the committee is especially grateful to the numerous additional IOM staff members who contributed to the study process, production, and dissemination of the report: Anton Bandy, Clyde Behney, Christie Bell, Porter Coggeshall, Bronwyn Schrecker Jamrok, Jim Jensen, William McLeod, Abbey Meltzer, Linda Meyers, Maria Oria, Christine Stencel, Lauren Tobias, Jackie Turner, and Jordan Wyndelts.

Preface

This report is the Institute of Medicine's (IOM) response to a congressional request to study whether the Department of Health and Human Services (HHS) is ideally organized to meet the public health and health care cost challenges that our nation faces. Congressmen Waxman and Davis asked for recommendations that are administratively feasible, could be implemented in a relatively short time frame, and would not require significant new resources. The IOM then framed the request into a broad committee charge to examine the mission, organization, and governance of the department.

Given the rapid pace of change in scientific knowledge and health care delivery, the fact that some priorities and funding levels may change as administrations change, and the reality that management styles and methods differ as new secretaries are appointed, the committee does not believe there is an "ideal" organization for the department. However, the committee does believe that HHS is ideally positioned to lead a coordinated national response to both enduring and new health challenges, and the committee's recommendations are intended to support that effort.

The committee also recognized that the department's management and program responsibilities are challenged by health care costs that are rising faster than national economic growth, differences in medical practice that are costly and undermine quality of care, and the growing number of uninsured. The unprecedented strain on resources means that other important roles beyond safeguarding federal health programs, such as supporting advances in medicine and technology or rapidly responding to emergencies, are also at risk.

The committee's recommendations would change the department in ways that allow it to leverage its purchasing power, relationships, workforce, and impartiality to affect both the future direction of our health care system and our population's health. The majority of recommendations reflect the experience and knowledge captured in the management literature—and validated by the experience of committee members—about creating high-performance organizations. Whether for-profit, nonprofit, or governmental, the principles for institutional success are similar.

For the committee then, it followed that HHS should first establish a vision, mission, and implementation strategy that unite all parts of the organization in achieving a specific set of measurable goals. The department should also align its agencies and programs in order to coordinate, cross-pollinate, and mutually reinforce currently separate efforts aimed at achieving similar or related goals. Once aligned, the department will be in a stronger position to support improvements in efficiency, effectiveness, and outcomes across the entire health care system. The committee also recognized that the positive impact of changing organization, systems, and cultures will occur only if qualified people are in place. Therefore, strengthening the HHS workforce, as well as the health care and public health workforces, is essential.

Ultimately, the committee was concerned that maximizing HHS's potential to bolster public- and private-sector efforts to reverse troubling trends in health measures and costs requires a different relationship with Congress. The committee envisioned a "new compact" with Congress that would require HHS to implement a rigorous decision-making process and have greater departmental accountability for informing Congress about progress toward its goals. In exchange, Congress would grant HHS the greater flexibility and management authority necessary to fulfill its mission.

The committee hopes that its report will be of interest to multiple audiences. However, we hope that our recommendations will provide specific value to Congress and the next secretary of HHS, as they work together to develop a road map for the department in meeting twenty-first century health challenges and improving the health of the nation.

I want to thank members of the committee for investing their time and energy in developing this report and producing recommendations based on sound research and reasoning. IOM staff was also deeply committed and supportive, and I especially appreciate Harvey Fineberg's encouragement. Our committee was diverse in experience and background and not always like-minded. Nonetheless, our deliberations, often energetic and spirited, were always characterized by the free exchange of ideas, creativity, and respect.

Leonard D. Schaeffer
Chair, Committee on Improving the Organization of the U.S. Department of Health and Human Services (HHS) to Advance the Health of Our Population

Contents

Tables, Figures, and Boxes

TABLES

FIGURES

BOXES

Summary[1]

OVERVIEW OF THE NATION'S HEALTH CHALLENGES

The U.S. Department of Health and Human Services (HHS), the largest department in the federal government in terms of budget, spends approximately $2 billion a day. The department's activities touch the lives of virtually all Americans—financing health care for elderly, disabled, and indigent individuals; protecting against domestic and global health threats; ensuring the safety of food and medications; advancing the science of fighting disease; and improving health care for everyone.

The department faces many serious and complex challenges:

- Health costs are rising, and a large number of Americans are uninsured and underinsured.
- Medicare is financially unsustainable and unprepared to meet the high costs that will result when tens of millions of baby boomers attain eligibility.
- The U.S. model of health care delivery does not ensure the efficient and effective prevention and management of chronic diseases, nor does it consistently apply principles of evidence-based medicine.
- The possibility of global pandemics, emerging infections, and bioterrorism threatens to harm many Americans and to strain limited resources further.

---

[1]This summary does not include references. Citations for the findings presented in the summary appear in the subsequent chapters.

- The public health infrastructure is weak and, in many locales, hard-pressed to meet current demands, much less those of the future.
- The United States trails many other countries in achieving desired health outcomes and longevity, despite having the world's highest level of per capita health care spending.

Unfortunately, HHS is not a high-performance organization, oriented to change and steady improvement. Over the years, change at HHS has been driven by the piecemeal accretion of programs legislatively mandated by various congressional committees, frequently without commensurate resources or regard for the department's capacity to manage them. One result is a department that is not optimally designed to meet the nation's current and future health challenges.

COMMITTEE CHARGE

The department's current structure, operations, and culture must be viewed against the backdrop of today's environment and the needs of the future. It is in this context that Representatives Henry A. Waxman and Tom Davis, the chair and ranking minority member, respectively, of the U.S. House of Representatives Committee on Oversight and Government Reform in the 110th Congress, asked the Institute of Medicine (IOM) to assess whether HHS is "ideally organized" to meet the enduring and emerging health challenges facing our nation. Box S-1 describes the statement of task with which the committee was charged.

BOX S-1
Statement of Task

To respond to Representatives Waxman's and Davis's request for a study of the organizational challenges facing HHS and a set of recommendations to address them, the IOM framed the following statement of task for the *Committee on Improving the Organization of the U.S. Department of Health and Human Services (HHS) to Advance the Health of Our Population*:

- What are the unifying elements of the mission of the department? What are the missions of its constituent agencies, and how do their activities relate to the public health, health care quality, and health care cost challenges facing the United States?

- Are the activities of its individual agencies aligned to optimally support the overall health mission of HHS? Should the operations of individual agencies be changed, consolidated, or realigned to make them collectively more effective in advancing the health of the nation?
- How can the governance of HHS be best organized to support and manage its responsibilities, function, and mission? How could the focus of individual agencies be improved to enhance their accountability and efficiency?
- How can relevant data be collected, integrated, and shared within and outside HHS in a way that is available, transparent, and useful for government and public decision making?

Assumptions and Approach

The 15-member IOM committee—all of whose members had either direct management experience in the department or significant expertise in relevant areas—used multiple resources to better understand the internal operational challenges that impede the department's efficiency and effectiveness. The members received a summary of interviews with the secretaries who led the department during the six most recent presidential transitions, an analysis of key statutory requirements for the department, relevant management literature, and reports on HHS's recent performance.

HHS has a staggering range of responsibilities. Addressing them is hampered by the diversity of its agencies' missions and goals, little discretionary funding, workforce shortages (and impending retirement of expert staff), fragmentation of responsibility for health issues across congressional committees, varying stakeholder priorities—including those of Congress and the White House—and difficulty in partnering effectively with states and the private sector. Such challenges partially explain the lack of progress in achieving the nation's health goals, enumerated in the best-known of several sets of departmental aims, the *Healthy People 2010* objectives.

The most critical conclusion that the committee came to (especially in light of the representatives' request that recommendations consider a shorter time frame and require minimal resources) was that *large-scale reorganization of the entire department was not the best way* to support key decision makers at HHS. The committee decided not to take the path of "moving around the boxes" for several reasons:

- There is no obvious or single way to restructure such a huge, complex organization.
- The time and energy required to make major changes would not only create distraction and paralysis, but also risks obsolescence owing to the rapidly changing environment and the possibility of health reform.
- Different secretaries and Presidents have different management styles, making specific organizational structures more or less appropriate over time.
- Management literature indicates that structure is only one element of successful organizational and managerial improvement, and that other elements such as strategy, systems, staff, skills, style, and shared values are also essential.

HHS AS A CHANGE AGENT FOR IMPROVING THE NATION'S HEALTH

Instead of wholesale reorganization, the committee made the following five interrelated recommendations for transforming the department into a powerful change agent, one that would create more value for the American people. The overarching themes of these recommendations are below. Many will require White House agreement and congressional support or action (see Appendix E), and all will require the secretary's commitment and active engagement:

- **Define a twenty-first century vision.** To meet twenty-first century challenges to America's health, the secretary of HHS should clearly articulate and actively promote a vision for the nation's health, ensure that the department's mission supports that vision, and establish a small number of measurable goals focused on critical challenges (Recommendation 1).
- **Foster adaptability and alignment.** To improve the public's health and achieve the department's goals, the secretary should align and focus the department on performance and encourage creative use of scientifically based approaches to meet new and enduring challenges (Recommendation 2).
- **Increase effectiveness and efficiency of the U.S. health care system.** The secretary should accelerate the establishment of a

collaborative, robust system for evaluating the health care system that would incorporate existing department and external research, stimulate new studies as needed, synthesize findings, and provide actionable feedback for policy makers, purchasers, payers, providers, health care professionals, and the public (Recommendation 3).

- **Strengthen the HHS and U.S. public health and health care workforces.** The secretary should place a high priority on developing a strategy and tools for workforce improvement within (1) HHS, (2) the public health and health care professions nationwide, and (3) the biosciences (Recommendation 4).
- **Improve accountability and decision making.** A "new compact" between Congress and the department is essential as HHS works toward achieving its vision for a healthy nation, departmental mission, and key health goals. Under this compact, the secretary would provide Congress and the nation regular, rigorous reports about departmental activities and assume greater accountability for improving performance and obtaining results; in return, Congress should allow the department greater flexibility in its internal operations and decision making (Recommendation 5).

The last recommendation, which the committee believes would enable development of a more effective working relationship—a new compact—between Congress and HHS, is essential to the implementation of all of these recommendations. This new compact would require a rigorous decision-making process and strengthened accountability, so that Congress is well informed of the department's goals and can measure its progress, while giving HHS the necessary flexibility and renewed management authority to fulfill its mission. Splintered congressional oversight and appropriations, increasingly prescriptive laws, and earmarked appropriations cause the department to be risk averse and slow to change. A new compact could enhance its ability to innovate and operate coordinated, productive programs that improve the quality of life for all Americans.

DEFINE A TWENTY-FIRST CENTURY VISION

The secretary should lead a process to identify and prioritize the nation's major health challenges that engages states, private-sector constituencies, congressional committees, other federal agencies, and global health leaders. With these agreed-upon priorities in hand, the department can proceed to other steps in setting clear direction—developing a compelling, well-articulated vision for the nation's health. It also must ensure that its mission statement adequately describes its role in achieving that vision.

To focus its resources and activities and allow its performance to be evaluated, the department also should identify a small number of measurable, time-specific goals that relate to the nation's major health priorities and its own internal challenges.

The need for health reform will require the secretary and the department's deep involvement. HHS has much to offer the reform process and, in any case, will be responsible for evaluating and eventually implementing many reforms.

Recommendation 1

To meet twenty-first century challenges to America's health, the secretary of HHS should clearly articulate and actively promote a vision for the nation's health, ensure that the department's mission supports that vision, and establish a small number of measurable goals focused on critical challenges.

a. **The secretary should lead a *thorough and thoughtful process* to identify and prioritize the nation's key health challenges.**
b. **The secretary should, in this process, *consult widely* with internal department leaders, others in the executive branch, Congress, governors and state-level officials, health care providers, scientific and professional organizations, and public interest and advocacy groups.**
c. **The secretary should establish a *vision, mission, and goals* that respond to twenty-first century challenges, enable greater programmatic continuity over time, and that can be used to *focus de-***

partment staff and activities on leading priorities, strengthen the public health infrastructure, facilitate assessment of impact, and lead to corrective action.

d. **The secretary, working closely with the White House and Congress, should** ***take a major role in promoting and achieving health reform nationwide.***

FOSTER ADAPTABILITY AND ALIGNMENT

The department must be able to meet the nation's health challenges, adapt quickly to changing circumstances, and solve problems creatively, using solid evidence and sound science. To accomplish this, all health and human services operations in the department need to be better aligned.

Under HHS's current structure, 30 official positions report directly to the secretary. This large number may impede coordination and efficient decision making. Management theory and research discourage such a wide span of control. Consideration of alternative management structures, which would establish a clear process for making policy and operational decisions, is desirable.

In addition to the secretary's leadership, the success of the department depends on the leadership and scientific integrity of several senior officials. For example, the surgeon general is responsible for providing scientifically valid information about health risks to the American public; heads of key scientific agencies—notably, the National Institutes of Health (NIH), Food and Drug Administration (FDA), and Centers for Disease Control and Prevention (CDC)—are responsible for preserving and advancing the scientific missions of the department. These officials should be appointed based on their experience and leadership skills, without regard to ideology. To help ensure insulation from political pressure, Congress should also consider establishing multiyear, fixed terms of office for these positions. To avoid gaps in leadership, all top HHS leaders should be identified and appointed expeditiously.

Public health focuses on the health of populations, rather than individuals. It protects the public from health risks, promotes beneficial health behavior, prevents disease and disability, and provides basic health services for vulnerable populations. HHS should integrate public health principles across its programs, including the major financing and research programs.

HHS policies and health and human services programs should incorporate current scientific knowledge and evidence-based practices. To accomplish this, the department needs to strengthen the science base of its programs and policy decisions. Political considerations cannot be allowed to override scientific evidence in the department's decision making. Further, research funding needs to be stabilized and become more predictable. The Agency for Healthcare Research and Quality (AHRQ) is a primary example of an agency in need of stable, predictable funding. It has not had its own budget allocation since 2002, despite its mission to support, conduct, and disseminate research that improves access to care and the outcomes, quality, cost, and utilization of health care services—in other words, to gain the types of information needed to create value in the U.S. health system.

Nowhere is the weakness of HHS's science base more apparent or potentially harmful to the public's health than in the area of food safety. Authority for food safety is diffused across several federal agencies, with FDA and the Food Safety and Inspection Service of the U.S. Department of Agriculture (USDA) both playing lead roles. Currently, U.S. food safety agencies are ill-equipped and understaffed and cannot keep pace with the globalization of the food supply or advances in food science and technology.

Recommendation 2
To improve the public's health and achieve the department's goals, the secretary should align and focus the department on performance and encourage creative use of scientifically based approaches to meet new and enduring challenges.

a. **The heads of all department units should ensure that their *activities and operations are aligned* with the department's vision, mission, and goals and marshal their resources to achieve them.**
b. **The secretary should reduce directly reporting senior-level officials to *a manageable number*. Although secretarial management styles differ, a rigorous decision-making process for both policy**

and operations must be established, along with accountability for results.

c. The secretary should ensure *a more prominent and powerful role* for the surgeon general, who, in addition to leading the Commissioned Corps, should be a *strong advocate for the health of the American people* and work actively to *educate Americans on important health issues*. The secretary should work with the President and Congress to *establish a process for identifying surgeon general candidates* for presidential appointment *that gives high priority to qualifications and leadership*, and Congress is strongly urged to consider a *longer term* for this office.

d. The secretary should work with the President and Congress to establish a selection process for the department's senior-level officials that *protects the scientific and administrative integrity of major departmental units, promotes progress toward departmental goals*, and is *based primarily on the candidates' qualifications and experience.* Congress again is strongly urged to consider *longer terms* for some of these officials—especially the directors of NIH and CDC, and the commissioner of FDA—which would provide critical continuity in the nation's public health and scientific endeavors.

e. The President should make timely appointments and Congress should expedite the confirmation process for key HHS officials, including the secretary, deputy secretary, surgeon general, and the heads of FDA and NIH. Secretarial appointments, such as the director of CDC, should also be expedited.

f. The secretary should ensure that *all department health programs, including the reimbursement programs, reinforce public health priorities and strategies* in order to provide a consistent framework for protecting the public from health risks, promoting health, preventing disease and disabil-

ity, and providing health services for vulnerable populations in the most efficient, cost-effective ways.

g. **To maximize value in the health care system, the secretary must** ***strengthen the scientific base and capabilities of the department*** **and ensure that** ***agencies' research findings*** **are shared department-wide and that** ***current best evidence is used for departmental decision making, including the Centers for Medicare and Medicaid Services (CMS) reimbursement policy.***

h. **Congress should allocate** ***sufficient, predictable funding for NIH, CDC, FDA, and AHRQ*** **in order to preserve and enhance these agencies' scientific missions. Congress should also establish a** ***specific budget line for AHRQ*** **that is** ***independent*** **of appropriations to other HHS agencies.**

i. **To address the growing threat of food-borne illnesses, Congress should** ***unify the USDA's Food Safety and Inspection Service and the food safety activities of FDA within HHS*** **and ensure provision of adequate resources for high-quality inspection, enforcement, and research.**

INCREASE EFFECTIVENESS AND EFFICIENCY OF THE U.S. HEALTH CARE SYSTEM

Health care accounts for nearly one-sixth of the U.S. gross domestic product, and Medicare and Medicaid account for 85 percent of HHS expenditures. These programs significantly contribute to rising national debt, and continued escalating costs threaten their sustainability.

Worse, our high national health care expenditures have not produced commensurate gains in the health of the nation or in the quality of care Americans receive. Research comparing the marked differences in care patterns (frequency of surgery, for example) provided in different parts of the country shows that not only are some patterns much more expensive, but residents of these high-cost areas have no better—and sometimes worse—health outcomes.

Many factors contribute to high health care costs, including provision of care that is not evidence based, lack of integration across providers and settings, overreliance on medical specialists, and inappropriate adoption of new technologies and procedures. Because Medicare and Medicaid have such a powerful influence on the U.S. health care system, these programs could be leaders in creating a value-driven health system and increasing evidence-based care.

Achieving a value-driven system will require analyses of the clinical- and cost-effectiveness of options for disease prevention and treatment and the way care is organized and delivered. These analyses should build on existing data collection efforts in agencies such as CDC, FDA, NIH, CMS, and AHRQ—as well as on external data sources—and will require transparent and credible analytic tools. The committee sees this type of research as providing useful guidance in clinical decision making, but recognizes it cannot be an absolute guide to the clinical care of *individual patients,* whose circumstances vary widely.

With new and better information available from comparative effectiveness analyses, CMS can develop a range of incentives for

- better management of high-cost chronic illnesses;
- use of primary, versus specialist, care;
- reduced geographic variation in care patterns;
- better integration of care, through, for example, establishment of a medical home or similar mechanism for assuring continuous, accessible, comprehensive, and coordinated care for Medicare and Medicaid patients; and
- more efficient practices, generally, including widespread adoption of electronic information exchange and electronic medical records.

Americans are becoming better informed about their health, health care technologies, and ways of navigating the health care system. They are also becoming increasingly responsible for managing their own health and illnesses. Today's consumers need access to unbiased, clearly worded, evidence-based, and up-to-date information about health concerns, prevention strategies, and the advantages and disadvantages of alternative tests, treatments, medications, and interventions. When they have full information, individuals often wisely make more conservative, less costly treatment choices.

At the patient level, the use of health information technology can help ensure the continuity and integration of care, improve health care quality, reduce costs, and expand access to affordable services. Secure electronic information exchanges among physicians—so that all necessary patient information is available at the point of care—can enable better, more informed treatment, and be designed to protect patient privacy.

For the public health system, health information technology can facilitate early detection of disease outbreaks and environmental hazards, improve monitoring of chronic diseases, and quickly identify adverse events involving drugs or other agents.

Recommendation 3
The secretary should accelerate the establishment of a collaborative, robust system for evaluating the health care system that would incorporate existing department and external research, stimulate new studies as needed, synthesize findings, and provide actionable feedback for policy makers, purchasers, payers, providers, health care professionals, and the public.

a. **The secretary should work with Congress to establish a capability for *assessing the comparative value—including clinical- and cost-effectiveness—* of medical interventions and procedures, preventive and treatment technologies, and methods of organizing and delivering care. The assessment of comparative value should begin by leveraging department-wide data sources in conjunction with supportive evidence from providers, payers, and health researchers.**[2]
b. **The secretary should work with Congress to ensure that the department's *programs and reim-***

[2]The committee did not reach consensus on recommendation 3a. Although the majority of the committee supports the language of the recommendation, David Beier, J.D., Senior Vice President of Global Government and Corporate Affairs, Amgen; Kathleen Buto, M.P.A., Vice President, Health Policy, Johnson & Johnson; and Myrl Weinberg, C.A.E., President, National Health Council, did not agree with the majority's view and provided dissenting opinions, which can be found in Appendix F. They were not able to agree on a common statement.

***bursement policies are outcomes based*, reflecting best available evidence of value and creating incentives for adoption of best practices, including integration of care, in order to improve quality and efficiency.**

c. **The department should *collaborate with state and local public health agencies and community-based organizations*, as both sources and users of practical program guidance.**
d. **The department should provide *authoritative, plain-language, and current evidence-based information* to the public regarding prevention and treatment options.**
e. **To assess the health of the American people and overall health system performance accurately, the department needs current data from the nation's health system. To facilitate collection of these data, the department should actively promote the universal adoption of *electronic information capabilities*—including health information exchange and electronic medical, personal health records—for administrative and clinical purposes.**

STRENGTHEN THE HHS AND U.S. PUBLIC HEALTH AND HEALTH CARE WORKFORCES

Analysts predict serious shortages of people with the right backgrounds, training, and skills in the department's senior levels, in the nation's health care workforce, in state and local public health agencies, and in the science establishment. These shortages can manifest themselves in the number, professional mix, geographic distribution, or composition of the workforces. The problems include

- an aging workforce, nearing retirement, in HHS and state and local health departments, especially among experienced scientists, managers, and professionals;
- a wide array of new health challenges that require strong new skills;

- shortages of primary care physicians and professionals in certain fields, such as oral health, mental health, and nursing;
- a shortage of talent in the biological and other health sciences; and
- underrepresentation of minority groups in the HHS workforce and among the nation's health professionals.

During the five-year period that began in 2007, half of all managers within HHS will be eligible to retire. Many are hard-to-replace, experienced senior managers and professionals. The committee believes that HHS will need to look for replacements not only within the department (using delayed retirements and appropriate advancement of current staff), but also toward more effective recruitment from the private sector and academic institutions. To make government service more attractive, federal hiring practices should be revised, and greater flexibility in fringe benefits and work patterns—such as telecommuting and flexible schedules—should be offered.

The health care workforce outside the department is also under strain. The balance between primary and specialist physicians continues to tip toward specialists, even though communities served by more primary care physicians have less costly care and better outcomes. Redressing this imbalance should be a key societal goal. Advanced practice nurses and physician assistants may help fill primary care gaps. Meanwhile, the aging of the U.S. population and associated increases in the prevalence of chronic diseases create growing demand for health care professionals skilled in geriatrics. Information technology may help alleviate some geographic or specialty shortages.

Constituting one-fourth of the nation's population, African Americans, Hispanic Americans, and Native Americans collectively account for only six percent of the nation's physicians. Certain Asian American groups experience similar underrepresentation. Minority professionals tend to practice in underserved minority communities and may be able to provide residents with more culturally competent care.

Federal support for health workforce training programs is uneven. Title VII support for public health, preventive medicine, and dental public health training was eliminated in the President's fiscal year (FY) 2009 budget, despite the difficulties recruiting staff in these disciplines, as reported by state and local health departments.

To continue advances in the health-related sciences, the nation needs biomedical scientists, health economists, other health service researchers, biostatisticians, and epidemiologists. The difficulty of attracting young people to these vital fields begins at the earliest grade levels, with poor math and science skills, and extends throughout the education pipeline.

Recommendation 4
The secretary should place a high priority on developing a strategy and tools for workforce improvement (1) in HHS, (2) in the public health and health care professions nationwide, and (3) in the biosciences.

a. **The secretary should immediately strengthen workforce planning in the department and develop a *comprehensive strategy to recruit highly qualified* public- and private-sector individuals in order to offset the large number of experienced staff expected to retire soon.**
b. **Congress should authorize the department, in cooperation with the Office of Personnel Management, to assemble a package of current and innovative programs and benefits designed to *encourage talented, experienced individuals to transition back and forth between government and private-sector service*, thereby identifying ways to leverage the best of both.**
c. **Congress should provide the secretary with additional authority to *reward performance, innovation, and the achievement of results*, through bonuses, merit-based pay, recognition awards, or other mechanisms of proven effectiveness.**
d. **The secretary, in concert with other public and private partners, should *develop a comprehensive national strategy to assess and address current and projected gaps* in the number, professional mix, geographic distribution, and diversity of the U.S. public health and health care workforces.**
e. **To help close projected gaps, the department should evaluate existing *health care professional training programs*, continued education programs, and graduate medical education funding**

and should encourage Congress to invest in programs with proven effectiveness.

f. **Congress should give the secretary authority to create new programs that invest in the *future generation of biomedical and health services researchers*, enabling the continued discovery of new, more effective methods of preventing, treating, and curing disease; promoting health; improving health care delivery and organization; and controlling health system costs.**

IMPROVE ACCOUNTABILITY AND DECISION MAKING

A strong system of accountability will provide information needed to improve HHS performance and will lead ultimately to better health for the American people. Accountability should begin with the development of measurable, time-specific goals[3] and should include

- clear lines of responsibility,
- quantifiable targets and time-specific milestones,
- strategies to overcome perceived barriers,
- regular reporting and assessments,
- a reward and recognition system that promotes achievement,
- a clear understanding of progress, and
- corrective action as needed.

To facilitate improved accountability, HHS needs a department-wide information system that would provide a panoramic view of how its health and human services programs work together to achieve departmental goals. Data supporting this system should come from within the department and from its key government partners. The information sys-

---

[3]HHS currently operates under a complex web of internally and externally generated goal-setting and reporting requirements, which includes *Healthy People 2010*, the department's five-year strategic plan, the Government Performance and Results Act, the Program Assessment Rating Tool, and the President's Management Agenda. Hundreds of discrete data points must be documented to satisfy these requirements; yet true accountability is still lacking, because these reports are not used to guide strategies for improved performance or for funding decisions.

tem should coordinate and integrate existing data collection efforts—such as those of the National Center for Health Statistics—and minimize creation of new ones. It should provide actionable feedback that would guide management decisions and facilitate preparation of an annual "State of the Nation's Health" report to Congress.

The committee determined that increased congressional involvement in HHS management and operations has hindered the department's flexibility. For example, during the past two decades, Congress has acted 125 times to give FDA increased regulatory responsibilities, but without providing the additional resources needed to meet them. Congressional responsibility and oversight for HHS are scattered across 12 Senate and House committees and six subcommittees, which hampers the department's coherence.

Greater management flexibility for the secretary is essential to improving the value obtained from HHS programs. With increased flexibility, the secretary could, for example, do the following:

- Rationalize Medicare and Medicaid reimbursement, in order to improve outcomes of care and produce savings.
- Combat fraud and abuse more effectively and recoup billions of dollars in improper payments.
- Make HHS programs more transparent and consistent across federal regions.

One way to provide greater flexibility would be to create a strategic initiative fund, drawn from the budgets of HHS agencies. Similar to the Department of Defense's Defense Advanced Research Projects Agency (DARPA) and the NIH common fund, this fund would allow the development of cross-agency and cross-departmental initiatives, as well as facilitate timely responses to public health threats.

Underlying the development of all of the committee's preceding recommendations is the recognition that an updated and streamlined relationship is needed between Congress and the department. Under this "new compact," HHS would provide greater accountability in exchange for more flexibility. The new compact would allow HHS and its future secretaries to achieve higher performance and provide more value to Americans, while improving Congress's ability to monitor the department's progress. In this way, a revitalized Department of Health and Human Services would be much better positioned to meet the nation's twenty-first century health care challenges.

Recommendation 5

A "new compact" between Congress and the department is essential as HHS works toward achieving its vision for a healthy nation, departmental mission, and key health goals. Under this compact, the secretary would provide Congress and the nation regular, rigorous reports about departmental activities and assume greater accountability for improving performance and obtaining results; in return, Congress should allow the department greater flexibility in its internal operations and decision making.

a. **To enable greater accountability, the secretary should oversee development and implementation of a *department-wide data, evaluation, and information system.* The system should be based on a broad analytic framework designed to aid in managing departmental operations, learning from program experience, evaluating the costs and impact of programs, and determining whether they provide sufficient value for the investment of public funds.**
b. **Congress should authorize the secretary to direct funding from the budgets of all departmental units to support the development of an HHS-wide information system. Funding for such a system would benefit all department units.**
c. **The department should use the data, evaluation, and information system to**

    - **enable the secretary to *provide Congress with regular reports* on progress toward achieving departmental goals,**
    - ***inform policy development*,**
    - ***facilitate cross-department activities*,**
    - **provide *operational information to program management* for quality improvement and midcourse corrections, and**
    - **support effective *long-range planning*.**

d. **For those outside the department, the system should**
    - ***be accessible, transparent, timely, and reliable*****, and**
    - **provide *useful, privacy-protected information* regarding department activities.**

e. **The department should *demonstrate accountability* through continuous critical assessment of program efficiency, equity, impact on health, and cost-effectiveness, and through corrective action for underperforming programs.**

f. **The secretary, in collaboration with the surgeon general, should present Congress and the public with an annual "State of the Nation's Health" report that describes progress toward achieving the vision for the nation's health and the department's key health goals.**

g. **Congress should establish *a new, strategic initiative fund* to enable the secretary to support cross-agency and cross-departmental activities that exhibit innovation in responding to twenty-first century challenges, and to respond quickly to new, unforeseen, or expanding public health threats.**

ENSURING A SMOOTH TRANSITION TO A NEW SECRETARY

Recognizing how important the transition period is to a new secretary and to the department, the committee provides informal advice for achieving a successful transition. It organized the preceding recommendations into a timetable, indicating what should be done in the first 90 days, the first year in office, and throughout the secretary's term (see Chapter 7). The committee has also translated some of its general thinking—about vision and goals, alignment and accountability, workforce, and its other recommendations—into specific suggestions for action.

This informal advice is not meant to be a rigid blueprint, but is intended to help a new secretary manage the political, budgetary, personnel, policy, and planning challenges that come with the appointment to this vital post.

1

Introduction

Men make history, and not the other way around. In periods where there is no leadership, society stands still. Progress occurs when courageous, skillful leaders seize the opportunity to change things for the better.

Harry S. Truman

The federal government's largest department in terms of budget, the Department of Health and Human Services (HHS) spends almost $2 billion a day. It spends more money than the Department of Defense or the Social Security Administration, and its budget dwarfs those of all other departments (see Figure 1-1). HHS has more than 65,000 full-time employees (OMB, 2008b), and actual spending in fiscal year (FY) 2007 was more than $658 billion—most of which (85 percent) was used for Medicare and the federal portion of Medicaid (OMB, 2008a).[1] The President's 2009 HHS budget request, which will undoubtedly be adjusted in various ways through the appropriations process, is for $737 billion (OMB, 2008a).

[1]Medicare is a federally administered entitlement program funded through payroll taxes that are set aside for that specific purpose and outside of the department's control; the Medicaid program is a federal-state partnership program for some categories of low-income Americans (with the largest share of payments going to the elderly and disabled individuals needing long-term care). The federal government provides a portion of the funds, and the states provide the remainder and administer the program.

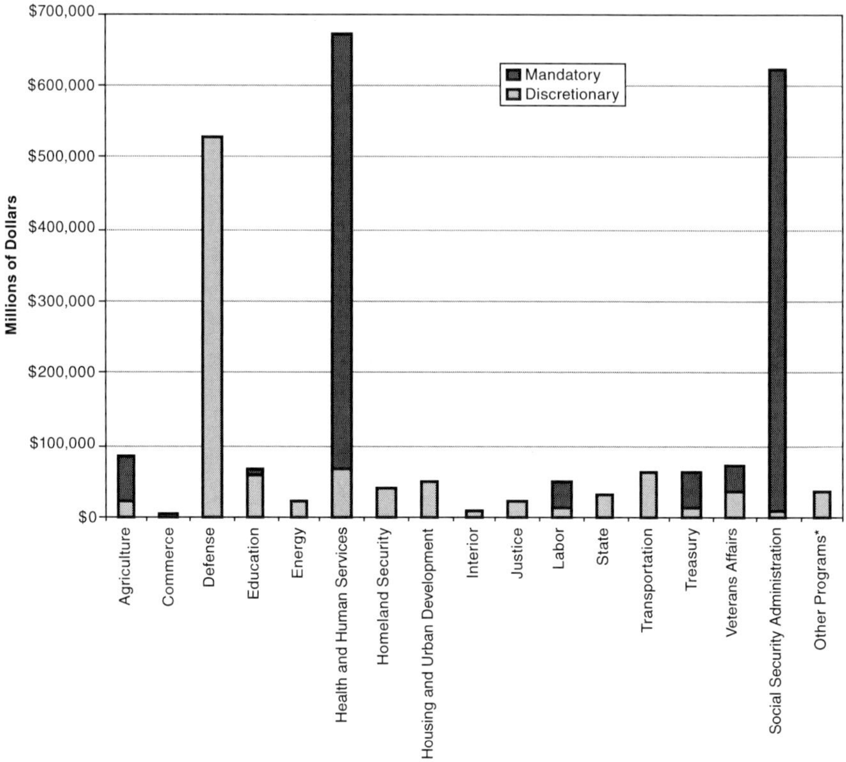

FIGURE 1-1 Federal budget by department: actual spending FY 2007 (showing mandatory and discretionary spending).
*This category includes the Corps of Engineers, Environmental Protection Agency (EPA), National Aeronautics and Space Administration (NASA), National Science Foundation (NSF), and Small Business Administration.
SOURCE: OMB (2008a).

More than sheer size determines the importance of a governmental activity. HHS touches the lives of virtually every American. Its agencies help pay for medical care for elderly, disabled, and low-income Americans; they protect our population against domestic and global health threats; they ensure the safety of our food and medications—regulating more than $1 trillion of the U.S. economy annually (FDA, 2008); they search for new scientific advances, tools, and techniques to prevent, manage, and cure diseases, including through grants that support the work of universities and scientists in all U.S. states and territories; they provide a safety net of services for the poor and special populations; and they work to make the entire health care system better for everyone.

In addition to its health activities described below, HHS is responsible for two significant human services programs—the Administration on Aging and the Administration for Children and Families. These programs support a variety of services including community-based programs for older persons, Temporary Assistance for Needy Families, Head Start, adoption and foster care services, and prevention of family violence. As is discussed in Chapter 3, an individual's health is determined by a variety of complex factors, including socioeconomic status, and the Administration on Aging and the Administration for Children and Families play an important role in assuring not only the financial well-being of their constituents, but also their health.

The sweep of the department and its many activities today is broad, though its beginnings were modest. For more than 200 years, the addition of new programs and agencies has created a patchwork of programs that is now the responsibility of HHS. Many units that began small are now large, complex enterprises in their own right. Carrying out these diverse roles involves agencies and people who represent multiple disciplines and organizational cultures. Biomedical researchers, regulators, service providers, payers, analysts, health education specialists—all have different priorities and ways of looking at the world and its problems. This makes it difficult to achieve organizational alignment—that is, to ensure that every agency, unit, and person in the organization is working toward a consistent set of goals.

If the department leadership had to deal only with achieving internal harmony, that in and of itself would be a significant challenge. However, it also must respond to the needs and desires of many other powerful players. The White House has health care priorities; so does Congress; and so do other departments, most notably, the Department of Homeland Security. HHS must consider the priorities and needs of the state and local health officials who implement its programs in communities; of advocacy groups that want attention to their issues; and of the health professions, provider groups, and institutions concerned about regulation and funding, as well as of a public that expects high-quality, affordable health care.

In today's globally connected world, the department's role and responsibilities do not end at the U.S. borders. People, knowledge, information, and goods travel across geographic boundaries more rapidly than ever. These transfers sometimes pose a risk to Americans: travelers may carry novel infections; food imports may be contaminated; products may be hazardous. Other times, information and knowledge gained elsewhere may help Americans, giving early warning of disease trends, suggesting how to prevent or treat medical problems, or providing more effective models of care. For reasons such as these, the department has an increasing role and expanding set of international relationships that it should pursue proactively.[2]

Responsibility for HHS activities is divided among many committees of Congress that oversee specific department activities, regularly legislate new programs and responsibilities, and control its funding. This type of oversight may address specific, current needs, but it militates against coordinated, efficient, cost-effective operations. The legislated requirements and budget mandates associated with specific programs also can inadvertently become a strait jacket—preventing deployment of resources for quick response to evolving circumstances and sustained investment in resolving enduring challenges.

Some observers of this patchwork of responsibility, structure, influence, and oversight occasionally wonder, at least rhetorically, whether such complexity can be managed at all (Shalala, 1998).

CHARGE TO THE COMMITTEE

In a letter to the Institute of Medicine (IOM), Representatives Henry A. Waxman and Tom Davis, chair and ranking minority member, respectively, of the House Committee on Oversight and Government Reform posed the question of whether HHS is "ideally organized" to meet the public health and health care cost challenges that require a focused national response (see Appendix B). They requested a study of this question, which the IOM framed as follows:

- What are the unifying elements of the mission of the department? What are the missions of its constituent agencies, and how

[2]The Institute of Medicine's Committee on the U.S. Commitment to Global Health recently evaluated the role for the United States in ensuring global health. The committee released a letter report in December 2008, titled *The U.S. Commitment to Global Health: Recommendations for a New Administration*, which outlined a vision for the U.S. government to improve the implementation of the U.S. global health enterprise. The committee's final report is expected to be released in the spring of 2009.

do their activities relate to the public health, health care quality, and health care cost challenges facing the United States?

- Are the activities of its individual agencies aligned to optimally support the overall health mission of HHS? Should the operations of individual agencies be changed, consolidated, or realigned to make them collectively more effective in advancing the health of the nation?
- How can the governance of HHS be best organized to support and manage its responsibilities, function, and mission? How could the focus of individual agencies be improved to enhance their accountability and efficiency?
- How can relevant data be collected, integrated, and shared within and outside HHS in a way that is available, transparent, and useful for government and public decision making?

THE NATION'S HEALTH CHALLENGES

As the congressmen note, threats to the health of Americans are increasingly diverse and urgent. They have both global and domestic origins. We see an aging population and climbing rates of costly chronic diseases, evolving risks of infectious diseases, the need for stronger emergency preparedness, weaknesses in the public health infrastructure, health risks from climate change, new outbreaks of food-borne diseases, and serious shortages of many key health professionals—all in the context of rising national health care costs, which limits the degrees of freedom to make system changes. Yet system changes are needed, in order to ensure that all Americans have access to basic health care and that the care we do receive is of high quality. Clearly, prompt action is needed to position HHS for these challenges.

MEETING CHANGING NEEDS FOR 210 YEARS

The roots of HHS stretch back to 1798, when Congress established a network of federal hospitals to care for merchant seamen. Piece by piece, the scope and importance of public health activities grew as new activities were added (see Box 1-1 for a definition of public health and related terms).

BOX 1-1
What Is Public Health?

The following definitions may help in distinguishing among several similar terms used in this report:

Public health (also "population health")–the science and practice dealing with the prevention of disease and injury and the protection and improvement of the health, safety, and well-being of *groups of people*, as contrasted with the individual care a person receives from a doctor, nurse, or other health care practitioner. Public health programs operate at the national, state, and local levels to, for example:

- Provide immunizations,
- Prevent tobacco use,
- Train communities in emergency preparedness,
- Better manage the costly consequences of chronic diseases,
- Ensure food safety,
- Track disease patterns,
- Prevent and control transmission of infectious diseases,
- Operate health programs for pregnant women and infants, and
- Research new disease prevention and treatment methods.

Health of the public–a broad construct that refers to the overall health of the American people, which is affected by public health actions as well as many other biological, social, and environmental factors–from individual genetic makeup, to the environments in which people live and work, to their own behavior, socioeconomic status, and the amount and kinds of health services they receive.

Public Health Service (PHS)–includes the Office of Public Health and Science, the department's 10 regional health administrators, which are under the oversight of the assistant secretary for health (ASH), and the health-related operating divisions of HHS, which are:

- National Institutes of Health (NIH),
- Health Resources and Services Administration (HRSA),
- Centers for Disease Control and Prevention (CDC),
- Indian Health Service (IHS),
- Substance Abuse and Mental Health Services Administration (SAMHSA),
- Food and Drug Administration (FDA),
- Agency for Healthcare Research and Quality (AHRQ), and
- Agency for Toxic Substances and Disease Registry (ATSDR).[a]

The PHS has been reshaped and expanded many times over the years, and a 1995 reorganization of its leadership resulted in direct reporting of PHS operating division heads to the secretary rather than, as formerly, to the ASH (Office of the Public Health Service Historian, 2004; Parascandola, 1998).

[a]CDC administers the ATSDR, which, although small, is considered a separate agency of the PHS.

In 1887, the federal government opened a one-room research laboratory within the Marine Hospital Service. This small Staten Island laboratory was the modest forerunner of the National Institutes of Health. The 1906 Pure Food and Drugs Act added regulatory authority to a small chemistry department—then in the Department of Agriculture—that we now know as the Food and Drug Administration. The Social Security program, enacted in 1935, was placed in the department, and in 1946, the Communicable Disease Center—parent of today's Centers for Disease Control and Prevention—was born, when a highly successful Public Health Service (PHS) program on malaria control was expanded to include other communicable diseases.

Congress created the cabinet-level Department of Health, Education, and Welfare (HEW) in 1953. Twelve years later, the department acquired two new programs—Medicare and Medicaid, which in the past 40 years have completely reshaped the U.S. health care system. Despite its growing size and multiplicity of responsibilities, the department's three-part mission remained intact until a separate Department of Education was created in 1979. Loss of the "E" in HEW prompted a name change, and the department became HHS the following year. In 1995 it lost much of the "W," when the Social Security Administration became an independent agency.

THE HHS BUDGET

Today, the department has 11 operating divisions, has 15 staff divisions, and implements more than 300 programs (HHS, 2008). Figure 1-2 shows how total department spending for FY 2007 was distributed across agencies and programs, and Figure 1-3 shows the trend in financial resources of the PHS agencies, with the National Institutes of Health (NIH) accounting for the largest share.

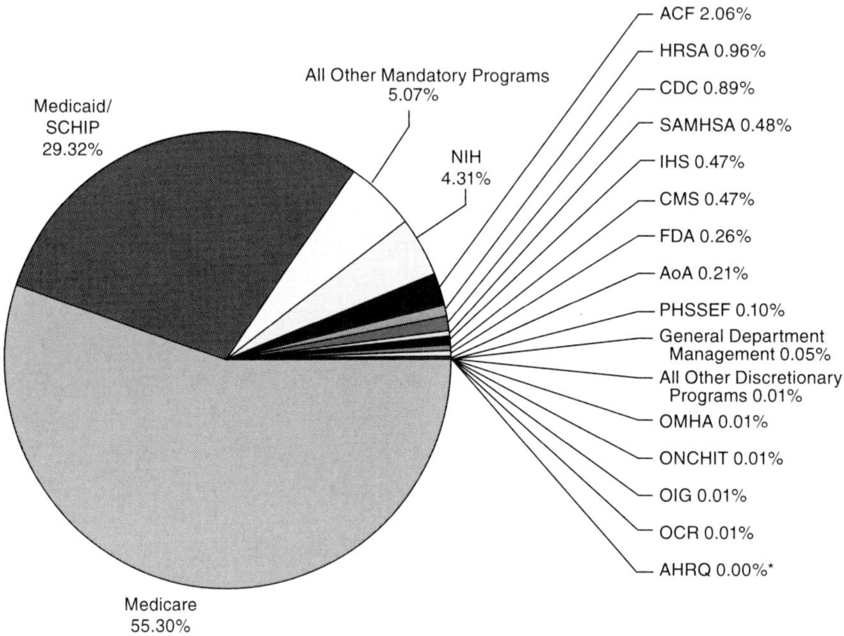

FIGURE 1-2 Distribution of HHS actual expenditures, FY 2007.
*The AHRQ is shown as representing 0 percent of the department's budget because it receives funds only from other PHS agencies through the PHS evaluation set-aside and has not had its own separate budget allocation since 2002. In fact, the President's budget request for AHRQ has been zero since 2001. Its 2009 program-level expenses were projected at $326 million, making it by far the smallest PHS agency.
NOTES: ACF = Administration for Children and Families; AHRQ = Agency for Healthcare Research and Quality; AoA = Administration on Aging; CDC = Centers for Disease Control and Prevention; CMS = Centers for Medicare and Medicaid Services; FDA = Food and Drug Administration; HRSA = Health Resources and Services Administration; IHS = Indian Health Service; OCR = Office for Civil Rights; OIG = Office of the Inspector General; OMHA = Office of Medicare Hearings and Appeals; ONCHIT = Office of the National Coordinator for Health Information Technology; PHSSEF = Public Health and Social Services Emergency Fund; SAMHSA = Substance Abuse and Mental Health Services Administration; SCHIP = State Children's Health Program, a component of Medicaid.
SOURCE: OMB (2008a).

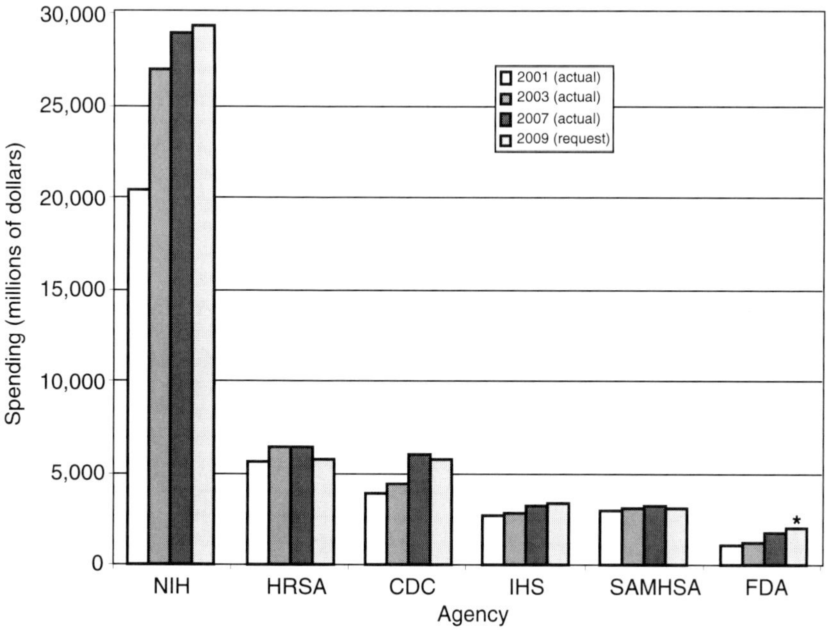

FIGURE 1-3 Public Health Service budgets, by agency (actual spending FY 2001, FY 2003, FY 2007, and President's budget request, FY 2009).
NOTES: This figure does not include data for the Agency for Toxic Substances and Disease Registry (ATSDR) or the Agency for Healthcare Research and Quality (AHRQ). Funding for ATSDR is included in CDC's budget. As noted above in Figure 1-2, AHRQ has not had its own separate budget allocation since 2002.
*Although the figure shows the President's budget request for FY 2009, an additional $300 million was included to reflect funds available to the FDA for FY 2009 as a result of the June 2008 Emergency Supplemental Appropriations Bill and the September 2008 Continuing Resolution.
SOURCE: OMB (2004, 2008a).

As demonstrated in Figure 1-2, HHS's budget is dominated by the Centers for Medicare and Medicaid Services, whose spending[3] grew from almost $350 billion in FY 2001 to $570 billion in FY 2007, with the President's budget request for FY 2009 standing at $635 billion—

[3]The CMS spending figures for 2001 and 2007 include discretionary spending as well as the mandatory outlays for Medicare and Medicaid/State Children's Health Insurance Program (SCHIP).

more than an 85 percent increase over the last eight years (OMB, 2004, 2008a).

As Figure 1-4 shows, the vast majority of the department's budget is designated for *mandatory* spending under entitlement and other service, training, and research programs. Only about 10 percent of the budget each year is discretionary (the largest share of which supports NIH).

STRUCTURE VERSUS RESTRUCTURING

Structure is a central contributor to the overall performance of any organization. It affects the movement of information up and down the chain of command, the level of cooperation between divisions, the development and implementation of policy, and workforce morale (Appendix G).

Over the years, organizational management literature has suggested many approaches to structuring large private-sector entities, and current analysis tends toward the view that "there is no single best way to organize" (Bradach, 1996). In the federal government context, numerous reorganization efforts have been attempted, but many have not achieved substantial or long-lasting change (Radin, 2000).

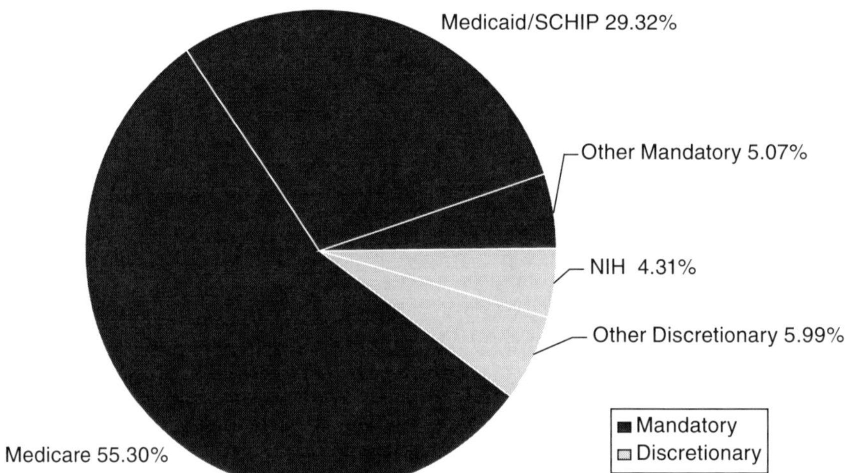

FIGURE 1-4 HHS mandatory and discretionary budget allocations, 2007.
SOURCE: HHS (2008).

The organizational difficulties of the Department of Homeland Security provide a cautionary tale. Since its formation in 2003, it—and its 16 operating components and more than 170,000 employees—has been internally reorganized at least twice (Appendix G). In addition, Congress stepped in with a legislative reorganization (the Post-Katrina Emergency Management Reform Act) in 2006. Despite the enormous national attention, priority, and resources placed on homeland security after 2001, it still was not easy to "get it right" the first time.

Since its creation in 1953, HHS has been led by 20 secretaries whose tenures in the earlier years tended to be relatively short. Since 1985, average tenures have more than doubled (see Appendix D). Successive HHS secretaries have favored markedly different approaches and degrees of reorganization and report mixed success (Balutis, 1979; Appendix G).

Interviews performed for the IOM committee with six former secretaries, who began their tenures at the beginning of the past six Presidencies, revealed varying views on the usefulness of a major departmental reorganization. However, these former secretaries unanimously agreed that the process of changing the underlying culture that influences day-to-day operations of individual units and the department as a whole is difficult, distracting, time consuming, and often unsuccessful (see Appendix G). If restructuring is to be attempted, it must begin immediately upon the secretary's taking office. The larger—and longer—the restructuring project, the more turmoil and the longer are the delays in acting on the agenda of the new President and secretary.

Upon deliberation, the IOM committee concluded that, given consensus among management experts, there is "no one best way" to organize a huge, complex entity such as HHS—a large-scale reorganization at this juncture would take too much time and attention away from pressing challenges that the department currently faces. Nor would it be timely, given the likelihood of at least some health reforms in the next few years, which themselves may necessitate some structural changes within the department.

The committee also recognized that success in large-scale reorganization is not guaranteed, and in any case would be difficult because of the short time the secretary has to act. In an interview, HHS Secretary Michael Leavitt explained the short time frame this way (Schaeffer, 2007):

> The government runs in four-year cycles, but it's really not four years. Because when it starts, there's about a six-month period when

no one's in place, and people are trying to find their way around. Then the last year, there's an election. So you've really got about two and a half years.

By contrast, the Government Accountability Office (GAO) has observed that it generally takes government entities *five to seven years* to successfully complete major change initiatives (GAO, 2004).

Although most recent secretaries caution against embarking on a major reorganization, even a secretary who wanted to do so would encounter the growing number of restrictions Congress has placed over departmental operations, job descriptions, and details of program delivery. Negotiating those restrictions—many of them statutory—would be another lengthy process of uncertain outcome (see Appendix G).

Opportunities for Change

Even without major structural change in the department, the committee saw many opportunities for improved alignment and performance and for building more value into departmental operations. As noted, HHS is a large, complex enterprise with many constituencies, each of which wishes that the department's activities and performance would meet its particular needs; collectively, these external forces create the complex environment that the secretary must skillfully navigate.

Organizational management literature is replete with advice and tools related to improving efficiency and effectiveness. A widely used management framework that the IOM committee found useful during its deliberations takes into account the following seven essential elements, distilled from research in the private sector (Waterman et al., 1980):

1. Strategy—the ways in which an organization achieves its ends
2. Structure—how tasks and people are organized to accomplish the work and what they are responsible for
3. Systems—the formal processes and procedures the organization uses to plan, allocate resources, measure performance, manage information, and so on
4. Staff—the organization's human resources
5. Skills—its distinctive attributes and capabilities
6. Style—how both top management and the overall organization operate

7. Shared values—the organization's fundamental, widely shared values that signal what is important to it (Bradach, 1996)

The committee believes that the department will derive great benefit from comprehensive organizational reform strategies that take into account fundamental structures and processes, such as those listed above.

While significant alterations in HHS structure would not be easy—or even possible—the *decision-making and management processes* at all levels of the department can change, and this is where the new secretary can make the most progress in responding to the concerns the House committee has raised.

The IOM committee's recommendations (see Box 1-2) are interrelated and mutually supportive. Many of them would require involvement and approval from Congress and the White House. They would ensure value in HHS operations and would focus the department squarely on purpose, which is essential to both performance and accountability. The committee believes that improved performance and accountability could strengthen the cooperation with Congress that the department urgently needs in order to move forward. The recommendations would

- focus the department on the most important health challenges for the nation (Recommendation 1),
- strengthen its organizational capacity to address these challenges (Recommendation 2),
- foster improved performance of the nation's health system overall (Recommendation 3),
- ensure the necessary workforce (Recommendation 4), and
- increase the department's accountability and give it more flexibility (Recommendation 5).

HHS has a long history of accomplishment and evolution to meet new needs, but it cannot afford to become stalemated by its own processes and precedents or by statutory restrictions that impede its ability to function effectively. Implementation of the committee's recommendations would better position HHS to meet both rapidly emerging and enduring health challenges in the twenty-first century.

BOX 1-2
Recommendations

1. To meet twenty-first century challenges to America's health, the secretary of HHS should clearly articulate and actively promote a vision for the nation's health, ensure that the department's mission supports that vision, and establish a small number of measurable goals focused on critical challenges.

a. The secretary should lead a *thorough and thoughtful process* to identify and prioritize the nation's key health challenges.
b. The secretary should, in this process, *consult widely* with internal department leaders, others in the executive branch, Congress, governors and state-level officials, health care providers, scientific and professional organizations, and public interest and advocacy groups.
c. The secretary should establish a *vision, mission, and goals* that respond to twenty-first century challenges, enable greater programmatic continuity over time, and that can be used to *focus department staff and activities on leading priorities, strengthen the public health infrastructure, facilitate assessment of impact, and lead to corrective action.*
d. The secretary, working closely with the White House and Congress, should *take a major role in promoting and achieving health reform nationwide.*

2. To improve the public's health and achieve the department's goals, the secretary should align and focus the department on performance and encourage creative use of scientifically based approaches to meet new and enduring challenges.

a. The heads of all department units should ensure that their *activities and operations are aligned* with the department's vision, mission, and goals and marshal their resources to achieve them.
b. The secretary should reduce directly reporting senior-level officials to *a manageable number.* Although secretarial management styles differ, a rigorous decision-making process for both policy and operations must be established, along with accountability for results.
c. The secretary should ensure *a more prominent and powerful role* for the surgeon general, who, in addition to leading the Commissioned Corps, should be a *strong advocate for the health of the American people* and work actively to *educate Americans on important health issues.* The secretary should work with the President and Congress to *establish a process for identifying surgeon general candidates* for Presidential appointment *that gives high priority to qualifications and leadership*, and Congress is strongly urged to consider a *longer term* for this office.
d. The secretary should work with the President and Congress to establish a selection process for the department's senior-level officials that *protects the scientific and administrative integrity of major departmental units, promotes progress toward departmental goals,* and is *based primarily on the candidates' qualifications and experience.* Congress again is strongly urged to consider *longer terms* for some of these officials–especially the directors of the National Institutes of Health (NIH) and the Centers for Disease Control and Prevention (CDC), and the commis-

sioner of the Food and Drug Administration (FDA)–which would provide critical continuity in the nation's public health and scientific endeavors.

e. The President should make timely appointments and Congress should expedite the confirmation process for key HHS officials, including the secretary, deputy secretary, surgeon general, and the heads of FDA and NIH. Secretarial appointments, such as the director of CDC, should also be expedited.

f. The secretary should ensure that *all department health programs, including the reimbursement programs, reinforce public health priorities and strategies* in order to provide a consistent framework for protecting the public from health risks, promoting health, preventing disease and disability, and providing health services for vulnerable populations in the most efficient, cost-effective ways.

g. To maximize value in the health care system, the secretary must *strengthen the scientific base and capabilities of the department* and ensure that *agencies' research findings* are shared department-wide and that *current best evidence is used for departmental decision making, including the Centers for Medicare and Medicaid Services (CMS) reimbursement policy.*

h. Congress should allocate *sufficient, predictable funding for NIH, CDC, FDA, and AHRQ* in order to preserve and enhance these agencies' scientific missions. Congress should also establish a *specific budget line for AHRQ* that is *independent* of appropriations to other HHS agencies.

i. To address the growing threat of food-borne illnesses, Congress should *unify the U.S. Department of Agriculture's (USDA's) Food Safety and Inspection Service and the food safety activities of FDA within HHS* and ensure provision of adequate resources for high-quality inspection, enforcement, and research.

3. The secretary should accelerate the establishment of a collaborative, robust system for evaluating the health care system that would incorporate existing department and external research, stimulate new studies as needed, synthesize findings, and provide actionable feedback for policy makers, purchasers, payers, providers, health care professionals, and the public.

a. The secretary should work with Congress to establish a capability for *assessing the comparative value–including clinical- and cost-effectiveness*–of medical interventions and procedures, preventive and treatment technologies, and methods of organizing and delivering care. The assessment of comparative value should begin by leveraging department-wide data sources in conjunction with supportive evidence from providers, payers, and health researchers.[a]

b. The secretary should work with Congress to ensure that the department's *programs and reimbursement policies are outcomes based*, reflecting best available evidence of value and creating incentives for adoption of best practices, including integration of care, in order to improve quality and efficiency.

c. The department should *collaborate with state and local public health agencies and community-based organizations*, as both sources and users of practical program guidance.

d. The department should provide *authoritative, plain-language, and current evidence-based information* to the public regarding prevention and treatment options.
e. To assess the health of the American people and overall health system performance accurately, the department needs current data from the nation's health system. To facilitate collection of these data, the department should actively promote the universal adoption of *electronic information capabilities*–including health information exchange and electronic medical, personal health records–for administrative and clinical purposes.

4. The secretary should place a high priority on developing a strategy and tools for workforce improvement (1) in HHS, (2) in the public health and health care professions nationwide, and (3) in the biosciences.

a. The secretary should immediately strengthen workforce planning in the department and develop a *comprehensive strategy to recruit highly qualified* public- and private-sector individuals in order to offset the large number of experienced staff expected to retire soon.
b. Congress should authorize the department, in cooperation with the Office of Personnel Management, to assemble a package of current and innovative programs and benefits designed to *encourage talented, experienced individuals to transition back and forth between government and private-sector service*, thereby identifying ways to leverage the best of both.
c. Congress should provide the secretary with additional authority to *reward performance, innovation, and the achievement of results*, through bonuses, merit-based pay, recognition awards, or other mechanisms of proven effectiveness.
d. The secretary, in concert with other public and private partners, should *develop a comprehensive national strategy to assess and address current and projected gaps* in the number, professional mix, geographic distribution, and diversity of the U.S. public health and health care workforces.
e. To help close projected gaps, the department should evaluate existing *health care professional training programs*, continued education programs, and graduate medical education funding and should encourage Congress to invest in programs with proven effectiveness.
f. Congress should give the secretary authority to create new programs that invest in the *future generation of biomedical and health services researchers*, enabling the continued discovery of new, more effective methods of preventing, treating, and curing disease; promoting health; improving health care delivery and organization; and controlling health system costs.

5. A "new compact" between Congress and the department is essential as HHS works toward achieving its vision for a healthy nation, departmental mission, and key health goals. Under this compact, the secretary would provide Congress and the nation regular, rigorous reports about departmental activities and assume greater accountability for improving performance and obtaining

results; in return, Congress should allow the department greater flexibility in its internal operations and decision making.

a. To enable greater accountability, the secretary should oversee development and implementation of a *department-wide data, evaluation, and information system.* The system should be based on a broad analytic framework designed to aid in managing departmental operations, learning from program experience, evaluating the costs and impact of programs, and determining whether they provide sufficient value for the investment of public funds.
b. Congress should authorize the secretary to direct funding from the budgets of all departmental units to support the development of an HHS-wide information system. Funding for such a system would benefit all department units.
c. The department should use the data, evaluation, and information system to
   - enable the secretary to *provide Congress with regular reports* on progress toward achieving departmental goals,
   - *inform policy development,*
   - *facilitate cross-department activities,*
   - provide *operational information to program management* for quality improvement and midcourse corrections, and
   - support effective *long-range planning.*
d. For those outside the department, the system should
   - *be accessible, transparent, timely, and reliable*, and
   - provide *useful, privacy-protected information* regarding department activities.
e. The department should *demonstrate accountability* through continuous critical assessment of program efficiency, equity, impact on health, and cost-effectiveness, and through corrective action for underperforming programs.
f. The secretary, in collaboration with the surgeon general, should present Congress and the public with an annual "State of the Nation's Health" report that describes progress toward achieving the vision for the nation's health and the department's key health goals.
g. Congress should establish *a new, strategic initiative fund* to enable the secretary to support cross-agency and cross-departmental activities that exhibit innovation in responding to twenty-first century challenges, and to respond quickly to new, unforeseen, or expanding public health threats.

---

[a]The committee did not reach consensus on recommendation 3a. Although the majority of the committee supports the language of the recommendation, David Beier, J.D., Senior Vice President of Global Government and Corporate Affairs, Amgen; Kathleen Buto, M.P.A., Vice President, Health Policy, Johnson & Johnson; and Myrl Weinberg, C.A.E., President, National Health Council, did not agree with the majority's view and provided dissenting opinions, which can be found in Appendix F. They were not able to agree on a common statement.

REFERENCES

Balutis, A. 1979. The reorganization of DHEW: What happened, why, and so what? *Journal of Health and Human Resources Administration* 1(4):504-525.

Bradach, J. 1996. *Organizational alignment: The 7-S model.* Boston, MA: Harvard Business School.

FDA (Food and Drug Administration). 2008. *Frequently asked questions (FAQs).* http://www.fda.gov/opacom/faqs/faqs.html (accessed October 8, 2008).

GAO (Government Accountability Office). 2004. *Centers for Disease Control and Prevention: Agency leadership taking steps to improve management and planning, but challenges remain.* Washington, DC: GAO.

HHS (Department of Health and Human Services). 2008. *Budget in brief: Fiscal year 2009.* Washington, DC: HHS.

Office of the Public Health Service Historian. 2004. *FAQs.* http://lhncbc.nlm.nih.gov/apdb/phsHistory/faqs.html (accessed September 22, 2008).

OMB (Office of Management and Budget). 2004. *Budget of the United States government, fiscal year 2005: Department of Health and Human Services.* http://www.whitehouse.gov/omb/budget/fy2005/hhs.html (accessed October 8, 2008).

OMB. 2008a. *Budget of the United States government, fiscal year 2009: Department of Health and Human Services.* http://www.whitehouse.gov/omb/budget/fy2009/hhs.html (accessed October 8, 2008).

OMB. 2008b. *Budget of the United States government: Federal employment and compensation tables fiscal year 2009: Federal civilian employment in the executive branch (table 24-1).* http://www.gpoaccess.gov/usbudget/fy09/sheets/24_1.xls (accessed October 8, 2008).

Parascandola, J. L. 1998. *A historical guide to the U.S. government.* Edited by G. T. Kurian. New York: Oxford University Press.

Radin, B. 2000. The Government Performance and Results Act and the tradition of federal management reform: Square pegs in round holes? *Journal of Public Administration Research and Theory* 10(1):111-135.

Schaeffer, L. 2007. Leading the way: A conversation with HHS secretary Mike Leavitt. *Health Affairs* 27:w52-w59.

Shalala, D. 1998. Are large public organizations manageable? *Public Administration Review* 58(4):284-289.

Waterman, R., Jr., T. Peters, and J. Phillips. 1980. Structure is not organization. *Business Horizons* 23(3):14-26.

2

Define a Twenty-First Century Vision

Where there is no vision, the people perish.
Proverbs 9:18

RECOMMENDATION 1

Define a Twenty-First Century Vision

To meet twenty-first century challenges to America's health, the secretary of the Department of Health and Human Services should clearly articulate and actively promote a vision for the nation's health, ensure that the department's mission supports that vision, and establish a small number of measurable goals focused on critical challenges.

a. **The secretary should lead a *thorough and thoughtful process* to identify and prioritize the nation's key health challenges.**
b. **The secretary should, in this process, *consult widely* with internal department leaders, others in the executive branch, Congress, governors and state-level officials, health care providers, scientific and professional organizations, and public interest and advocacy groups.**
c. **The secretary should establish a *vision, mission, and goals* that respond to twenty-first century challenges, enable greater programmatic continuity over time, and that can be used to *focus department staff and activities on leading priorities, strengthen the public***

health infrastructure, facilitate assessment of impact, and lead to corrective action.

d. **The secretary, working closely with the White House and Congress, should *take a major role in promoting and achieving health reform nationwide.***

CHARTING THE DEPARTMENT'S COURSE

To provide greater value to the American people for its $700 billion in annual health expenditures, the Department of Health and Human Services (HHS) requires clear direction. The first step is to identify and prioritize key health challenges, which would then be used *to guide the development of a compelling, well-articulated vision for the nation's health, to ensure that the department's mission statement adequately describes its role in achieving the vision, and to identify a relatively small number of explicit, measurable goals that are geared to meeting the nation's greatest health challenges.*

The secretary should launch a formal process for establishing these guidelines for action, building on, as appropriate, the department's current mission and commitments, as well as its long history of ensuring health and human services, and special attention should be paid to the needs of vulnerable populations served by the department. The process not only should involve the many important constituencies whose advice is essential to moving forward but also should be one that can be completed in a timely way.

The First Step: Identify the Nation's Top Health Challenges

The uppermost challenge facing the nation at present is the fundamentally flawed health care system and the need for health reform. Additional challenges include

- the rising prevalence of costly chronic diseases;
- developing prevention and treatment methods for diseases that currently lack them;
- persistent poverty (affecting more than 37 million Americans in 2007) (U.S. Census Bureau, 2008);

- global threats to health (including pandemics, emerging infections, bioterrorism, natural disasters, and climate change);
- workforce shortages;
- the crumbling public health infrastructure;
- social, environmental, and behavioral factors affecting health; and
- health disparities and the needs of vulnerable populations.

The review of the nation's top health challenges cannot begin with a blank slate; it must take into account HHS's ongoing responsibilities and legislated commitments and should incorporate contributions from many quarters. It should include the White House and Congress, state government, the private sector, and a small number of individuals with unique perspectives, such as the head of the World Health Organization, or leading scientists and innovators.

Within the administration, the process of identifying the nation's top health challenges needs to be a team effort involving the White House and leaders of other cabinet-level departments (Warshaw, 1996). Many federal departments have major health programs (see Box 2-1), and some health challenges—such as improving the response to national emergencies—cross traditional department jurisdictions. Much is to be gained by closer collaboration between HHS and other departments—such as Homeland Security—and agencies, such as the Social Security Administration or Environmental Protection Agency—whose actions greatly affect the health of the public.

The opinions of leaders of the congressional committees with oversight or appropriations responsibility for HHS must be solicited. This would include members of the 12 Senate and House committees and 6 subcommittees that currently oversee the department or its component agencies (see Box 2-2). Participation in the priority-setting process might improve the department's responsiveness to public concerns while also helping members of Congress take into account the enormous number of challenges the department faces, stem the number of legislatively mandated programs layered on the department, and persuade members to allow the department more flexibility in program implementation (see Chapter 6).

BOX 2-1
Other Federal Departments with Major Health Programs

A number of other federal departments and agencies are responsible for important health-related activities:

- The Department of Veterans Affairs has an undersecretary for health in charge of hospitals, clinics, and other health services for eligible military veterans.
- The Department of Defense has an assistant secretary for health affairs and separate surgeons general for the Army, Navy, and Air Force, who oversee health care services for active military service members and their families, and a joint staff surgeon, who serves as medical advisor to the chairman of the Joint Chiefs of Staff.
- The Department of Homeland Security has an assistant secretary for health affairs, who also serves as the department's chief medical officer and is responsible for advising the DHS secretary and the Federal Emergency Management Agency administrator on health-related issues.
- The Department of Labor oversees ERISA (the Employee Retirement Income Security Act), the statute that governs employer-sponsored health insurance.
- The Office of Personnel Management manages the Federal Employees Health Benefits Program, which is often cited as a possible model for the expansion of health care coverage.

State involvement in setting priorities is crucial, because Medicaid, health care financing innovations, and most public health activities—such as disease control and surveillance, emergency preparedness, and public information campaigns about tobacco and obesity—are carried out not just at the federal level, but in states and communities, as well. Greater inclusion of states in HHS strategic planning would be an important step forward, as states, despite their vital role in implementing HHS programs, frequently perceive that they are treated as an "interest group just like any other" (Boufford and Lee, 2001).

Health care experts outside government—such as professional associations, researchers and scientists, care providers, product manufacturers, business and labor, insurers, and health care associations—also should be consulted, as should consumer groups and organizations representing people with chronic diseases and disabilities and their family caregivers.

BOX 2-2
Committees That Oversee HHS and Related Appropriations

Senate Committees
Appropriations
- Subcommittee on Agriculture, Rural Development, and Related Agencies
- Subcommittee on Labor, HHS, and Education

Budget
Finance
Health, Education, Labor, and Pensions
Homeland Security and Governmental Affairs
Labor and Human Resources
- Subcommittee on Public Health and Safety

House Committees
Appropriations
- Subcommittee on Agriculture, Rural Development, Food and Drug Administration, and Related Agencies
- Subcommittee on Labor, HHS, and Education

Budget
Education and the Workforce
Energy and Commerce
- Subcommittee on Health and Environment

Oversight and Government Reform
Ways and Means

SOURCES: IOM (1998); see www.kaiserEDU.org; see www.frac.org.

Such a broad effort to obtain input about the nation's key health challenges and priorities would ensure that the result will reflect a comprehensive awareness of the problems, promote acceptance of the goals the department ultimately chooses, facilitate implementation of related programs, generate partnerships, encourage longer-term investments, and foster continuity.

Related Recommendations

a. **The secretary should lead a *thorough and thoughtful process* to identify and prioritize the nation's key health challenges.**

b. **The secretary should, in this process, *consult widely* with internal department leaders, others in the executive branch, Congress, governors and state-level officials, health care providers, scientific and professional organizations, and public interest and advocacy groups.**

Vision

The analysis of current, emerging, and potential health challenges and priorities facing the nation would provide the department with consensus-based background information—a type of "environmental scan"—necessary to construct a twenty-first century vision for the nation's health. It would describe what the department sees as a compelling vision for the future state of the nation's health, and it should combine elements of aspiration and inspiration—not only desire, but also motivation to work toward that desire:

- *"I have a dream today"* (Martin Luther King, Jr., March on Washington, August 28, 1963)
- *"These united colonies are, and of right ought to be, free and independent states"* (Declaration of Independence, 1776)
- *"With confidence in our armed forces, with the unbounding determination of our people, we will gain the inevitable triumph—so help us God"* (Franklin D. Roosevelt, Address to Congress, December 8, 1941)

A clear, central *vision* of a desired future state is essential to high performance (Peters, 1988). The articulation of a vision can reflect many possible outcomes. HHS's vision for the nation's health might, for example, express a determination to make the United States one of the world's healthiest nations or orient the nation toward health promotion and disease and injury prevention.

Although the choice of a vision is not always obvious, without it, organizations become diffuse and distracted, spend time on noncritical activities, and fall short of their potential effectiveness. Ideally, HHS's vision for the nation's health would be compelling enough to endure beyond a single secretary's tenure.

Mission

A *mission statement* describes what the organization does, why it exists, and its role in achieving the vision. It defines success for the organization. The current HHS mission statement, which encompasses both its health and human services roles, accomplishes these purposes well (HHS, 2008b):

> to enhance the health and well-being of Americans by providing for effective health and human services and by fostering strong, sustained advances in the sciences underlying medicine, public health, and social services.

With a newly articulated vision in mind, HHS should assess whether this mission is well designed to achieve the vision.

Goals

To establish accountability and to monitor performance, both internally and externally, a set of time-specific, *measurable goals* is required, in addition to the vision and mission statements (see Chapter 6).[1] Goals should be few in number, reflecting hard and firm choices, since "to govern is to choose" (Shalala, 1998). They should be measurable, so that progress toward them can be tracked. In addition, they should be published and accessed easily, similar to the objectives of *Healthy People 2010.* An example of a goal that was easily measured *and* inspiring was the National Aeronautics and Space Administration's (NASA's) goal of getting a man to the moon and returning him safely to Earth by 1970, which generated agency efforts so focused that it was achieved a year ahead of schedule.

In general, HHS goals should do the following:

- Support its vision and mission statements.
- Reflect challenges raised in the internal and external assessments.
- Focus its activities.

[1]HHS currently has a large number of goals that are discussed in Chapter 6. These goals include four very broad goals that are not time specific; the secretary has nine priorities, and *Healthy People* has 467 objectives for the nation.

- Be consistent with each other, across the department's health and human services programs.
- Balance ongoing responsibilities and new demands.
- Be challenging, realistic, and achievable.

Setting goals makes the secretary's job even more complicated, because the choices are so many and current responsibilities are so great. The goals should align with the vision and mission statement and should be designed to meet the established priorities. Some of the department's goals should respond to the nation's *greatest health challenges*, as the secretary and other key advisers perceive them. Other goals may need to address *internal challenges* related to the department's organization and operations.

The department faces an array of internal challenges that impede its efficiency and effectiveness. Some of the challenges listed below are general problems—such as the department's likely workforce shortage; some are specific to certain departmental units; and some reflect organizational approaches that were better designed to deal with the health problems of yesterday, not today—and much less tomorrow. Progress in responding to these internal challenges will require attention and action from some combination of the secretary, Congress, and the White House. For example:

- They must address the extraordinary diversity in the goals of the department's individual health and human services programs, coupled with the need to customize programs to make them effective.
- The personal nature of health care and health maintenance requires that policies and programs take into account diversity among patients and tailor interventions to individuals.
- The dominance of entitlement programs and other mandatory spending in the department's annual budget leaves department leaders little flexibility in spending, while federal budget constraints limit new funding.
- At present, there is no mechanism to finance an effective response to public health emergencies (Lister, 2008).
- Establishing effective partnerships with state and local governments and the private sector is desirable, but difficult.
- Currently, the secretary has significant management demands, providing direct oversight of 11 operating divisions and 15 staff

divisions, without positions such as undersecretaries or assistant secretaries with line authority.

- The department's data and information systems inadequately support decision making and program assessment.
- Responsibility for key issues is fragmented across agencies, making it difficult to leverage resources for maximum impact; for example, obesity—now generally considered one of the nation's foremost health issues—is addressed by programs in nearly every health and human services agency.
- The once-powerful position of assistant secretary for health (ASH) no longer has authority over the department's major public health agencies and, consequently, has little capacity to generate or inspire change in the public health sector. Instead, the ASH oversees 16 offices, many focused on socially sensitive areas—such as biomedical ethics, reproductive health, HIV/AIDS policy, and minority and women's health (HHS, 2008a).
- The department has made insufficient progress toward achieving the nation's current health goals—for example, of the *Healthy People 2010* objectives set a decade ago, only one-third have seen progress (HHS Office of Disease Prevention and Health Promotion, 2005).
- The HHS workforce needs major strengthening.

Each such internal issue should be evaluated to determine whether the secretary has authority to remedy it or whether the involvement of Congress is required.

VISION, MISSION, AND GOALS AS MANAGEMENT TOOLS

The process of establishing vision, mission, and goals relates to the seven elements of organizational success noted in Chapter 1—most notably, strategy, systems, and shared vision (Bradach, 1996). All three of these expressions of purpose are essential for the effective functioning of any organization.

This report does not recommend what the department's vision for the nation, its own mission, or its goals should be. Instead, the committee firmly believes that these choices belong to the President and the secretary, that they must be articulated clearly and forcefully and promulgated widely, and that the department's activities must be aligned to achieve them (see Chapter 3).

A focus on purpose—vision, mission, and goals—is preferable to a focus on structure, because attention paid to purpose should result in a strategic cohesiveness within the entire department, while attention paid to structure and reorganization is likely to yield more limited benefits, at high cost (Waterman et al., 1980). The vision and mission statements should be intended to *endure*. They should provide program continuity in the face of presidential transitions and when new secretaries and new executive leadership comes aboard. Also, the vision and mission statements should encourage rather than stifle creativity and innovation.[2]

Clear purpose can help inform budget decisions and focus attention on long-term needs, including how to achieve sustainability in the department's programs, especially Medicare and Medicaid. Guided by department goals, the budgets of the leading Public Health Service agencies—the National Institutes of Health (NIH), Centers for Disease Control and Prevention (CDC), and Food and Drug Administration (FDA), in particular—could be more predictable, rather than showing wide year-to-year fluctuations (see Chapter 3). If more predictable funding arrangements could be worked out with Congress, this budgetary continuity not only would aid federal public health efforts, but could also stabilize federally funded community-based programs.

Clear purpose facilitates program evaluation, discussed in Chapter 6. Evaluation results should help refine goals, while the vision and mission remain intact.

Finally, clear purpose helps others—in Congress, throughout government, throughout the health sector, and in the nation at large—understand the role and importance of the department's work.

Just as words are no substitute for action, vision and mission statements are no substitute for leadership. The department needs an effective leader to set it on course and keep it there, to achieve real progress. Within the limits imposed by Congress, *ultimately, it will be the secretary's responsibility to ensure department-wide integration of the vision, mission, and goals into HHS daily activities and operations.*

Related Recommendation

---

[2]In the HHS Human Capital Survey (HHS, 2007), less than half of respondents agreed with the statement, "Creativity and innovation are rewarded."

c. **The secretary should establish a *vision, mission, and goals* that respond to twenty-first century challenges, enable greater programmatic continuity over time, and that can be used to *focus department staff and activities on leading priorities, strengthen the public health infrastructure, facilitate assessment of impact, and lead to corrective action.***

SECURING HEALTH REFORM

A major theme of this report is about building value into the work of HHS, and it is equally vital to build greater value into our nation's health system. HHS is deeply affected by current problems in the system and can be a major force in their solution. High health care costs, lack of access to care, poor quality and outcomes—a Venn diagram of overlapping influences—are the major sources of mounting pressure for health reform—among the public, health professionals and providers, and policy makers.

When Congress requested this report, it asked that the Institute of Medicine (IOM) consider the department's preparedness to meet the nation's greatest health care challenges: advancing health and controlling health care costs. The consensus of many experts—and the IOM committee—is that these challenges cannot be met without comprehensive health reform.

Comprehensive reform would result in a health system that produces more value for Americans. It would be characterized by improved access to care *and* coverage; it would promote higher quality care, including all the attributes identified by the IOM (safe, effective, patient centered, timely, efficient, equitable) (IOM, 2001), and it would emphasize health promotion and prevention of disease and disability. Efforts at health reform should take this comprehensive approach, the committee believes, so that a reformed system is sustainable and accountable, has the necessary and appropriate workforce, and again, creates value in response to the massive investments of the American people.

As far back as the 1930s, attempts have been made to rationalize the U.S. health care system by proposing changes in the way the nation pays for health care (Committee on the Costs of Medical Care, 1932), but powerful interest groups and opponents of federal and state government solutions have pointed out the risks of change, and reform has repeatedly stalled. Inaction may not be possible for much longer, as increases in health care costs, which were $2.1 trillion in 2006 (Catlin et al., 2008), are rising faster than the gross domestic product, prompting one group of prominent analysts to predict that "By the early 2030s, assuming health care costs grow at their historical rate, the three major entitlement programs [Medicare, Medicaid, and Social Security] will absorb *all* of the federal government's projected revenues" [emphasis added] (Frenzel et al., undated).

Health care costs also are prime contributors to escalating national debt and pervade economists' concerns about the state of the entire economy. A September 2008 Congressional Budget Office (CBO) report concluded that current trends in federal spending and revenues are "unsustainable." The CBO identified health care spending and, "to a lesser extent," the aging population (which requires Social Security spending, as well as increased health care spending) as two of the largest ongoing contributors to growing demand for federal resources (CBO, 2008).

Dismay about high health care costs (see Box 2-3) is deepened by evidence that the money being spent on health care does not produce commensurate gains in population health. Much research comparing expenditures and care patterns in different areas of the country has shown that "spending more" does not improve health outcomes (Wennberg et al., 2008). Additional dismay stems from revelations regarding severe quality problems in individuals' health care—problems that every year cost tens of thousands of lives, much needless suffering, and untold dollars (IOM, 2001).

BOX 2-3
The Results of Increasing Health Care Costs

- Nearly 46 million Americans were uninsured in 2007–15.3 percent of the population (U.S. Census Bureau, 2008).
- Eighty percent of the uninsured live in families with at least one employed individual, and a third have family incomes above 200 percent of poverty (Kaiser Commission on Medicaid and the Uninsured, 2008).
- Some 18 million mostly poor and uninsured Americans now rely on publicly funded community health centers for their care (NACHC, 2008a).
- These centers' patient populations grew 56 percent between 2000 and 2006 (NACHC, 2008b).
- A third of U.S. adults spend at least 10 percent of their income on health services or health insurance.
- Medical debt is a factor in nearly half of personal bankruptcy filings (IOM, 2002).

The leadership for reform may emerge from various congressional committees, private-sector interests, a new working group established by the President, or various other organizational arrangements. Lessons from the failed 1993 reform effort—including the need for greater transparency—would undoubtedly underpin the design of a new reform process. Regardless of the entity that takes the lead, the secretary and the department inevitably will be required to give sustained attention to the development and assessment of reform options.

Any health reform strategy ultimately put forward will affect every aspect of department activities:

- Reform will affect departmental priorities and whether and how well it can meet its mission and goals.
- Reform will influence the structure, alignment, and interrelationships of departmental agencies and units.
- Reform will affect many aspects of HHS agencies' daily operations and the expertise their staff will need.
- Reform will change the outcomes for which the department is accountable.

In fact, reform will have an impact on all of the seven elements of organizational success: strategy, structure, systems, staff, skills, style, and shared values.

If only because health reform would have such a major impact on the department, the secretary cannot afford to be merely a passive observer of the process. The department has both motivation and opportunity to play a significant role in creating a high-value health system because of the enormous costs—and powerful leverage—of Medicare and Medicaid and its role in setting quality standards across government health programs (IOM, 2003).

The department also has important expertise and information to contribute, too. Because it is the principal advocate within the federal government for public health and advancing the health of the population, it may be up to the secretary to make the critical case that "health reform" is more than just reforming the insurance coverage and payment systems. HHS has paramount operational knowledge about the complex workings of the health sector, and the secretary will want to use the extensive data available from Medicare, Medicaid, CDC, FDA, the Health Resources and Services Administration, the Agency for Healthcare Research and Quality, and other federal, state, and private-sector agencies to help shape and assess options. HHS will want to leverage its relationships with many important constituencies that also can contribute to the reform process.

A successful health reform process would require transparency and strong communication and would undoubtedly be collaborative, cross-governmental, and involve many public- and private-sector entities. The department should clarify its role early in the process and marshal its resources to contribute its unique data resources and the perspectives gained from long and diverse experience.

Specific ways in which the department should participate in a reform process include the following:

- Set up a capacity to quickly conduct or coordinate external research on proposals offered by the White House, Congress, and others.
- Pull together cross-department work teams on key issues as they arise.
- Communicate knowledge to the public about what is known regarding important aspects of reform.
- Organize new forms of demonstration or state waiver programs to test specific aspects of reform proposals.
- Ensure health promotion and disease prevention are adequately included in reform efforts.
- Assess the adequacy of the workforce to support reform proposals.
- Ensure that the new system can be both sustainable and accountable.
- Generally, emphasize creation of more value in the health system.

The combination of a health system that is widely considered fundamentally flawed, competing external demands, internal organizational complexity, and impending large workforce losses due to retirement presents HHS with serious challenges, as well as opportunities for new thinking about the important themes the IOM committee considers in this report: *vision, focus, alignment, effectiveness, and accountability*.

Related Recommendation

d. **The secretary, working closely with the White House and Congress, should *take a major role in promoting and achieving health reform nationwide.***

REFERENCES

Boufford, J., and P. Lee. 2001. *Health policies for the 21st century: Challenges and recommendations for the U.S. Department of Health and Human Services.* New York: Milbank Memorial Fund.

Bradach, J. 1996. *Organizational alignment: The 7-S model.* Boston, MA: Harvard Business School.

Catlin, A., C. Cowan, M. Hartman, S. Heffler, and the National Health Expenditure Accounts Team. 2008. National health spending in 2006: A year of change for prescription drugs. *Health Affairs* 27(1):14-29.

CBO (Congressional Budget Office). 2008. *The budget and economic outlook: An update.* Washington, DC: CBO.

Committee on the Costs of Medical Care. 1932. *Medical care for the American people: The final report of the Committee on the Costs of Medical Care.* Chicago, IL: University of Chicago Press.

Frenzel, W., C. W. Stenholm, G. W. Hoagland, and I. V. Sawhill. undated. *Taming the deficit: Forge a grand compromise for a sustainable future.* Washington, DC: Brookings Institution.

HHS (Department of Health and Human Services). 2007. *HHS human capital survey—2007.* Washington, DC: HHS.

HHS. 2008a. *Office of public health and science.* http://www.hhs.gov/ophs/ (accessed October 15, 2008).

HHS. 2008b. *Performance highlights.* Washington, DC: HHS.

HHS Office of Disease Prevention and Health Promotion. 2005. *Healthy people 2010: Midcourse review.* Washington, DC: HHS.

IOM (Institute of Medicine). 1998. *Scientific opportunities and public needs: Improving priority setting and public input at the NIH.* Washington, DC: National Academy Press.

IOM. 2001. *Crossing the quality chasm: A new health system for the 21st century.* Washington, DC: National Academy Press.

IOM. 2002. *Health insurance is a family matter.* Washington, DC: The National Academies Press.

IOM. 2003. *Leadership by example: Coordinating government roles in improving health care quality.* Washington, DC: The National Academies Press.

Kaiser Commission on Medicaid and the Uninsured. 2008. *Five basic facts on the uninsured.* Palo Alto, CA: Henry J. Kaiser Family Foundation.

Lister, S. 2008. *Public health and medical preparedness and response: Issues in the 110th Congress.* Washington, DC: Congressional Research Service.

NACHC (National Association of Community Health Centers). 2008a. *Access transformed: Building a primary care workforce for the 21st century.* Bethesda, MD: NACHC.

NACHC. 2008b. *A sketch of community health centers: Chartbook 2008.* Bethesda, MD: NACHC.

Peters, T. 1988. *Thriving on chaos: Handbook for management revolution.* New York: HarperCollins.

Shalala, D. 1998. Are large public organizations manageable? *Public Administration Review* 58(4):284-289.

U.S. Census Bureau. 2008. *Health insurance coverage status and type of coverage by selected characteristics: 2007.* http://pubdb3.census.gov/macro/032008/health/h01_001.htm (accessed September 9, 2008).

Warshaw, S. 1996. *Powersharing: White House–cabinet relations in the modern American presidency.* Albany, NY: State University of New York Press.

Waterman, R., Jr., T. Peters, and J. Phillips. 1980. Structure is not organization. *Business Horizons* 23(3):14-26.

Wennberg, J., E. Fisher, D. Goodman, and J. Skinner. 2008. *Tracking the care of patients with severe chronic illness.* Hanover, NH: Dartmouth Atlas of Health Care.

3

Foster Adaptability and Alignment

There should be an unremitting effort to improve those health, education, and social security efforts, which have proved their value. . . . But good intent and high purpose are not enough; all such programs depend for their success upon efficient, responsible administration.

Dwight D. Eisenhower (1953)

RECOMMENDATION 2

Foster Adaptability and Alignment

To improve the public's health and achieve the department's goals, the secretary should align and focus the department on performance and encourage creative use of scientifically based approaches to meet new and enduring challenges.

a. **The heads of all department units should ensure that their *activities and operations are aligned* with the department's vision, mission, and goals and marshal their resources to achieve them.**
b. **The secretary should reduce directly reporting senior-level officials to *a manageable number.* Although secretarial management styles differ, a rigorous decision-making process for both policy and operations must be established, along with accountability for results.**
c. **The secretary should ensure *a more prominent and powerful role* for the surgeon general, who, in addition to leading the Commissioned Corps, should be a *strong advocate for the health of the American people* and work actively to *educate Americans on important health issues.* The secretary should work with the President and Congress to *establish a process for identifying surgeon***

***general candidates for Presidential appointment that gives high priority to qualifications and leadership*, and Congress is strongly urged to consider a *longer term* for this office.**

d. **The secretary should work with the President and Congress to establish a selection process for the department's senior-level officials that *protects the scientific and administrative integrity of major departmental units, promotes progress toward departmental goals*, and is *based primarily on the candidates' qualifications and experience.* Congress again is strongly urged to consider *longer terms* for some of these officials—especially the directors of the National Institutes of Health (NIH) and the Centers for Disease Control and Prevention (CDC), and the commissioner of the Food and Drug Administration (FDA)—which would provide critical continuity in the nation's public health and scientific endeavors.**

e. **The President should make timely appointments and Congress should expedite the confirmation process for key HHS officials, including the secretary, deputy secretary, surgeon general, and the heads of FDA and NIH. Secretarial appointments, such as the director of CDC, also should be expedited.**

f. **The secretary should ensure that *all department health programs, including the reimbursement programs, reinforce public health priorities and strategies* in order to provide a consistent framework for protecting the public from health risks, promoting health, preventing disease and disability, and providing health services for vulnerable populations in the most efficient, cost-effective ways.**

g. **To maximize value in the health care system, the secretary must *strengthen the scientific base and capabilities of the department* and ensure that *agencies' research findings* are shared department-wide and that *current best evidence is used***

for departmental decision making, including the Centers for Medicare and Medicaid (CMS) reimbursement policy.

h. **Congress should allocate *sufficient, predictable funding for NIH, CDC, FDA, and the Agency for Healthcare Research and Quality (AHRQ)* in order to preserve and enhance these agencies' scientific missions. Congress should also establish a *specific budget line for AHRQ* that is *independent* of appropriations to other HHS agencies.**

i. **To address the growing threat of food-borne illnesses, Congress should *unify the U.S. Department of Agriculture's (USDA's) Food Safety and Inspection Service and the food safety activities of FDA within HHS* and ensure provision of adequate resources for high-quality inspection, enforcement, and research.**

SCOPE OF THE CHALLENGES

As the organization charged with primary responsibility for ensuring the health and well-being of Americans, HHS must keep pace with rapid advances in many fields—biomedical sciences, health care technologies, the organization of health care, information technologies, health and social services research, and quality improvement. It also must keep abreast of emerging global threats to health, rising consumer expectations, and pressure for cost control and greater efficiency.

As Chapter 2 shows, substantial evidence indicates problems in HHS's structure and alignment. However, even with an optimal structure and admirable alignment across its many units, HHS would face an array of challenges that were unimaginable when the department was created in 1953. First, like any large American organization, it must adapt to new and overarching trends, including many described by the former comptroller general:

- the need to respond to terrorism and other threats to security,
- a population marked by increasing diversity and older age,
- an accelerating pace of advances in science and technology,
- rapid evolution of information and communications technology,

- new challenges and opportunities to maintain and improve quality of life,
- variable and diverse governmental tools and structures (Walker, 2003), and
- the many serious and long-standing threats to health that may be resolved, in part, only through additional research.

Second, globalization—the growing interdependence among enterprises, economies, and governments—complicates any effort to improve or protect health, placing many risk factors beyond the department's control. For example, the globalization of the food supply has the potential to introduce a wide range of contaminants. Organisms that produce infectious diseases can now move rapidly through air travel and the movement of people across countries. Changing demographics, including high levels of immigration into the United States from every continent, introduce a greater range of health behavior and present cultural differences that create communication and health education challenges.

Third, the burdens imposed by disease and disability do not lend themselves to the equal or "fair" distribution of government protections that citizens influenced by almost a half century of advances in civil rights and consumer advocacy now expect. Some diseases of great severity, prevalence, and emotional cost have as yet no known treatment, so their victims suffer disproportionately. Some populations are at greater risk of certain diseases or complications, so they too suffer more than others. Children, the mentally ill and developmentally disabled, and other vulnerable groups cannot readily advocate for better health care for themselves. And, access to care is not uniformly available nationwide, since health professionals generally gravitate to larger, more prosperous communities, leaving many rural and low-income communities underserved.

Fourth and finally, HHS has an extraordinarily broad reach throughout the U.S. health care system and many types of relationships:

- Through its payment programs, HHS exerts regulatory influence over virtually all acute care hospitals, most physician practices, and many other health care providers. It affects more than 80 million Medicare and Medicaid beneficiaries (U.S. Census Bureau, 2008) and influences the flow of health information they receive.

- Through grants and contracts, HHS relates to health departments in every state and territory and to the nation's 2,800 local health departments (NACCHO, 2006).
- Through service, research, and payment programs, HHS responds to hundreds of organizations advocating for people with low incomes or who have specific diseases or disabilities and their families, children in Head Start, and the elderly who need meals at home or supportive services.
- Through its operation of over 700 health facilities, HHS provides a vital source of health care to American Indians and Alaska Natives, groups who suffer disproportionately from the burden of chronic disease.
- Through regulation, HHS reaches the manufacturers and suppliers of pharmaceuticals and medical devices, food processors and cosmetics manufacturers, and health care providers and professionals of all kinds and in all localities.
- Through its research agenda, HHS supports the nation's biomedical and health research community, health insurers, and health plans.
- Finally, through its funding for health professions training, HHS interacts with the medical schools and other health professions educational programs that represent the future health care workforce.

In short, HHS is an integral and central figure in a technology-intensive sector that now makes up nearly one-sixth of the nation's economy (Catlin et al., 2008), which continues to grow rapidly, and that vitally concerns every individual, family, employer, and community in the nation. HHS must be able to adapt to changing circumstances in a timely manner, take an active part in reforms of the health system, and solve problems creatively, using solid evidence and sound science.

AN IMPROVED ALIGNMENT

Alignment, or unification of strategy and activities throughout an organization, has become extraordinarily important in progressive parts of the private sector, infusing employees of large firms with a sense of common purpose and a common approach to the future. Alignment also has been working its way into some parts of the public sector, such as the

Department of Defense. HHS should go further in embracing this concept across its health and human services agencies. When programs are uncoordinated or operate at cross-purposes, less value is obtained.

It will not be possible to align all department activities with the recommended small number of goals, owing to agencies' and programs' existing responsibilities and commitments, many of which are congressionally mandated. However, a concerted effort should be made, especially within the department's major units, to evaluate their current missions, goals, responsibilities, and available resources to ensure that, insofar as possible, they are aligned with the department's overarching vision, mission, and goals.

Related Recommendation

a. The heads of all department units should ensure that their *activities and operations are aligned* with the department's vision, mission, and goals and marshal their resources to achieve them.

LIMIT THE NUMBER OF PEOPLE REPORTING TO THE SECRETARY

Many of this report's recommendations begin with "The secretary" not because the committee believes that every decision should emanate from the secretary's office, but simply because the person in that position bears ultimate responsibility for departmental operations. While the secretary needs a good rapport with the President, in addition to strong leadership and management skills, the committee places equal importance on the need for these skills among agency heads, who also must possess strong scientific and technical expertise and be able to work as a team led and coordinated, through some internal arrangement, by the secretary's office.

Currently, 30 official positions report directly to the secretary (HHS, 2008). These positions are as powerfully endowed as the administrator of the Centers for Medicare and Medicaid Services, which is responsible for 85 percent of all HHS expenditures, and as narrowly focused as the director of the Center for Faith-Based and Community Initiatives. The surgeon general is not among those who report directly to the secretary and possibly should be.

Management theory and research generally suggest that the larger the organization, the fewer the number of people who should report directly to its chief executive officer (Hattrup and Kleiner, 1993). With such a wide a span of control, the secretary has little time to work with individuals on their plans for new and existing programs, implementing strategies, or improving operations. The secretary's role should be to concentrate on major emerging problems, or controversies, and on a handful of major initiatives, such as health reform, on the department's budget and key appointments, and to serve as "ambassador" for the department to other cabinet agencies, Congress, and the private health sector.

To create a new level of senior officials—including perhaps an undersecretary, powerful assistant secretaries, or some other configuration—might require congressional approval, but would follow the norm of other cabinet-level departments. HHS now has no undersecretary; by contrast, most departments have about three. While the committee endorses the need for streamlined reporting to the secretary, it does not make recommendations about specific configurations of positions and responsibilities, noting that such choices may be a matter of style or preference. To illustrate how such officials could possibly be deployed:

- A subcabinet-level position could be created for each of HHS's four main "business lines": reimbursement, regulation, research, and direct services provision. The difficulty with the business lines approach is that many agencies are deeply involved in some combination of these activities. However, there are advantages in clustering agencies by their primary function.
- Such an official could oversee cross-cutting departmental functions around policy, operations, information technology, communications, and budget.
- A subcabinet-level official could oversee all of the agencies of the Public Health Service (PHS), whose functions should complement and reinforce each other. This would have the advantage of bringing more coherence to the various agencies. This model was used for a number of years when the assistant secretary for health (ASH) oversaw these agencies.
- A subcabinet-level official could oversee cross-department activities, envisioned in Recommendation 5.

- Alternatively, the department's major health-related line functions, including key agency heads (such as NIH, FDA, CDC, CMS) and the surgeon general, could report directly to the secretary, while other agency heads and staff functions could report to a single subordinate, such as the deputy secretary.

Having a smaller number of senior subcabinet-level officials reporting directly to the secretary would enable better management and coordination of agency directors, aid in the development of cross-cutting policies, facilitate collaboration, and ensure consistency (alignment) across agencies, while allowing individual agency directors to focus on their agency responsibilities and pay less attention to political pressures. While day-to-day operations could be managed by a new senior official (or officials), agency heads should, of course, always have direct access to the secretary for major policy decisions, budget planning, and in times of crisis. The committee also recognized a number of disadvantages to this approach, strongest among them that it could dissuade some talented individuals from accepting appointment to high-profile and influential posts—such as the directorships of FDA, NIH, and CDC—if it moved them a level down the chain of command and limited direct access to the secretary. The scope of responsibilities of the agency heads would remain the same with this streamlined approach, but the coherence of agency activities to the department's mission would be enhanced. Talented and experienced individuals will be attracted to top HHS positions because of their confidence in the leadership and direction of the department.

The committee recognizes—and recent experience indicates—that individual secretaries will have different management styles and that some will want to centralize management in their office, while others will rely more heavily on subcabinet officials, such as an ASH, to manage the department. There are instances in which both styles have worked well. In either case, secretaries generally should encourage initiative and creativity at the program level. Often the best ideas come from the agency heads who are most deeply involved in the specifics of their unit's work.

Whatever internal configuration is chosen for the secretary's office, the objective should be to encourage feedback loops across departmental units, so that they communicate with and learn more readily from each other, can align policies and programs more effectively, and work toward common goals. Whether that coordination rests with one or two people in the secretary's office or by closer collaboration among a larger group of senior officials, it needs to happen.

Similarly, regardless of the secretary's management style, it is essential that there be in place a process for making policy and operational decisions that is *rigorous*, so that decisions are made based on the best evidence; *clear*, so that the department's many agencies and programs can stay in alignment; and *efficient*, so that the processes are not redundant and that decisions are responsive and timely. This process includes consideration of how the organization will be *accountable for the results* of the decision and how it will measure or evaluate the decision's results.

Related Recommendation

b. The secretary should reduce directly reporting senior-level officials to *a manageable number.* Although secretarial management styles differ, a rigorous decision-making process for both policy and operations must be established, along with accountability for results.

AN EMPOWERED SURGEON GENERAL

Americans have learned to look to, and trust, the U.S. surgeon general for impartial, scientifically valid information about health risks and health improvement:

- In 1964 Surgeon General Luther L. Terry issued the landmark report declaring smoking hazardous to health.
- In the 1970s Surgeon General Julius B. Richmond advanced childhood immunizations and many other health promotion and disease prevention measures.
- In the 1980s Surgeon General C. Everett Koop, living up to his iconic status as a "straight talker," demanded greater attention to HIV/AIDS.
- In the 1990s Surgeon General David Satcher advocated action to provide mental health parity, reduce health disparities, and end discrimination based on sexual orientation, and reinvigorated the campaign to control tobacco.

Since the Office of Surgeon General was established in 1871, only 17 individuals have held the office on a permanent (not "acting") basis. The surgeon general holds the three-star rank of vice admiral, reports to the ASH, and serves a four-year term, which can be renewed for a second term. Since the expiration of Richard Carmona's four-year term in July 2006, the United States has not had a permanent surgeon general.

The surgeon general also oversees the operation of the 6,000 public health professionals in the Commissioned Corps of the Public Health Service, who serve in full-time capacities in agencies and programs throughout the federal government. Commissioned Corps members are available around the clock to meet public health emergencies anywhere in the United States and, sometimes, the world. Because of the emergency nature of these assignments, the surgeon general must have a smoothly operating management structure and good communication with the ASH, the assistant secretary for preparedness and response, and other HHS agencies involved in emergency response, in order to enable rapid mobilization.[1]

The President appoints the surgeon general, subject to Senate confirmation, and on occasion these appointments have proved controversial. Surgeon General Joycelyn Elders held an expansive view of sex education, which made her a lightning rod for criticism and led to her exit from office (Elders, 1996). After Surgeon General Richard Carmona left office, he accused the administration of silencing him on embryonic stem cell research, abstinence-only sex education, contraception, climate change, prison health, and mental health, and discouraging him from supporting the Special Olympics (Harris, 2007).

In July 2007 testimony before the House Committee on Oversight and Government Reform, former Surgeon General C. Everett Koop said that, when working on his report on HIV/AIDS and a subsequent mailer, he and the secretary had to maintain strict secrecy throughout the process. If they had "followed protocol and had every word scrutinized by the secretary's secretariat," he said, "these reports, because of their nature and plain speaking, would not have seen the light of day" (Koop, 2007). Although the nation's senior health advocate should speak with discretion, the surgeon general should be free to openly discuss important

---

[1]In recent years, the surgeon general has deployed these well-trained individuals to respond to the terrorist attacks of 9/11 and to natural disasters, including Hurricanes Katrina and Rita and the Indian Ocean tsunami, where they provided medical and public health services and humanitarian assistance.

health topics and educate the public on evidence-based prevention and health promotion strategies.

To ensure the independence of this uniquely trusted office—and the politically unfettered advocacy for improved health of the American people—the surgeon general should not be subject to an appointment process influenced by partisan pressures.[2] Alternatives to help guarantee the surgeon general's independent voice include the following:

- Establish the custom that a prestigious committee oriented to science and health would identify and review candidates and recommend a panel of three or four highly qualified candidates, from which the President could choose (similar to the appointment process for the undersecretary for health in the Department of Veterans Affairs; the process, specified in law [38 USC §305], also stipulates that the appointment should be "without regard to political affiliation or activity").
- Establish a tradition that such a committee would authoritatively evaluate the President's choice of a prospective surgeon general's credentials before the appointment is sent to the Senate.
- Secure bipartisanship support prior to an appointment, for example, by consultation with the chair and ranking member of the Senate Committee on Health, Education, Labor, and Pensions.

These types of processes would respond to most of the reforms recommended by a recent National Academies committee as ways to ensure the best science and technology appointments for government by addressing the need to attract the best leadership; make appointments speedily; provide continuity; improve the process by which candidates are nominated, cleared, and confirmed; and broaden the pool of potential candidates (NRC, 2008). Such processes could be equally well employed in filling other top departmental positions, such as those discussed in the next section.

Related Recommendation

[2]The role of the surgeon general has been taken up by some members of the 110th Congress, including proposed legislation that would strengthen the role of the surgeon general as America's health advocate (the Surgeon General Restoration Authority Act [S. 1777] and the Surgeon General Independence Act [H.R. 3447]).

c. **The secretary should ensure *a more prominent and powerful role* for the surgeon general, who, in addition to leading the Commissioned Corps, should be a *strong advocate for the health of the American people* and work actively to *educate Americans on important health issues*. The secretary should work with the President and Congress to *establish a process for identifying surgeon general candidates* for Presidential appointment *that gives high priority to qualifications and leadership*, and Congress is strongly urged to consider a *longer term* for this office.**

A PROTECTED CORPS OF SCIENTIFIC LEADERS

Continuity, competence, and scientific integrity will be enhanced to the extent that heads of HHS's science agencies—primarily NIH, CDC, FDA, and AHRQ—are appointed without regard to politics and may remain in their positions for fixed terms that may straddle presidential transitions. Given the importance of these positions to protecting the public's health, they should be filled quickly after vacancies occur. Indeed, any new secretary's team should be put in place without undue delays.

When the White House and the secretary select top departmental officials—and when Congress considers their confirmation—they should not impose an ideological test, but should look for leadership and management qualifications, as well as scientific or technical expertise. The latter is of particular importance because the secretary's primary skills are likely to be focused on management and leadership. These departmental officials must be able to

- assess competing scientific opinions and recognize when the science remains inconclusive,
- balance scientific interests and uncertainty with the practicalities of resource limitations,
- authoritatively fend off doctrinaire demands while respecting diverse human values, and
- have a strategic perspective to enable them to anticipate and shape the evolution of cutting-edge research, public health and human services program initiatives, and regulatory oversight.

As a previous IOM committee remarked, "Healthy organizations require effective and stable leadership" (IOM, 2007). Once key officials are selected, they need to be in place long enough to appreciate fully the challenges, pressures, and opportunities their agencies face; to understand the strengths and weaknesses of major units and staff leaders; to effectively plan ways to build on strengths and shore up deficits; to become effective advocates for their agencies; to build productive relationships with the secretary, key agency staff, and important players outside the agency; and, in general, to carry out the administration's, department's, and agency's immediate and long-term priorities. Such facility is not acquired overnight, which is one reason the committee endorses prompt filling of key scientific agency positions.

The committee is also persuaded that it would be helpful for Congress and the secretary to consider whether longer fixed-term appointments would be beneficial in establishing continuity and improving performance. Previous reports from the Government Accountability Office (GAO) and the National Academy of Sciences have reported that turnover in government agency leaders "is linked with a focus on short-term goals and uncertain accountability and that fixed terms ... help to ensure stability and strengthen an agency's leadership" (IOM, 2007).

The committee recognizes that an administration or secretary may have strong candidates of their own for these positions and that solid, trusting working relationships between the secretary and agency heads are essential. However, if agency head appointments are, as recommended, based on leadership, management skills, and scientific expertise, with minimal political considerations, then incumbents to these positions may well survive a change in administration. The committee recommends that multiyear, fixed terms be considered,[3] because it would support greater management and intellectual continuity—especially for research projects with long trajectories—avoid at least some turnover that may be unnecessary, decrease the amount of time that top leadership posts are vacant, and might attract more individuals to serve, particularly when a vacancy occurs in the latter stages of an administration.

Nothing in this recommendation is meant to suggest that the President or secretary would not have the authority to remove individuals for

[3]Note that the director of the National Science Foundation and the commissioner of the Social Security Administration currently have six-year terms; that commissioners of the Federal Communications Commission have five-year terms; and that past IOM committees likewise recommended a six-year term for the NIH Director and FDA Commissioner.

cause, at any stage in their tenure. A potential problem with this approach, in a new administration, could be that the incumbent would be seen as an "outsider" in an almost wholly new department team and not integrate well with the new staff. Of course conflicts among staff members can occur regardless of whether they are holdovers or brand new, and such impediments to teamwork are a not uncommon management problem.

Related Recommendations

d. **The secretary should work with the President and Congress to establish a selection process for the department's senior-level officials that *protects the scientific and administrative integrity of major departmental units*, *promotes progress toward departmental goals*, and is *based primarily on the candidates' qualifications and experience.* Congress again is strongly urged to consider *longer terms* for some of these officials—especially the directors of NIH and CDC, and the commissioner of FDA—which would provide critical continuity in the nation's public health and scientific endeavors.**
e. **The President should make timely appointments and Congress should expedite the confirmation process for key HHS officials, including the secretary, deputy secretary, surgeon general, and the heads of FDA and NIH. Secretarial appointments, such as the director of CDC, also should be expedited.**

AN INTEGRATED PUBLIC HEALTH AGENDA

HHS's challenges are especially profound in the public health arena. *Public health, in contrast to health care, focuses on disease and injury prevention rather than treatment, and on measures to improve and safe-*

guard the health of entire populations rather than individual patients.[4] Flexibility, adaptability, and creativity will allow HHS to respond effectively to urgent public health challenges as they arise and make progress toward solving persistent public health problems facing the American people.

HHS's ultimate role is to improve and safeguard the health and well-being of the American people. "Good health" at the personal level depends on the individual's biology and genetics, behavior, lifestyle, and social, economic, and physical environment, as mediated by public health, social, economic, and environmental factors, and health care over the course of an individual's life (Figure 3-1). "Population health" depends on the same factors, but at the "30,000-foot level." Population health also can be influenced by conditions determined by governmental public health and social services infrastructure (both federal and state), communities, health care delivery systems, employers and business, the media, and academia (IOM, 2002a). This means that many important factors affecting health—at either level—lie outside the control of the department's health and human services agencies, and that the department influences several other factors only indirectly. Exercising so little direct influence, HHS must be focused in its health promotion efforts and evolve with changing circumstances, and it must be the leading advocate within the federal government, and with the American people, for achieving population health.

The federal government provides financial support for the nation's health in a variety of ways, which include providing direct payment for about a quarter of the nation's health care services (mostly through Medicare and Medicaid), tax breaks on premiums that are paid by employers, and funding for most of the country's public health activities. Its investments in health care services dwarf spending on public health. Less than three percent of combined government and private health expenditures, and only six percent of government health expenditures, are directed to public health (Catlin et al., 2008). With so few resources, the public health system must be efficient and well aligned, *as well as* flexible and creative, to serve the American people adequately. Federal programs must learn and share all they can from on-the-ground experiences at the state and local levels to promote quality improvements.

---

[4]A 1988 Institute of Medicine report articulated core public health functions at the federal, state, and local level (IOM, 1988).

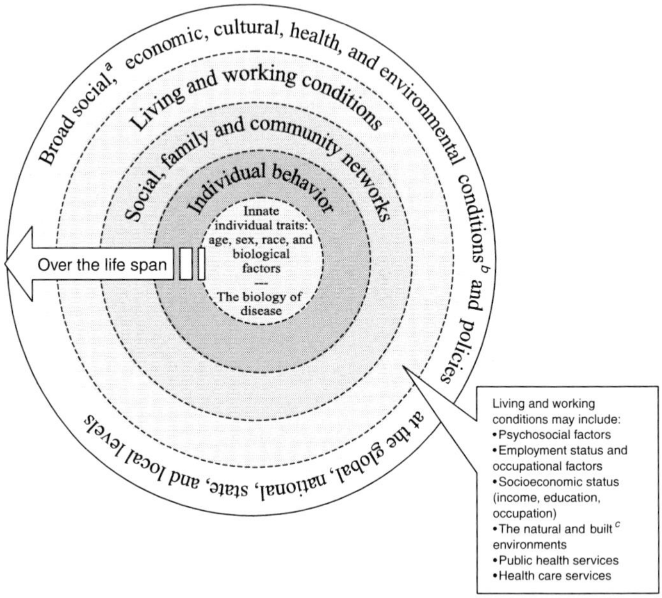

FIGURE 3-1 Key factors in personal and population health.
[a]Social conditions include economic inequality, urbanization, mobility, cultural values, and attitudes and policies related to discrimination.
[b]Other national conditions might include major sociopolitical shifts, such as recession, war, and government collapse.
[c]The built environment includes transportation, water and sanitation, housing, and urban planning (Worthman, 1999).
SOURCE: Adapted from Dahlgren and Whitehead (1991), as printed in *The Future of the Public's Health in the 21st Century* (IOM, 2002b).

Some prominent former HHS leaders have advocated that a population-health model be implemented across the department (Boufford and Lee, 2001). In 2002, the Institute of Medicine recommended adoption of "a population health approach that considers the multiple determinants of health." That committee also recommended strengthening the governmental public health infrastructure (both federal and state), building partnerships across diverse communities, enhancing communication within the public health system, and, like the authors of this report, recommended improved systems of accountability and strengthening evidence for decision making (IOM, 2002a).

The committee believes that evidence-based public health strategies should infuse all departmental programs, including the reimbursement and research programs. This model would, for example: emphasize prevention in Medicare and Medicaid and in NIH, enabling these different types of programs to positively reinforce each other; recognize the importance of supporting services, such as the nutrition programs provided by the Administration on Aging that in the past 36 years have served seniors more than six billion meals, or the vital work of Head Start, which produces not just educational outcomes for participating children, but improvements in their health and beneficial effects on parents.

Attributes of an integrated public health agenda, in addition to helping create an aligned and coherent mission, as discussed above and in Chapter 2, would include the following:

- *Insistence that public health interventions, as well as medical services, create value*—they should produce improvements or benefits for the greatest number of individuals, to the most vulnerable populations, to the greatest degree possible, and at the lowest cost.
- *Calculation of the full value of public health services*—value should not be determined by just measuring the costs and benefits to the health sector, but should also include estimates of societal costs and benefits. For example, public health programs to urge the use of child car seats can prevent injuries that would not only require expensive medical care (health costs), but also special education (education costs) and lifelong disability payments (social welfare costs and lost productivity).
- *An emphasis on health behavior, disease prevention, and health literacy*—health literacy requires that individuals have the capacity to obtain, process, and understand basic health information and services so they can make appropriate health decisions (HHS, 2000); at the same time, it requires that the information provided be culturally and linguistically appropriate.
- *Interdepartmental and cross-departmental approaches*—representatives of diverse units of HHS—and in some cases, other departments[5]—should coordinate related activities to avoid

[5]The Departments of Agriculture, Defense, Education, Energy, Homeland Security, Interior, Labor, Transportation, Treasury, Veterans Affairs, and the Environmental Protection Agency all play a role in some aspect of health policy (see Box 2-1).

gaps, duplication, and contradictory or inconsistent federal policies.

- *Fostering effective partnerships*—partnerships may be with state and local health and human services departments, health care providers and professionals, consumer groups, organizations that represent and serve people with chronic diseases or disabilities and their family caregivers, and other community-based organizations.
- *Strict avoidance of partisan politics* in program design and in selection of personnel (Shalala, 1998).
- *Adopting only those policies that are supported by evidence of effectiveness* or are consistent with established public health or health services research findings.
- *Focusing on, and investing in, human capital*—attention to improving the workforce within and outside the department is necessary, to ensure high performance within HHS, the public health sector, and the health care system in general (Walker, 2003; see also Chapter 5).

Effective leadership by the secretary is essential to charting and integrating the public health agenda. As Secretary Leavitt has said (Schaeffer, 2007):

> My job as "the leader" is to decide where we ought to go, to be effective in persuading other people that that's the right destination, organizing all of the elements to conspire toward that end, and then making sure that there's a system and a series of incentives that enable it.

Related Recommendation

f. **The secretary should ensure that *all department health programs, including the reimbursement programs, reinforce public health priorities and strategies* in order to provide a consistent framework for protecting the public from health risks, promoting health, preventing disease and disability, and providing health services for vulnerable**

populations in the most efficient, cost-effective ways.

A STRENGTHENED SCIENCE BASE

A recent report examining presidential appointments affirms (NRC, 2008):

> The nation requires exceptionally able scientists and engineers in top executive positions and on federal advisory committees to weigh available data, to consider the advice of scientists and technical specialists, and in the case of presidential appointees to make key management, programmatic, and policy decisions.

In HHS, the kinds of scientific expertise needed are broad: they include biomedical scientists doing laboratory and clinical research, behavioral scientists, statisticians and epidemiologists, health services researchers, policy analysts, economists, and others applying their skills to solving problems that range from the size of a molecule to the size of the health care system.

Although much of this report dwells on the applied sciences, especially health services research and systems analysis, the committee recognizes that basic biomedical research is essential to achieving continued medical progress. Many significant diseases still do not have effective prevention or treatment options. Prime examples are Alzheimer's disease, pancreatic cancer, autism, amyotrophic lateral sclerosis, schizophrenia, and many genetic conditions. These are not the "new threats" to which this report often refers, but rather well-known problems that require new knowledge or new approaches to solve.

The department explicitly acknowledges the importance of scientific research. As one of four goals in its five-year strategic plan, its "scientific research and development" goal aims to "advance scientific and biomedical research and development related to health and human services" (HHS, 2007). The objectives supporting this goal would

- strengthen the pool of qualified health, biomedical, and behavioral science researchers;

- increase basic scientific knowledge to improve human health and human development;
- conduct and oversee applied research to improve health and well-being; and
- communicate and transfer research results into clinical, public health, and human service practice (HHS, 2007).

To the greatest extent feasible, HHS policies and programs should incorporate and be informed by current scientific knowledge and evidence-based practices. Using results of applied research on program effectiveness and valid evaluations, as discussed in Chapter 4, HHS also should promote best practices in health care, public health, and program management. For this to happen, the department needs to strengthen its science base across the board. A credible, transparent process should also be developed to resolve scientific disputes that arise when evidence does not provide definitive answers or when there are disagreements among experts in the interpretation of that evidence.

Especially when scientific findings are inconclusive, the door is opened for policy decisions that are based on nonscientific grounds and "political pressure" from various sources. But in all cases, policy should rely most heavily on best available scientific evidence. There are many examples, from the current and previous administrations, in which political interference has influenced policy and diverged from sound, available evidence. These include decisions relating to fundamental HHS responsibilities:

- *Biomedical research funding* has been affected, such as the elimination of federal funding for embryonic stem cell research on cell lines established after 2001, despite the potential value of such research (IOM, 2005).
- Federal funding for needle-exchange programs, a *proven HIV/AIDS prevention strategy*, has been withheld since 1988, although these programs are effective in reducing the spread of HIV without increasing illegal drug use or encouraging new users (IOM, 1995).
- *Effective family planning methods*, such as contraceptives, have not been promoted, but instead, an "abstinence-only" approach has been embraced (Union of Concerned Scientists, 2004), despite its ineffectiveness in reducing sexually transmitted infec-

tions and unintended pregnancies (DiCenso et al., 2002; Underhill et al., 2007).

- *Findings contained in scientific reports* have been compromised and scientists muzzled. Former Surgeon General Richard Carmona said that "top officials delayed for years and tried to 'water down' [his] landmark report" on the effects of secondhand smoke (Harris, 2007). Former Surgeon General David Satcher's initial attempts to publish a report on sexual health in the late 1990s were thwarted by the White House in light of increased political sensitivity to these issues (Satcher, 2007).
- *Testimony before congressional committees*. CDC Director Julie Gerberding's statement before a Senate committee on the health effects of global warming was cut in half by the White House, with references to the health effects of climate change removed (Revkin, 2007).

The department's policy-making role is credible only to the extent that it is based on sound science. In the regulatory sphere, for example, the link between valid, reliable information and policies must be strong enough to meet legal challenges, as well as critiques by members of Congress, the news media, organizations representing various HHS constituencies, and the public. In short, decision makers must have access to scientific findings, transparent methods of reviewing them, free of influence by the regulated industries, and plausible ways to resolve questions when scientific findings conflict or are inconclusive (Wagner and Steinzor, 2006).

Basing policy on the best science can directly serve patient interests and protect the public's health. Through the years, policies developed by Medicare have played a leadership role in clinical areas by, for example

- mandating the replacement of hospital wards with semiprivate rooms, which helps control the spread of infection;
- ending racial segregation of hospitals, which led to better care for African Americans;
- covering influenza immunizations (CDC, 1993);
- providing data that permitted analysis of both costs and effectiveness of selected new medical technologies (Coye and Kell, 2006; Hlatky et al., 2005);
- using quality rankings to promote certain best practices in inpatient care and group practice by physicians;

- using evidence-based quality measures in producing hospital and state report cards and in pay-for-performance (P4P) quality incentive initiatives (IOM, 2006); and
- implementing "coverage with evidence development," a new concept of making evidence generation a condition of coverage.

Related Recommendation

g. To maximize value in the health care system, the secretary must *strengthen the scientific base and capabilities of the department* and ensure that *agencies' research findings* are shared department-wide and that *current best evidence is used for departmental decision making, including the CMS reimbursement policy.*

STABILIZED RESEARCH FUNDING

Scientific research projects typically extend well beyond a single fiscal year. Predictability in funding is important, and delays in budget approvals can be especially injurious to the large, multiyear, multi-institutional, multidisciplinary projects that now distinguish scientific inquiry (IOM, 2003), from which so much has been learned about disease risk factors and treatments (NHLBI, 2007).

HHS's use of, and support for, science can be impeded by uncertainties about the department's annual budget, especially during extended congressional consideration. For example, the 2009 HHS budget appears unlikely to be adopted until February 2009, with the government operating under a continuing resolution bill enacted in September 2008. Under previous continuing resolutions, NIH has given investigators with ongoing projects 80 percent of their approved budgets for the continuing resolution period, typically a few months. Unfortunately, when a budget is delayed until over a third of the fiscal year has elapsed, this can have a significant impact on research funding. Because of the below-inflation percentage increase in the 2009 proposed President's budget for NIH, if the agency is funded at that level, it may be forced to award fewer grants in fiscal year 2010 (Bhattacharjee et al., 2008).

Budget delays—and any perception that HHS is a less-than-hospitable environment for scientists—compound difficulties in recruiting and retaining the quality and quantity of scientists needed to support agency missions—whether in the biomedical sciences, social sciences, biostatistics and epidemiology, or health services research.

Budgets of HHS science agencies have fluctuated greatly in recent years. NIH and CDC experienced large increases after 2000 (see Figure 1-3 in Chapter 1) and then saw little growth or experienced actual reductions in funding. Multiyear budget planning for these vital agencies would be helpful. Serious concerns also have been raised about the *adequacy* of funding of HHS science agencies, with the news media reporting that recent budget cuts threaten gains in the public's health (Fox, 2008; Harris, 2008; Trapp, 2008).

Since 2002, AHRQ has not had its own separate budget allocation, but receives funds from other PHS agencies through a PHS evaluation set-aside. This has left the agency's budget an order-of-magnitude smaller than every other major PHS agency except FDA, whose budget is still five times that of AHRQ.[6] AHRQ's mission is to support, conduct, and disseminate research that improves access to care and the outcomes, quality, cost, and utilization of health care services—in other words, to increase the value of the health care services Americans receive. Research projects in AHRQ's diverse portfolio investigate nearly every aspect of the U.S. health care system, and AHRQ works with both the public and the private sectors to conduct and sponsor research and translate its research findings into improved clinical practice. The agency also attempts to refine decision-making techniques and practices, such as comparative effectiveness studies and evidence-based medicine.

To make progress in developing and applying critical analytic tools to today's health care organization, delivery, and financing challenges, AHRQ requires a more reliable and viable funding stream. Giving AHRQ an independent budget, adequate to its task, is essential to achieving the accountability and the value-based health system the committee envisions.

---

[6]In 2007, the program level budget for AHRQ was $319 million and for FDA just over $2 billion.

Related Recommendation

h. Congress should allocate *sufficient, predictable funding for NIH, CDC, FDA, and AHRQ* in order to preserve and enhance these agencies' scientific missions. Congress should also establish a *specific budget line for AHRQ* that is *independent* of appropriations to other HHS agencies.

A FORTIFIED STRUCTURE OF FOOD SAFETY REGULATION

There are many opportunities for reorganization within HHS—and indeed across federal departments—that would bring more coherence, reduce overlaps and redundancy, and create more efficiency. Changes of this sort can be extremely difficult, time consuming, and highly controversial. They involve obtaining new authorizing legislation, the reassignment of large budgets and significant numbers of people, the opposition of powerful special interest groups, both expected and unexpected disruptions in work, and other implementation difficulties. Creation of the new Department of Homeland Security was a case in point: Only at a time when Congress and the nation felt a sense of severe crisis could such a massive reorganization have occurred so swiftly, but even with that utmost sense of urgency, the transition was far from smooth.

For these reasons, the IOM committee so far has avoided suggesting the reorganization of agencies within HHS or across departments. However, the seriousness of the food safety issue prompted the committee to use it as an example of a public health issue that HHS *cannot address adequately within its current structure*, which is the reason some reorganization would be both logical and advantageous, despite the difficulties. Proposed consolidation of the food safety activities of FDA and the USDA's Food Safety and Inspection Service (FSIS) is not merely illustrative, however, since its potential to benefit the health of the American public is so great that it is included among the committee's recommendations.[7]

Nowhere is the weakness of HHS's science base more apparent or potentially harmful than in FDA's food safety regulatory activities. A candid report recently prepared for the FDA Science Board found (FDA Subcommittee on Science and Technology, 2007):

> The nation's food supply is at risk. Crisis management in FDA's two food safety centers, Center for Food Safety and Applied Nutrition and Center for Veterinary Medicine, has drawn attention and resources away from FDA's ability to develop the science base and infrastructure needed to efficiently support innovation in the food industry, provide effective routine surveillance, and conduct emergency outbreak investigation activities to protect the food supply. *FDA's inability to keep up with scientific advances means that American lives are at risk.*[8] [Emphasis added.]

In part, this state of affairs reflects deficits in both the number and the expertise of FDA's scientific workforce: "[D]espite the significant increase in workload during the past two decades, in 2007 the number of appropriated personnel remained essentially the same—resulting in major gaps of scientific expertise in key areas.... The turnover rate in FDA science staff in key scientific areas is twice that of other government agencies" (FDA Subcommittee on Science and Technology, 2007). In fact, in the past three years, one-fifth of the science staff and 600 inspec-

---

[7]Food safety issues have garnered a great deal of attention in Congress. A search for bills in the 110th Congress related to "food safety" returns over 100, with some calling for improved coordination and unification of the food safety inspection activities (e.g., H.R. 2297 and H.R. 7143), which the Senate Committee on Governmental Affairs concluded was necessary over 30 years ago when it called for a single food safety agency (Senate Committee on Governmental Affairs, 1977).

[8]The Subcommittee on Science and Technology concluded that "science at the FDA is in a precarious position: the Agency suffers from serious scientific deficiencies and is not positioned to meet current or emerging regulatory responsibilities." The report indicates that the science base of the entire agency is lacking, not just in the area of food safety, and is in need of reinforcement (FDA Subcommittee on Science and Technology, 2007). A discussion earlier in this chapter calls for a strengthened science base for HHS, including FDA.

tors have left FDA's Center for Food Safety and Applied Nutrition (TFAH, 2008).

Within the department, the organization of food safety responsibilities and information technology infrastructure is inadequate (FDA Subcommittee on Science and Technology, 2007). There are three separately managed components of FDA with major food safety responsibilities—the Center for Food Safety and Applied Nutrition, the Center for Veterinary Medicine, and the Office of Regulatory Affairs, which oversees FDA's field force and controls the majority of the agency's food safety resources. FDA has established an assistant commissioner for foods "to provide advice and counsel to the Commissioner on strategic and substantive food safety and food defense matters" (FDA, 2007a). However, there is no FDA official whose full-time job is food safety *and* who has line and budget authority over the three food safety operating components. Moreover, monitoring any food-related outbreaks that occur—the vital food safety epidemiology function—is managed and operated by CDC.

Ensuring the safety of the food supply is an expanding—and visible—governmental responsibility.[9] In the era of globalization, when the United States increasingly uses foreign sources for raw and processed foods, contamination of food sources has become much more common. Sixty percent of the fresh fruits and vegetables and 75 percent of the seafood that Americans consume is imported, but FDA inspects only an estimated one percent of these imports (TFAH, 2008), and some analysts estimate that tests for U.S.-produced foods dropped nearly 75 percent between 2003 and 2006 (Bridges, 2007).

Bacteria and other potentially injurious organisms are transported easily across the nation or between countries in containers or through human travel; chemical contamination can occur in processing, storage, or transport, especially in nations with lax inspection systems. These problems have been illustrated in recent, widely publicized outbreaks of food-borne illnesses, such as the 2008 *Salmonella* outbreak, involving imported raw jalapeño and serrano peppers, which affected some 1,400 individuals (CDC, 2008).

---

[9]The USDA, which is responsible only for meat, poultry, and processed egg products, spends twice as much on food safety as does FDA, which is responsible for all other foodstuffs. USDA's FSIS has a budget of more than $1 billion (USDA, 2008a) and a workforce of more than 9,000 (USDA, 2008b), many of whom are deployed at inspection sites around the country.

What the Government Accountability Office has called "the patchwork nature of the federal oversight of food safety" compromises the federal government's ability to keep up with fast-evolving food safety challenges (GAO, 2007). Food regulation is diffused across at least 12 agencies, including FDA, USDA's FSIS, the National Marine Fisheries Service of the Commerce Department, the Environmental Protection Agency (regulating pesticides) (IOM, 1998), and the Department of Homeland Security (coordinating federal food security activities). Costly duplication and potentially dangerous inconsistencies result, affecting such jointly regulated aspects as importation facilities (GAO, 2007).

As one of many examples of costly duplication and inefficiency, USDA and FDA inspect different types of imported food, but they do not share resources. USDA officials are present every day in import inspection facilities, many of which also receive and store FDA-regulated products. But FDA inspectors appear less frequently, so foods often "remain at the facilities for some time," since USDA has no jurisdiction over them (Walker, 2007).

Although many agencies are involved in food safety, none "has ultimate authority or responsibility, so accountability for the total system is limited. No one person in the federal government has the oversight and accountability for carrying out comprehensive, preventive strategies for reducing food-borne illness" (TFAH, 2008).

Further, FDA's food safety authority, like its authority over drugs, was constructed decades ago and does not reflect current manufacturing and distribution processes (IOM, 2007). The system remains ill equipped to meet emerging challenges—as an Institute of Medicine (IOM) report concluded a decade ago (IOM, 1998), even before the terrorist events of 2001 heightened concerns about the security of our food supply. Congress should assess the large collection of food safety laws regulating various commodities to determine whether they should be updated and coordinated, in light of an evolving industry, improved science for detecting hazards, trends in contamination, and globalization of food products and ingredients. The goal should be to mount a public health-oriented regulatory program that not only would prevent food-borne illnesses, but also would make rational use of federal food safety resources.

Because of shortcomings and gaps in the existing regulatory structure, the IOM committee recommends uniting the food safety responsibilities of the two largest agencies involved—FDA and FSIS—within HHS, as the most appropriate locus for comprehensive regulation. The committee considered other alternatives including maintaining the current division of responsibility or uniting food safety responsibilities within FSIS. The recent and problematic food safety issues described in this chapter strongly indicate the need for strengthening our ability to monitor the safety of our food supply. The committee believed that the problems cannot be solved within the current structures. There are at least five major reasons for the choice of unifying food safety responsibilities within HHS:

1. The department is dedicated solely to protecting the public, in contrast to USDA, which has additional, industry-fostering purposes, and it is important to immunize food safety regulation from potential undue industry influence.
2. The department is oriented to disease prevention, health promotion, and public health generally. Placing food safety responsibilities within HHS could more effectively link those functions to the overall mission of the department. For example, within HHS, food inspection functions would be closer to the surveillance functions carried out by the CDC.
3. The Committee recognizes the strengths of the FSIS program and the scientific expertise it provides (currently, FDA relies on USDA for much of the science base of food safety regulation). A thoughtful and careful transfer of FSIS functions to HHS and its multiple science-based resources could enhance the capability to more effectively coordinate the use of science to enhance food safety.
4. HHS has full regulatory authority over drugs, and the distinction between foods and drugs is diminishing. We have the advent of "nutriceuticals" and greater acceptance of "health foods" and supplements, and foods are increasingly exposed to antibiotics, irradiation, pesticides, and other chemical interventions, as well as genetic modification.
5. Recognizing the need to strengthen its food safety regulatory operations, FDA recently developed a Food Protection Plan, an integrated strategy to protect the food supply through prevention, intervention, and response (FDA, 2007b).

The IOM committee understands that transferring FSIS functions to the department is likely to be difficult and that similar proposals in the past have been met with resistance:

- It would be a large move, in both budgetary and personnel terms.
- Major revisions to authorizing legislation for FSIS would be needed.
- It would weaken the voice of public health within USDA—obviating the need for the position of USDA undersecretary for food safety, who is currently required by law to have food safety or public health credentials.
- Without additional action, it would sever the food regulatory responsibility from its research base.

For the unification to be effective, it therefore would have to include provisions for (1) ongoing collaboration or relocation of USDA food safety research programs to HHS, and (2) maintaining relationships with USDA programs that work to prevent food contaminations on farms. Bringing FSIS—and closer ties to USDA's science programs—into HHS would strengthen U.S. food safety efforts overall.

Finally, because drug regulation so dominates the current FDA,[10] the committee was not persuaded that the unified food safety function should be lodged automatically within that agency. Creation of a new, focused food safety entity might be preferable. In any case, the advantages to the public of unifying food safety regulatory authority within a health-focused department far exceed the disadvantages. The nation no longer should have to rely on excessively compartmentalized, fragmented, and inconsistent regulatory procedures to ensure that the food Americans eat is safe for human consumption.

Related Recommendation

i. **To address the growing threat of food-borne illnesses, Congress should *unify the USDA's Food Safety and Inspection Service and the food safety activities of FDA within HHS* and ensure provision of adequate resources for high-quality inspection, enforcement, and research.**

---

[10]Internally, the ratio of FDA's budget spent on food, compared to that spent on human drugs, has shrunk markedly—from 0.89:1 in 2000 to 0.73:1 in 2009 (FDA, 2008). (That is, in 2000, for every dollar spent on human drugs, the agency spent 89 cents on food safety; in 2009, though budgets for both activities have increased, it spent only 73 cents on food safety for every dollar spent on drugs.)

REFERENCES

Bhattacharjee, Y., J. Kaiser, E. Kintisch, A. Lawler, and J. Mervis. 2008. U.S. science faces a flat 2009. *ScienceNOW* September 29.

Boufford, J., and P. Lee. 2001. *Health policies for the 21st century: Challenges and recommendations for the U.S. Department of Health and Human Services.* New York: Milbank Memorial Fund.

Bridges, A. 2007. Food safety. *Associated Press Archive* February 26.

Catlin, A., C. Cowan, M. Hartman, S. Heffler, and the National Health Expenditure Accounts Team. 2008. National health spending in 2006: A year of change for prescription drugs. *Health Affairs* 27(1):14-29.

CDC (Centers for Disease Control and Prevention). 1993. Perspectives in disease prevention and health promotion final results: Medicare influenza vaccine demonstration—selected states, 1988-1992. *Morbidity & Mortality Weekly Report* 41(August).

CDC. 2008. *Investigation of outbreak of infections caused by* Salmonella saintpaul. http://www.cdc.gov/salmonella/saintpaul (accessed August 20, 2008).

Coye, M., and J. Kell. 2006. How hospitals confront new technology. *Health Affairs* 25:163-173.

Dahlgren, G., and M. Whitehead. 1991. *Policies and strategies to promote social equity in health.* Stockholm, Sweden: Institute for the Futures Studies.

DiCenso, A., G. Guyatt, A. Willan, and L. Griffith. 2002. Interventions to reduce unintended pregnancies among adolescents: Systematic review of randomised controlled trials. *British Medical Journal* 324(7351):1426.

Eisenhower, D. 1953. Special message to the Congress creating the Department of Health, Education, and Welfare. Washington, DC.

Elders, J. 1996. *From sharecropper's daughter to Surgeon General of the United States of America.* New York: William Morrow & Co.

FDA (Food and Drug Administration). 2007a. *FDA commissioner announces new food protection position.* http://www.fda.gov/bbs/topics/NEWS/2007/NEW01622.html (accessed November 6, 2008).

FDA. 2007b. *Food protection plan: An integrated strategy for protecting the nation's food supply.* Washington, DC: FDA.

FDA. 2008. *FY 2009 congressional justification table of contents.* http://www.fda.gov/oc/oms/ofm/budget/2009/TOC.htm (accessed October 27, 2008).

FDA Subcommittee on Science and Technology. 2007. *FDA science and mission at risk.* Washington, DC: FDA Science Board.

Fox, M. 2008. CDC head feels budget bite; Predicts worse. *Reuters*, February 4, 2008.

GAO (Government Accountability Office). 2007. *High-risk series: An update.* Washington, DC: GAO.

Harris, G. 2007. Surgeon General sees 4-year term as compromised. *New York Times*, July 11.

Harris, G. 2008. Panel's bipartisan view—FDA is underfinanced. *New York Times*, April 16.

Hattrup, G., and B. Kleiner. 1993. How to establish the proper span of control for managers. *Industrial Management* 35:28-29.

HHS (Department of Health and Human Services). 2000. *Healthy people 2010.* Washington, DC: HHS.

HHS. 2007. *HHS strategic plan—FY 2007-2012.* http://www.hhs.gov/strategic_plan/ (accessed August 22, 2008).

HHS. 2008. *Department of Health & Human Services organizational chart.* http://www.hhs.gov/about/orgchart.html (accessed September 25, 2008).

Hlatky, M., G. Sanders, and D. Owens. 2005. Evidence-based medicine and policy: The case of the implantable cardioverter defibrillator. *Health Affairs* 24:42-51.

IOM (Institute of Medicine). 1988. *The future of public health.* Washington, DC: National Academy Press.

IOM. 1995. *Preventing HIV transmission: The role of sterile needles and bleach.* Washington, DC: National Academy Press.

IOM. 1998. *Ensuring safe food from production to consumption.* Washington, DC: National Academy Press.

IOM. 2002a. *The future of the public's health in the 21st century.* Washington, DC: The National Academies Press.

IOM. 2002b. *Health insurance is a family matter.* Washington, DC: The National Academies Press.

IOM. 2003. *Enhancing the vitality of the National Institutes of Health: Organizational change to meet new challenges.* Washington, DC: The National Academies Press.

IOM. 2005. *Guidelines for human embryonic stem cell research.* Washington, DC: The National Academies Press.

IOM. 2006. *Rewarding provider performance: Aligning incentives in Medicare.* Washington, DC: The National Academies Press.

IOM. 2007. *The future of drug safety: Promoting and protecting the health of the public.* Washington, DC: The National Academies Press.

Koop, C. E. 2007. *Testimony of C. Everett Koop, M.D., Sc.D., before the House Committee on Oversight and Government Reform, June 10, 2007.* http://oversight.house.gov/documents/20070710111012.pdf (accessed November 4, 2008).

NACCHO (National Association of County and City Health Officials). 2006. *2005 national profile of local health departments.* Washington, DC: NACCHO.

NHLBI (National Heart, Lung, and Blood Institute). 2007. *The Framingham heart study: Research milestones.* http://www.nhlbi.nih.gov/about/framingham/timeline.htm (accessed August 25, 2008).

NRC (National Research Council). 2008. *Science and technology for America's progress: Ensuring the best presidential appointments in the new administration.* Washington, DC: The National Academies Press.

Revkin, A. C. 2007. White House cuts to climate testimony raise questions. *New York Times*, October 25.

Satcher, D. 2007. *Testimony by David Satcher, M.D., Ph.D., before the House Committee on Oversight and Government Reform, June 10, 2007.* http://oversight.house.gov/documents/20070710111034.pdf (accessed November 5, 2008).

Schaeffer, L. 2007. Leading the way: A conversation with HHS Secretary Mike Leavitt. *Health Affairs* 27:w52-w59.

Senate Committee on Governmental Affairs. 1977. *Study on federal regulation, regulatory organization.* Washington, DC: Government Printing Office.

Shalala, D. 1998. Are large public organizations manageable? *Public Administration Review* 58(4):284-289.

TFAH (Trust for America's Health). 2008. *Fixing food safety: Protecting America's food supply from farm to fork.* Washington, DC: TFAH.

Trapp, D. 2008. 2008 NIH budget nearly flat—again. *American Medical News*, January 21.

Underhill, K., P. Montgomery, and D. Operario. 2007. Sexual abstinence only programmes to prevent HIV infection in high-income countries: Systematic review. *British Medical Journal* 335(7613):248.

Union of Concerned Scientists. 2004. *Abstinence-only education.* http://www.ucsusa.org/ scientific_integrity/abuses_of_science/abstinence-only-education.html (accessed October 17, 2008).

U.S. Census Bureau. 2008. *Health insurance coverage status and type of coverage by selected characteristics: 2007.* http://pubdb3.census.gov/macro/032008/health/h01_001.htm (accessed September 10, 2008).

USDA (U.S. Department of Agriculture). 2008a. *Food Safety and Inspection Service FY 2008-2013 strategic plan.* Washington, DC: USDA.

USDA. 2008b. *FY 2009 budget summary and annual performance plan.* Washington, DC: USDA.

Wagner, W., and R. Steinzor, eds. 2006. *Rescuing science from politics*. New York: Cambridge University Press.

Walker, D. 2003. *Executive reorganization authority: Balancing executive and congressional roles in shaping the federal government's structure.* Washington, DC: GAO.

Walker, D. 2007. *Federal oversight of food safety: High-risk designation can bring needed attention to fragmented system.* Washington, DC: Government Accountability Office.

Worthman, C. 1999. Epidemiology of human development. In *Hormones, health, and behavior: A socio-ecological and lifespan perspective*. Edited by C. Panter-Brick and C. Worthman. Cambridge, UK: Cambridge University Press.

4

Increase Effectiveness and Efficiency of the U.S. Health Care System

No matter how much costs and decision making are shifted to consumers, they cannot succeed unless providers and health plans have to compete on results and the right information and advice are available.

Porter and Teisberg (2006)

RECOMMENDATION 3

Increase Effectiveness and Efficiency of the U.S. Health Care System

The secretary should accelerate the establishment of a collaborative, robust system for evaluating the health care system that would incorporate existing department and external research, stimulate new studies as needed, synthesize findings, and provide actionable feedback for policy makers, purchasers, payers, providers, health care professionals, and the public.

a. **The secretary should work with Congress to establish a capability for *assessing the comparative value—including clinical and cost-effectiveness—* of medical interventions and procedures, preventive and treatment technologies, and methods of organizing and delivering care. The assessment of comparative value should begin by leveraging department-wide data sources in conjunction with supportive evidence from providers, payers, and health researchers.**[1]

[1]The committee did not reach consensus on recommendation 3a. Although the majority of the committee supports the language of the recommendation, David Beier, J.D., Senior Vice President of Global Government and Corporate Affairs, Amgen; Kathleen Buto, M.P.A., Vice President, Health Policy, Johnson & Johnson; and Myrl Weinberg, C.A.E., President, National Health Council, did not agree with the majority's view and provided

b. **The secretary should work with Congress to ensure that the department's *programs and reimbursement policies are outcomes-based*, reflecting best available evidence of value and creating incentives for adoption of best practices, including integration of care, in order to improve quality and efficiency.**
c. **The department should *collaborate with state and local public health agencies and community-based organizations*, as both sources and users of practical program guidance.**
d. **The department should provide *authoritative, plain-language, and current evidence-based information* to the public regarding prevention and treatment options.**
e. **To assess the health of the American people and overall health system performance accurately, the department needs current data from the nation's health system. To facilitate collection of these data, the department should actively promote the universal adoption of *electronic information capabilities*—including health information exchange and electronic medical, personal health records—for administrative and clinical purposes.**

HHS'S ROLE IN A VALUE-BASED SYSTEM

Medicare and Medicaid exert powerful influence on the U.S. health care system beyond the impact of the large dollars they expend. Because their rules and coverage decisions often are adopted by private payers, these two public programs—although limited to covering specific population groups—affect the entire health care system and all Americans. Also, some of their reimbursement strategies—especially those supporting traditional fee-for-service care—have inadvertently contributed to the rapid growth in health care costs. As the Institute of Medicine (IOM) committee considered its charge to examine how the Department of Health and Human Services (HHS) could be more effective in "advanc-

dissenting opinions, which can be found in Appendix F. They were unable to agree on a common statement.

ing the health of the nation," it saw an important potential role for the Centers for Medicare and Medicaid Services (CMS) in providing leadership on issues of evidence-based care and creating a value-driven system—arguably the most promising current approach to the problems of rapidly rising health care costs and shortfalls in quality.

KNOWING WHAT WORKS: ESTABLISHING VALUE IN HEALTH CARE

An IOM committee has recommended a multipart national program to identify which diagnostic, treatment, and prevention services really work and under what conditions (IOM, 2008).[2] This work originates from recognition that many health care practices need closer scrutiny. On one hand, patients often do not receive services that are known to be effective and appropriate.[3] On the other, new technologies or certain patterns of care may be adopted without knowing whether they are the most effective.

Evidence is compelling that Americans receive a substantial amount of care that is inappropriate. Two decades of studies by a team of Dartmouth College researchers have shown large differences from one geographic area to another in care patterns, such as the frequency with which patients receive certain surgical operations or are admitted to intensive care units (ICUs). These differences are not associated with characteristics of the patients themselves but attributable almost entirely to differences in the way local doctors practice and the supply of clinical resources—hospital beds, ICUs, high-tech equipment, and specialist phy-

---

[2]Legislation on this topic is currently pending in the 110th Congress, including the Comparative Effectiveness Research Act of 2008 (S. 3408, introduced August 2008), which would establish a nonprofit corporation, the Health Care Comparative Effectiveness Research Institute; the Children's Health and Medicare Protection Act (H.R. 3162, Sec. 904, passed the House August 2007), which would establish a Center for Comparative Effectiveness Research within the Agency for Healthcare Research and Quality (AHRQ); and the Enhanced Health Care Value for All Act (H.R. 2184, introduced May 2007), which charges a Comparative Effectiveness Advisory Board, led by the director of AHRQ, to determine whether one or more AHRQ-sponsored federally funded research and development centers should be created to conduct and review comparative effectiveness research within two years of the act's passage.

[3]An often-cited study showed that, in general, Americans receive only about 55 percent of the care recommended for their condition or situation (McGlynn et al., 2003).

sicians. For example, for the average patient in Miami, Medicare spends about two and a half times the amount it spends for the average patient in Minneapolis (Wennberg et al., 1999), even after adjusting for age, illness severity, and comorbidities; in recent years, Medicare spent an average of almost $60,000 on New Jersey patients in the last 24 months of their lives, but only half that amount on similar patients in North Dakota (Wennberg et al., 2008). At the same time, effective preventive services, such as mammography or pneumonia vaccinations, are underutilized in *both* high- and low-cost geographic areas (Wennberg et al., 1999).

Ironically, a greater intensity of services does not necessarily mean that patients fare better. Sometimes, they fare worse. Mortality rates for patients with the same personal characteristics and the same disease are often *higher* in locales where more health care services are routinely provided (Wennberg et al., 2008).

Significant resources could be saved throughout the health system if the least efficient providers mimicked the practices of the most efficient (Antos and Rivlin, 2007). If all patients nationwide had the kind and intensity of care that patients receive in the least-intensive, most conservative settings (notably Mayo Clinic in Rochester, Minnesota, and Intermountain Healthcare in Salt Lake City), Medicare—and perhaps other—spending could be reduced by about 30 percent (Wennberg et al., 2002). There may always be patients who do benefit more from an intensive approach, but the costs of paying for extra care for these few would be more than balanced by reducing the intensity of services for the larger number who receive too much care (Wennberg et al., 2008).

Figure 4-1 presents state-level data showing what Medicare spends, on average, per beneficiary, compared to how the quality of care for beneficiaries is rated in that state. Each dot represents a state, and the figure clearly shows the absence of a relationship between spending and quality. If the two were related, low-spending states would be clustered in the lower left of the figure and higher-spending states would rise on the quality scale. Instead, beneficiaries in some states on the low end of the spending scale receive high-quality care, whereas beneficiaries in some states on the high end of the spending scale receive low-quality care. In fact, the state with the *highest*-quality care is at the low-cost end, with annual costs of about $6,000 per beneficiary, whereas the two states where care is most expensive (close to $9,000 per year) have among the lowest quality ratings.

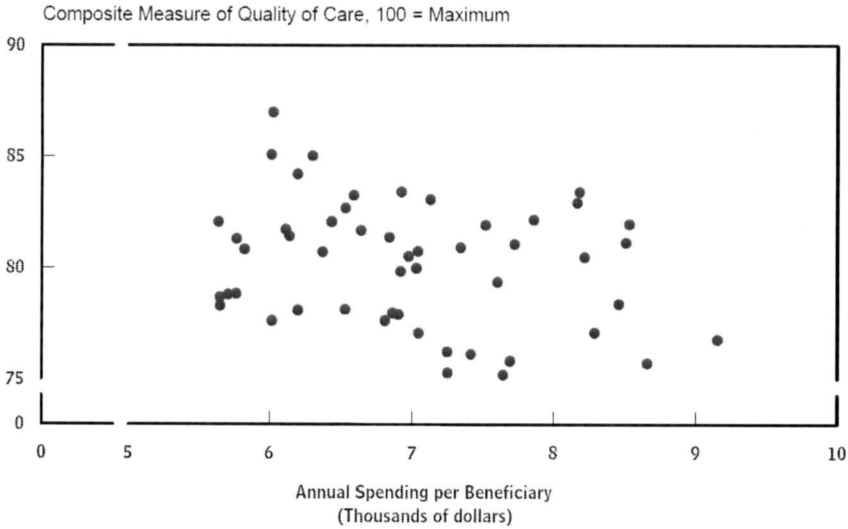

FIGURE 4-1 Relationship between quality of care and Medicare spending, by state (2004).
NOTES: The composite measure of the quality of care, based on Medicare beneficiaries in the fee-for-service program who were hospitalized in 2004, conveys the percentage who received recommended care for myocardial infarction, heart failure, or pneumonia. Spending figures are average amounts for each state.
SOURCE: Congressional Budget Office (Orszag, 2008), based on data from CMS and AHRQ's National Healthcare Quality Report, 2005.

Even in the nation's "best" hospitals—those that are integrated academic medical centers and members of the Council of Teaching Hospitals and Health Systems—costs of care vary markedly. Figure 4-2 shows that among 93 such hospitals, the cost of care for Medicare patients with specific chronic diseases ranges from about \$24,000 to almost \$92,000 in the last two years of life—nearly a four-fold difference. Again, this suggests that changing physician and hospital practice patterns could drastically reduce costs and still mirror the care found among the nation's leading hospitals.

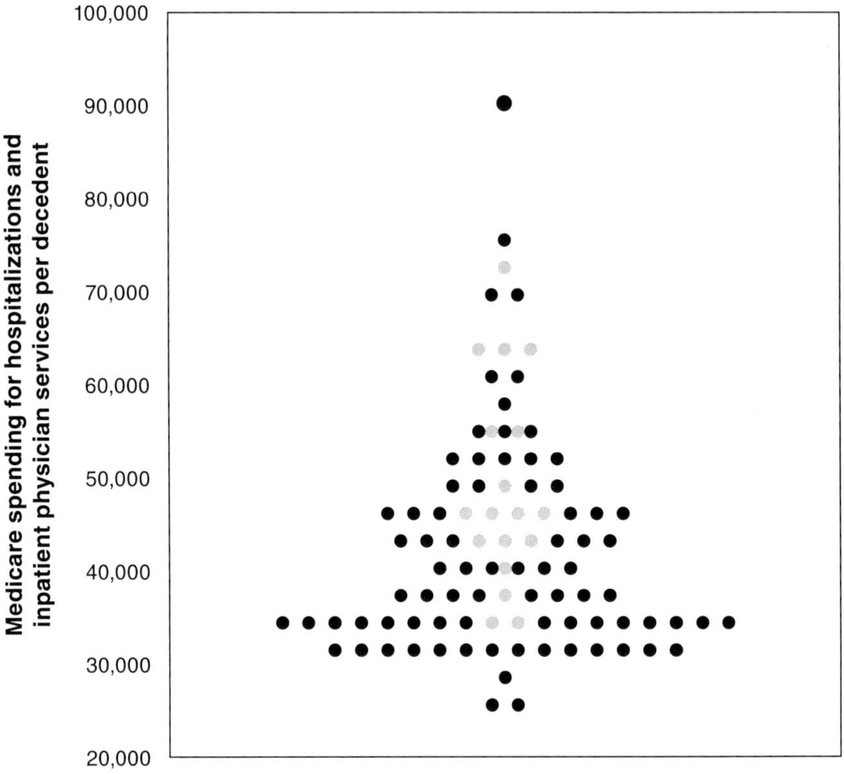

FIGURE 4-2 Medicare spending for hospitalizations and inpatient physician services per decedent in the last two years of life among patients with at least one of nine chronic conditions receiving most of their care from selected Council of Teaching Hospitals (COTH) integrated academic medical centers (deaths occurring 2001–2005).
NOTE: The 18 hospitals on *U.S. News & World Report*'s Honor Roll for 2007 are noted in the lighter shade of gray.
SOURCE: Wennberg et al. (2008).

Patient outcomes are affected by the clinical content of care, as well as by whether care is integrated and how it is organized, delivered, and paid for. "Integrated care" is guided by a plan that takes into account the individual's personal needs and goals, and reflects patient preferences after being informed of the benefits, risks, and availability of alternative treatments. Integrated care is coordinated across all providers and settings over time, is culturally and linguistically appropriate, and uses interactive electronic medical and personal health records. The *organization and delivery of care* relates to whether it is provided in private offices or multispecialty group practice, financed through fee-for-service or under managed care or an alternative payment method, is provided principally by primary care physicians or specialists, with or without participation of nurse practitioners, physician assistants, nutritionists, health educators, or other health professionals. The *way care is paid for* profoundly affects outcomes. Fee-for-service payment systems give providers financial incentives to do more tests, procedures, and treatments, in order to maximize income. Just as there may be no "one best way" to organize a large federal department, it is likely that there is no "one best way" to provide health care, and that different approaches may work best in different circumstances.

Analyses of all these factors clearly are beyond the capacity of individual physicians or hospitals. Nor are insurers or payers likely to invest in such analyses if they will benefit competitors equally. Also, none of these entities is likely to commission significant new research to fill in any gaps in understanding. Government should provide significant national leadership, through support for a variety of intra-agency and cross-agency efforts, to describe more effective health care. The astronomical cost of Medicare and Medicaid is a powerful incentive to do so.[4]

Related Recommendation

a. **The secretary should work with Congress to establish a capability for *assessing the comparative value—including clinical and cost-effectiveness—* of medical interventions and procedures, preventive and treatment technologies, and methods of organizing and delivering care. The assessment of comparative value should begin by leveraging department-wide data sources in conjunction**

[4]The Centers for Medicare and Medicaid Services projects that by 2017, national health expenditures will double to more than $4 trillion annually. With the leading edge of the baby boom generation beginning to become eligible for Medicare in 2011, that program would more than double its 2006 size, to reach $884 billion, as would Medicaid, reaching a projected $402 billion. In total, government sources alone would be responsible for $2 trillion of the national health bill (Keehan et al., 2008).

with supportive evidence from providers, payers, and health researchers.[5]

EMPLOYING EVIDENCE FOR IMPROVED OUTCOMES

Better coordination is needed to leverage the comprehensive data collected by the CMS, Food and Drug Administration (FDA), National Institutes of Health (NIH), Centers for Disease Control and Prevention (CDC), and other government agencies, as well as the data collected by nongovernmental payers, providers, and researchers. Improved coordination would allow existing data to be used more effectively in assessing the value (costs and benefits) of health services. Consideration also must be given to the methodological limitations of studies. For example, study designs such as randomized controlled trials and observational studies provide valuable population-level information but do not always provide definitive direction for care at the individual patient level. Despite these limitations, best available evidence can be used to inform policy decisions and the development of clinical guidelines. This can result in a better understanding of which policies produce improved outcomes and fewer unnecessary costs—ultimately increasing the value of the health care system.

Assessing the comparative clinical and cost-effectiveness of different health services and organizational and delivery arrangements need not create a rigid system that limits choices for patients, providers, and health systems. Indeed, the particular situations of individual patients and communities *always* have to be taken into account in making decisions about clinical care and organization of services.[6] (See Box 4-1 for a brief description of "value" in health care.)

---

[5]The committee did not reach consensus on recommendation 3a. Although the majority of the committee supports the language of the recommendation, David Beier, J.D., Senior Vice President of Global Government and Corporate Affairs, Amgen; Kathleen Buto, M.P.A., Vice President, Health Policy, Johnson & Johnson; and Myrl Weinberg, C.A.E., President, National Health Council, did not agree with the majority's view and provided dissenting opinions, which can be found in Appendix F. They were unable to agree on a common statement.

[6]For patients, this means consideration not just of their clinical situation, but also of their unique preferences, concerns, and expectations that are brought to a clinical encounter and that must be integrated into clinical decisions if the patient is to be well served.

BOX 4-1
Value in Health Care

Patient value ... is the compass that must guide the strategic and operational choices of every provider group, hospital, clinic, and physician practice
Porter and Teisberg (2006)

IOM Roundtable on Evidence-Based Medicine's Definition of Value:

...*Value in health care is expressed as the physical health and sense of well-being achieved relative to the cost.* This means getting the right care at the right time to the right patient for the right price.... Value in health care ... depends on vantage point and circumstance. Perceived value will vary according to one's view as a patient, caregiver, family member, neighbor, community leader, employer, health care manager, innovator, or policy official.

Sometimes the determination of value is complicated by the fact that a benefit received is the result of a cost shared or borne elsewhere. This is typical of activities in which there is advantage or necessity to arrange for pooling of resources to make it possible for groups of people to benefit. . . . In these cases, the gain is considered from two perspectives: the individual gain for one person's investment and the social gain from the collective investment. *Value from pooled arrangements is expressed as the aggregate gains relative to the aggregate costs.*

Rewarding caregivers who deliver high-value care . . . should be a central goal of incentives embedded in health care financing. Accomplishing this aim will require analytic tools and capacity beyond those currently available, including development of the capacity to study relative safety and effectiveness; to inform, assess, and integrate patient preferences; to better characterize and target groups at particular risk; to understand and balance the various elements of cost; to fashion the principles needed to ensure an appropriate balance between an individual's value proposition and that of the aggregate for a population; to systematically track the results of health care interventions; and to identify the system elements most conducive to high-value health care (IOM Roundtable on Evidence-Based Medicine, 2008).

To this committee, research related to establishing value creates *actionable information* about the relative benefits and costs of preventive and treatment technologies, procedures, and methods of organizing, delivering, and paying for services. Assessments of value should include measures of both individual and societal costs and benefits (quality of life, productivity) and would be useful to policy makers, payers, purchasers, providers, health care professionals, and the public.

This preeminence of *value* in comparing professionals and providers (individual physicians, hospitals, and the like) applies equally to comparisons of medical treatments used in treating a disease, of alternative preventive measures, or varying organizational structures for care. As Porter and Teisberg (2006) conclude, "If value for patients truly governed every provider choice, the health outcomes per dollar expended in the U.S. health care system would improve dramatically."

Better evidence on comparative effectiveness must be a priority, but we also need to acknowledge the challenges in obtaining *timely, patient-relevant* evidence. For example, patients currently receive recommended, effective treatments only about half of the time (McGlynn et al., 2003). Thus far, having evidence on what works has not resulted in closing the substantial gaps between evidence development and its application at the bedside; one study estimates that 17 years pass before published research is translated into practice (Balas and Boren, 2000). We must find new, more effective ways to move the results of research into clinical practice.

Undertaking assessments of the value of services to treat specific diseases could be accomplished by an existing government agency, a newly formed one, a quasi-government organization, or some type of public-private partnership (CBO, 2007). The effort should leverage current private and public agency research efforts, such as those of the Agency for Healthcare Research and Quality (AHRQ), which already supports some studies comparing technologies and styles of medical practice, and for which the committee recommends a larger budget in recommendation 2. There are many management choices regarding governance and oversight, but the first step is to support research on "what works" as the best hope for improving quality and efficiency in the near future and certainly an important component of long-term system reform.

AHRQ is working closely with other units of HHS to fulfill the goals of HHS Secretary Leavitt's Value-Driven Health Care Initiative. This initiative requires federal agencies that administer or support health insurance programs to provide information on the cost and quality of health care and collaborate on strategies to do the following:

- Connect data throughout the system, by adopting interoperable health information technologies and strategies.
- Measure and make available information on the quality and costs of health care services.
- Align incentives so that payers, providers, and patients benefit when care delivery is focused on achieving the best value of health care at the lowest cost.

Medicare and Medicaid officials (and those of other government payment programs) should use the results of comparative effectiveness studies to inform, but not dictate, their coverage decisions. CMS leadership will positively influence other payers to gravitate to evidence-based practices, and payers can create incentives for health care providers and professionals to adopt evidence-based practices, as well. In such a potentially contentious arena, the analyses that support coverage decisions must be absolutely independent, methodologically sound, and perfectly transparent.

Although information is rarely perfect and controversies may arise, in the long run it seems fundamental that payers should reward care for which there is evidence of value and discourage care that is either too costly for the benefit received or too low in benefit, regardless of cost. At present, the science is far from able to translate this general principle into care decisions for individual patients with their unique needs; nor would an absolute application of general rules to individual cases be ethically acceptable.

To take full advantage of the findings from effectiveness research, CMS reimbursement practices will have to change. With new and better information from these analyses, CMS should be able to focus on creating value in the system, by developing a range of policy incentives for

- better management of high-cost chronic illnesses, including proactive management by providers and self-management by patients (practices discouraged by some current reimbursement policies);
- use of primary, versus specialist, care;
- reduced geographic variation in care patterns;
- better integration of care, through, for example, establishment of a medical home or similar mechanism for assuring continuous, accessible, comprehensive, and coordinated care; and
- more efficient practices, generally, including adoption of electronic information exchange and clinical records.

Comparative effectiveness research, like any sharp tool, needs to be used carefully. It does not provide the answer to every question. Most thought leaders acknowledge that it can reduce uncertainty, but there will rarely be black-and-white choices that can guide coverage decisions. In other words, when it comes to care for individual patients, we must accept a gray area. However, this type of research would provide information that patients and physicians need to make choices that offer them the greatest value, as they define it.

The committee believes strongly that the department's activities must rest on a strong science base, that it should foster ongoing learning of many types, and that it needs more effective ways to assess its performance, for accountability purposes. Comparative effectiveness analyses fit nicely into this overall learning theme—for both the department and our health system as a whole.

Related Recommendation

> **b. The secretary should work with Congress to ensure that the department's *programs and reimbursement policies are outcomes-based*, reflecting best available evidence of value and creating incentives for adoption of best practices, including integration of care, in order to improve quality and efficiency.**

The department has strong relationships with state and local government entities that deliver services and manage programs, and with community-based organizations that are grantees. These groups, too, should align their services with the comparative effectiveness study results, in order to increase system value at the community level. If these entities had appropriate electronic links to the federal government, they could provide real-time feedback to program administrators regarding the functioning of grant and contract programs and their effects on the populations served.

Related Recommendation

> **c. The department should *collaborate with state and local public health agencies and community-based organizations*, as both sources and users of practical program guidance.**

PUBLIC INFORMATION

The era when Americans were passive recipients of health services and physicians were unquestioned authorities is fast fading—in part because of societal trends and patients' own desires, influenced by new information technologies, and in part because of trends in the health care system itself.

An uneasy shift in terminology often defines patients as "consumers." They certainly act like consumers when they take advantage of self-help medical volumes at the local bookstore; access information about their symptoms, conditions, or treatments on the Internet; participate in online "chats" about symptoms and therapies; and join support groups. Health topics are among the most popular on the web: WebMD, the most often-consulted health site, averages 17.3 million unique users per month, according to web marketing analysts (comSource, 2008). This collection of resources of varying reliability is obviously filling a need, but people should have guidance to locate easy-to-understand and immediately accessible information from authoritative sources as well. Several government-sponsored websites aim to direct people toward those more reliable sources.[7]

At the same time, changes in health care delivery push Americans toward becoming better informed about their health, medical treatments, and ways of navigating the health care system. Outpatient surgery and faster hospital discharges send patients home needing significant attention and infection control; an increasing number of home care technologies—heart disease monitoring, diabetes and asthma management, kidney dialysis, analgesia pumps, and many others—require greater knowledge of both the disease and how to work with sophisticated equipment; home-based hospice teaches families to handle emergencies and to manage pain and symptoms; parents of children with severe disabilities learn to deal with respirators and feeding tubes, and to watch for early signs of impending crises.

Families dealing with elderly members aging in place are presented with a constellation of care choices and decisions, sometimes having to be made for a loved one no longer capable of participating in health-related decisions. For these families, it is essential that they have confidence in the choice they make on behalf of their loved one and the adequacy of the information on which it is based. In hospitals, the trend toward larger patient rooms with accommodation for family members is facilitating instruction of families about follow-up care and even encouraging some patient care by family members.

---

[7]See, for example, http://www.health.gov; http://nnlm.gov/hip/; and http://www.cancer.gov/cancertopics/factsheet/information/internet.

Americans have long held substantial personal responsibility for preventing disease and injury—obtaining immunizations and checkups, eating properly, driving safely, exercising, not smoking—but today, they are becoming increasingly responsible for carrying out their treatments, too—well beyond taking medications and returning to the doctor every six months.

In general, greater involvement in one's own care is a positive trend. Extensive research has shown that involving patients effectively in decision making increases their knowledge of their choices, gives them a realistic understanding of what to expect, and helps them be comfortable with the choice made. For example, when patients were given appropriate help in deciding whether to have major elective surgery, about 25 percent fewer chose the more invasive surgical option, with no adverse effects on health outcomes or satisfaction with care. Further, when patients are involved in decision making, some evidence suggests they tend to choose lower-cost options and have better results (O'Connor et al., 2007).

In weighing treatment options, Americans must be able to easily find unbiased, accurate, and up-to-date information that describes in plain language the pros and cons of available treatments. Also, with trends toward reduced insurance coverage and higher out-of-pocket payments, this information should include an indication of costs, as well. Public education efforts may also be necessary to demonstrate that "more expensive" is not necessarily better, and is sometimes worse.

Related Recommendation

d. The department should provide *authoritative, plain-language, and current evidence-based information* to the public regarding prevention and treatment options.

FULFILL THE PROMISE OF HEALTH INFORMATION TECHNOLOGY

Among the many potential benefits of increased use of health information technology are several that relate directly to the committee's recommendation regarding increased health care system effectiveness and efficiency. The use of health information technology can improve the continuity and integration of care the committee espouses, by facilitating exchanges of information when a patient is referred from one physician to another, goes to a different hospital, fills prescriptions at different pharmacies, seeks care while traveling, or obtains health-supporting services from social workers, mental health specialists, or other health care professionals.

Such technology would make health care more accessible for patients if more physician offices allowed patients to schedule appointments and obtain test results online, send their physician e-mail queries, receive electronic reminders, and provide helpful clinical information. Early efforts to facilitate the exchange of health information, so that health professionals and patients can access electronically all necessary information at the point of care, should be strengthened to improve patient safety, improve the quality of care, and reduce the costs of missing information and duplicated services. Yet adoption of electronic records at the physician-office level has been slow—in 2006, only 29 percent of physicians reported using any type of electronic medical record in their office-based practices (Hing et al., 2007)—mostly because of high infrastructure costs, uncertainty about which system to buy, the need for training and integration with other office systems, concerns about patient privacy, and the lack of incentives to do so.

Although only a small proportion of medical records are fully electronic today, many important elements of medical care exist in electronic form—insurance status; claims for services; pharmacy, laboratory, and other reports—that can give insights into the operations of the health care system. In the future, systems that allow selective information exchange, while maintaining patient privacy, will eventually provide the databases for systematic review and synthesis of the clinical effectiveness and cost-effectiveness of various treatments and help establish their relative value. The results can be used to create "rapid learning" for providers and payers, enable large-scale national research projects with robust results in shorter time frames, facilitate technology assessment, and monitor and improve system performance overall (Etheredge, 2007). Electronic distribution of the findings from these analyses, in forms suitable for different audiences—health care professionals, payers, and the public—would fill current information gaps.

HHS has identified many of the previously cited benefits for patients of expanded use of health information technology as well as predicting that it would make care more accessible, increase administrative efficiencies, and decrease paperwork.

Health information technology can produce many public health benefits, as well, enabling

- early detection of outbreaks of infectious diseases or bioterrorism and tracking short- and long-term effects of exposures to environmental hazards,
- improved monitoring and proactive management of chronic disease patterns,
- more coordinated care for clients of publicly funded clinics, and
- identifying adverse events once drugs are in real-world use.

In the IOM's widely referenced report on achieving health care quality, *Crossing the Quality Chasm*, the authors say that achievement of every one of the health care attributes they describe as essential to quality care—that it be safe, effective, patient-centered, timely, efficient, and equitable—would be aided by improved information technology (IOM, 2001). However, financial and technical assistance may be necessary to help small physician practices and safety-net providers adopt these systems. Progress has been slow in many areas: standards development, private physician adoption, achieving interoperability across systems and within institutions, and achieving confidentiality—areas in which government carrots (financial incentives) and sticks (penalties) could move the field forward more quickly, such as those set forth in the Medicare Improvements for Patients and Providers Act (MIPPA) of 2008. This act provides phased incentive payments for doctors who begin e-prescribing, and eventually, penalties for those who don't comply.

Health information technology is a tool that can facilitate change. However, it cannot create change. The potential benefits of health information technology, in terms of quality and cost-effectiveness, cannot be realized without substantial changes in the organizational arrangements of the health system. Otherwise, the new information capacity will only perpetuate and further institutionalize the built-in problems we have today (Diamond and Shirky, 2008).

Having available timely electronic data from both the public and the private sectors will enable the secretary to provide Congress and the American people with a more complete picture of the state of Americans' health, unmet needs, the costs and effectiveness of health services, and opportunities for improvement. Used appropriately, it will facilitate the greater accountability this IOM committee recommends (see Chapter 6).

Related Recommendation

e. To assess the health of the American people and overall health system performance accurately, the department needs current data from the nation's health system. To facilitate collection of these data, the department should actively promote the universal adoption of *electronic information capabilities*—including health information exchange and electronic medical, personal health records—for administrative and clinical purposes.

REFERENCES

Antos, J., and A. Rivlin. 2007. Slowing the growth of health spending: We need mixed strategies, and we need to start now. In *Opportunity 08: Independent ideas for America's next president*. Edited by M. O'Hanlon. Washington, DC: Brookings Institution. Pp. 303-320.

Balas, E., and S. Boren. 2000. Managing clinical knowledge for health care improvement. In *Yearbook of medical informatics*. Bethesda, MD: National Library of Medicine. Pp. 65-70.

CBO (Congressional Budget Office). 2007. *Research on the comparative effectiveness of medical treatments: Issues and options for an expanded federal role.* Washington, DC: Congress of the United States.

comSource. 2008. *Online health information category grows at rate four times faster than total Internet.* http://www.comscore.com/press/release.asp?press=2436 (accessed November 17, 2008).

Diamond, C. C., and C. Shirky. 2008. Health information technology: A few years of magical thinking? *Health Affairs* 27(5):w383-w390.

Etheredge, L. 2007. A rapid-learning health system. *Health Affairs* 26:w107-w118.

Hing, E. S., C. W. Burt, and D. A. Woodwell. 2007. *Electronic medical record use by office-based physicians and their practices: United States, 2006.* Atlanta, GA: National Center for Health Statistics.

IOM (Institute of Medicine). 2001. *Crossing the quality chasm: A new health system for the 21st century.* Washington, DC: National Academy Press.

IOM. 2008. *Knowing what works in health care: A roadmap for the nation.* Washington, DC: The National Academies Press.

IOM Roundtable on Evidence-Based Medicine. 2008. *Learning healthcare system concepts, v. 2008.* Washington, DC: The National Academies Press.

Keehan, S., A. Sisko, C. Truffer, S. Smith, C. Cowan, J. Poisal, and M. K. Clemens. 2008. Health spending projections through 2017: The baby-boom generation is coming to Medicare. *Health Affairs* 27(2):w145-w155.

McGlynn, E., S. Asch, J. Adams, J. Keesey, J. Hicks, A. DeCristofaro, and E. Kerr. 2003. The quality of health care delivered to adults in the United States. *New England Journal of Medicine* 348:2635-2645.

O'Connor, A. M., J. E. Wennberg, F. Legare, H. A. Llewellyn-Thomas, B. W. Moulton, K. R. Sepucha, A. G. Sodano, and J. S. King. 2007. Toward the "tipping point": Decision aids and informed patient choice. *Health Affairs* 26(3):716-725.

Orszag, P. 2008. *Increasing the value of federal spending on health care.* Washington, DC: CBO.

Porter, M., and E. Teisberg. 2006. *Redefining health care: Creating value-based competition on results*. Boston, MA: Harvard Business School Press.

Wennberg, J., J. D. Birkmeyer, K. K. Bronner, T. A. Bubolz, D. E. Campbell, E. S. Fisher, G. T. O'Connor, J. F. Poage, S. M. Sharp, J. S. Skinner, T. A. Stukel, and D. E. Wennberg. 1999. *The quality of medical care in the United States: A report on the Medicare program.* Hanover, NH: Dartmouth Atlas of Health Care.

Wennberg, J. E., E. S. Fisher, and J. S. Skinner. 2002. Geography and the debate over Medicare reform. *Health Affairs* Suppl Web Exclusives: w96-w114.

Wennberg, J., E. Fisher, D. Goodman, and J. Skinner. 2008. *Tracking the care of patients with severe chronic illness.* Hanover, NH: Dartmouth Atlas of Health Care.

5

Strengthen the HHS and U.S. Public Health and Health Care Workforces

The single biggest constraint on the success of (any) organization is the ability to get and to hang on to enough of the right people.

Jim Collins (2001)

RECOMMENDATION 4

Strengthen the HHS and U.S. Public Health and Health Care Workforces

The secretary should place a high priority on developing a strategy and tools for workforce improvement (1) in HHS, (2) in the public health and health care professions nationwide, and (3) in the biosciences.

- a. **The secretary should immediately strengthen workforce planning in the department and develop a *comprehensive strategy to recruit highly qualified* public- and private-sector individuals in order to offset the large number of experienced staff expected to retire soon.**
- b. **Congress should authorize the department, in cooperation with the Office of Personnel Management, to assemble a package of current and innovative programs and benefits designed to *encourage talented, experienced individuals to transition back and forth between government and private-sector service*, thereby identifying ways to leverage the best of both.**
- c. **Congress should provide the secretary with additional authority to *reward performance, innovation, and the achievement of results*, through**

bonuses, merit-based pay, recognition awards, or other mechanisms of proven effectiveness.

d. **The secretary, in concert with other public and private partners, should *develop a comprehensive national strategy to assess and address current and projected gaps* in the number, professional mix, geographic distribution, and diversity of the U.S. public health and health care workforces.**

e. **To help close projected gaps, the department should evaluate existing *health care professional training programs*, continued education programs, and graduate medical education funding and should encourage Congress to invest in programs with proven effectiveness.**

f. **Congress should give the secretary authority to create new programs that invest in the *future generation of biomedical and health services researchers*, enabling the continued discovery of new, more effective methods of preventing, treating, and curing disease; promoting health; improving health care delivery and organization; and controlling health system costs.**

SCOPE OF THE CHALLENGES

The Institute of Medicine (IOM) committee was charged with considering how the activities of the department and its constituent agencies relate to the public health, health care quality, and health care cost challenges facing our nation. In each of these arenas, the Department of Health and Human Services (HHS) must interact with other organizations and, of course, their people. As this chapter documents, there appear to be impending shortages of people with the right backgrounds, training, and skills within the department's senior levels, within the nation's health care workforce generally, within state and local public health agencies, and within the science establishment. These shortages will cripple the ability of the department to carry out its work and negatively affect health care delivery, even as demands are increasing.

An array of new health challenges—not to mention the ongoing triad of access, quality, and cost control—confront the department just as a large portion of its own workforce is near retirement. A similar pattern is also occurring in state and local public health agencies. Outside the public health world, problems in the number, mix, and composition of the nation's health workforce also have a negative impact on the department and its agenda:

- The United States has an overall imbalance between specialist and primary care physicians, and the higher costs that result from an overreliance on specialist care fall heavily on Medicare and Medicaid.
- It would take 16,261 additional primary care physicians to meet the need in currently underserved areas, where federally funded safety net programs struggle to fill the gaps (HRSA, 2008).
- A recent survey of medical school students revealed that a mere two percent are planning a career in general internal medicine (Hauer et al., 2008).
- Nationally, minority groups are underrepresented among doctors, nurses, and other clinical disciplines, which affects access to care, especially for the vulnerable populations that are a high department priority (Sullivan Commission on Diversity in the Healthcare Workforce, 2004).
- Rural areas and low-income communities are especially affected by shortages of health professionals, so, again, publicly funded health clinics try to pick up the slack.
- At a time when there is a greater emphasis on improving the science base in many federal agencies, the nation faces a shortage of talent in the biological and other health sciences (National Science Board, 2008b).

These examples show how public programs and publicly funded services are affected by workforce shortages in the private sphere. As a consequence, as it attempts to address some of the nation's key health challenges described in this report, the department must look beyond its own resources to the health workforce capacity of the entire nation. Developing and maintaining the health professions workforce will require broad-based strategies that include participation by the states, the private sector, the academic community, and other federal departments with substantial health system involvement.

THE HHS WORKFORCE

Structure and systems are vital to organizational health, but "success depends on having the right employees with the right competencies at the right time" (HHS Office of Human Resources and ASMB, 1999). A major stumbling block to strengthening the public health infrastructure is a shortfall in the number, and in some cases the qualifications, of the HHS and public health workforces.

Within the five-year span that began in 2007, about half of all HHS managers are or will be eligible for retirement (HHS, 2007). Such a large loss of experienced managers, scientists, and other professionals in the HHS workforce will create a tremendous challenge to the secretary for many years to come. While bringing in new people with new skills and ideas may make it easier to refocus department priorities and align people to purpose, it may also make sense to devise benefit programs and work arrangements that encourage some potential retirees to stay, perhaps with shorter, more flexible hours, job sharing, or other arrangements. Shortages of person-power clearly place a tremendous burden on remaining staff, reduce efficiency and productivity, and make government less responsive to constituents.

To recruit professionals with the appropriate managerial experience and scientific expertise, the department will have to engage in creative recruitment of at least some people with deep private-sector experience, as well as cultivate talented employees within the department who have the ability to move into more senior roles. It will also need to establish a robust recruitment program for experienced, well-qualified economists, health services researchers, statisticians and epidemiologists, clinical scientists, biomedical engineers, computer scientists, information systems engineers, and other such disciplines.

Loss of Senior Leadership

Since 2001, the HHS budget has included between 63,000 and 66,000 full-time equivalent employees, supplemented by a significant number of contract employees. On average, the age of the HHS workforce is increasing and is slightly older than federal government employees in general. For these reasons, anticipated retirement rates have been a concern for at least a decade, as reflected in the department's workforce planning guide (HHS Office of Human Resources and ASMB, 1999).[1]

In 2001, 1,067 individuals retired from HHS, 1.7 percent of its workforce; the average age at retirement was 60.3 years. These retirees were an experienced group, with 28 years' service, on average; 22 were from the Senior Executive Service (SES); 370 were categorized as "professional." Three years later, in 2004, a somewhat larger number—1,700—of employees retired, 2.9 percent of the department's workforce. On average, these retirees were a little younger (59.9 years), but had served a little longer (29.5 years). Twenty-eight were from the SES, and a much larger number—470—were "professionals."

Experienced senior managers and professionals are not easy for government agencies to replace. Retirees around age 60 are part of the generation born from 1946–1964—the baby boom—and the following generation provides a pool of potential workers that is not only somewhat smaller, but also less interested in public service careers (Light, 2007). This underscores the need for the secretary to establish "moon landing" type goals that inspire a new generation of Americans—one representing our nation's diversity—to enter public service.

> The situation of the Centers for Disease Control and Prevention (CDC) offers a case in point. CDC had about 9,000 employees in 2007. In 2008, the Government Accountability Office estimated that 27 percent of CDC's workforce, which includes a great many highly skilled employees—statisticians, epidemiologists, and laboratory scientists—would be eligible to retire within five years, as would more than a third of its hard-to-replace medical officers. (GAO, 2008a)

Several nonprofit, nonpartisan organizations have emerged that attempt to encourage public-sector careers (see, for example, Partnership for Public Service, http://www.ourpublicservice.org/OPS/; the Demos Center for the Public Sector, http://www.demos.org, which encourages a "reenvisioning" of the public sector; and the Council for Excellence in Government, http://www.excelgov.org/). Academic institutions could also play a critical role in encouraging public service.

---

[1]The Office of Personnel Management projects that 18.5 percent of the government-wide full-time permanent workforce will have retired between 2006 and 2010.

As a potential partial response to the shortfall in personnel in the senior ranks of government, Congress and the executive branch have initiated a number of small recruitment and retention initiatives. For example, a 2003 Presidential Executive Order (13318) authorized a Senior Presidential Management Fellows program, intended "to provide for the recruitment and selection of outstanding employees for service in public-sector management" for terms of up to three years (Bush, 2003).[2] Individuals were to be selected through a merit-based system from among people with "extensive work experience" and "exceptional leadership or analytic ability." Five years later, the program awaits implementation guidance from the Office of Personnel Management before it can begin. However worthy in intent, fellowship programs make a small contribution, considering the size of the overall need.

In addition to identifying highly qualified people within the department for promotion to senior ranks,[3] recruitment of the next generation of department leaders will have to look outside. The loss of scientific talent is particularly severe in some agencies. For example, a 2007 Institute of Medicine report reviewing the future of drug safety recommended increasing the scientific capacity of the Food and Drug Administration (FDA) staff (IOM, 2007a):

> The IOM committee concluded that, in order to better plan and evaluate research on drug risks and benefits, the FDA's Center for Drug Evaluation and Research needs "more expert staff, deeper expertise in the staff it already has, and different kinds of expertise." (p. 127)

Findings such as these suggest the need for a concerted effort at recruitment from academia and the private sector to obtain the depth and level of necessary expertise. In a survey, 23 percent of HHS staff themselves believed that their work units were not "able to recruit people with the right skills" (HHS, 2007).

---

[2]A separate Presidential Management Fellows program, intended for individuals with recent graduate degrees, is operational and provides HHS with about 50 Fellows annually. The similar Emerging Leaders Program (ELP) also recruits among graduate students.

[3]Promoting leadership and management skills could be accomplished through training opportunities offered through the HHS University or the expansion of internal programs, such as the Department's Senior Executive Service Candidate Program.

> Again, the CDC experience is germane. HHS agencies were asked to reduce the number of administrative management and support positions by 15 percent, moving some of these workers into frontline public health work. However, these former administrative and support staff did not necessarily have the requisite public health education and experience. (GAO, 2004)

The accountability and improved performance strategies envisioned by the committee and described in Chapter 6 would make the present shortfall in senior-level staff in the department even more acute. Improving performance would require personnel with greater expertise in managing large organizations, deep familiarity with organizational quality improvement strategies, skill in managing and motivating staff, and expertise in program assessment and evaluation. In addition, the committee's recommendations regarding greater use of information technology, noted especially in Chapter 4, will require a range of personnel who are trained in medical informatics. Medical informatics experts are in short supply across the nation, and HHS may need to take steps to ensure that these experts become available to both the public and private sectors.

Congress and the Office of Personnel Management have taken steps to allow agencies more hiring flexibility, and these tools (including recruitment bonuses and special needs appointments above minimum salaries) should be fully utilized in recruiting the department's next generation of managers.

Streamlining cumbersome federal hiring practices would be another substantial aid to recruitment (Partnership for Public Service, 2008). According to GAO, in recent years, the time required to hire a new employee averaged between 73 and 92 days. One motivation for hiring contract workers is that this avoids the lengthy hiring process and allows the agency to bring workers on board more quickly to meet immediate needs (GAO, 2008a).

To attract experienced professionals working in the private sector to a period—or a career—in public service will require administrative and congressional consideration of more competitive, innovative approaches to employment benefits, perhaps starting with discovery of what benefits and features this category of workers most values (McKinsey & Company, 2005). At the same time, portable benefits and job security would enable public-sector employees to work for a time outside the federal government. Consideration should be given to work arrangements and benefits that appeal to mature workers, such as flexible work schedules and other arrangements, telecommuting, phased retirement with pension protection, and family and medical leave programs.

Related Recommendations

a. **The secretary should immediately strengthen workforce planning in the department and develop a *comprehensive strategy to recruit highly qualified* public- and private-sector individuals, in order to offset the large number of experienced staff expected to retire soon.**
b. **Congress should authorize the department, in cooperation with the Office of Personnel Management, to assemble a package of current and innovative programs and benefits designed to *encourage talented, experienced individuals to transition back and forth between government and private-sector service*, thereby identifying ways to leverage the best of both.**

Rewarding Performance

Congress has taken measures to help combat the problem of lower federal salaries that impedes efforts to recruit and retain experienced personnel and has directed the administration to create several different pay systems, separate from the 15 grades in the traditional General Schedule (GS) system. The intent is to give agencies more flexibility in setting employees' salaries, especially the ability to base pay increases on performance rather than merely tenure. Still, most federal employees are paid under the more rigid GS system.

Just over 400 HHS employees are members of the SES, which now uses a performance-based pay system. Results of a survey of SES employees, published in May 2008, indicated some skepticism about the effects of this program. While more than 90 percent of the department's SES employees support the notion of performance-based pay, only 44 percent believe it has improved their organization's performance, and only 65 percent say they understand how their own recent salary increase was determined (OPM, 2008). This suggests that the new performance-based pay system may need strengthening and clarification in order to achieve its desired effects.

For HHS, efforts to ensure the *quantity* and *quality* of the workforce should support the other fundamental organizational activities already touched upon in this report—the alignment of vision, mission, and goals, monitoring performance, and assuring effectiveness.

Related Recommendation

c. **Congress should provide the secretary with additional authority to *reward performance, innovation, and the achievement of results*, through bonuses, merit-based pay, recognition awards, or other mechanisms of proven effectiveness.**

THE U.S. HEALTH WORKFORCE

The total U.S. health workforce includes all the categories of workers and professionals who provide services related to the care of individual patients; the state and local public health workforce; and the scientists who perform basic biomedical, health services, and other research related to the prevention, tracking, and treatment of disease and disability. A number of problems in the number, mix, and distribution of the various components of this total workforce are straining today's health system, and the trends bode ill for the future.

The Clinical Care Workforce

The following problems in the clinical care workforce affect access to health services:

- 63 million Americans live in a primary care practitioner shortage area.
- 47 million live in a dental practitioner shortage area.

- 76 million live in a mental health care practitioner shortage area (HRSA, 2008).
- Shortages are particularly acute in rural and low-income areas.
- In 2004, community health centers had vacancy rates for family practice and internist positions of 13 and 21 percent, respectively; 19 percent vacancy rates for dentists; and 11 percent vacancy rates for nurses and pharmacists (NACHC, 2007).

These problems in the workforce affect the quality of care and patient outcomes:

- Numerous studies indicate a population's health outcomes, including mortality, improve as the number of primary care physicians—but not specialty physicians—increases (Starfield et al., 2005a).
- Yet, the supply of primary care physicians is not keeping up with demand, while the proportion of medical specialists in the U.S. grew from 32 to 38 percent between 1996 and 2004, the proportion of primary care physicians decreased from 39 to 37 percent over those same years (Tu and O'Malley, 2007).
- Much research links higher hospital registered nurse (RN) staffing with improved patient outcomes and even reduced costs (AcademyHealth, 2006), but recent predictions suggest that the national shortage of RNs in the nursing workforce will be between 220,000 and 450,000 in 2020 (Buerhaus et al., 2009).

If today's health workforce supply problems weren't serious enough, demands for health care are rising quickly. The leading edge of the baby boom generation will turn 65 in 2011, and the population of Americans 85 and older continues to grow. Between 40 and 50 percent of all Americans have at least one chronic condition, such as hypertension, asthma, arthritis, diabetes, or a psychiatric disorder. The number and severity of chronic conditions increase with age, and people over 65 generally have more than one chronic disorder. Treatment of chronic conditions is expensive, accounting for almost 80 percent of the nation's $2 trillion in annual health care expenses (Kovner and Knickman, 2008).

While the aging population will require many kinds of health services, it will encounter a severe shortage of professionals prepared to provide specialized geriatric care. A new IOM report recommends an array of measures to improve the health workforce's competency in geriatrics (IOM, 2008).

For many years, health care experts have called for an increase in primary care practitioners. These generalist physicians—general internists, family practitioners, obstetrician-gynecologists, and pediatricians—provide holistic, patient-centered care that should be patients' "first line of defense" in preventing and treating many illnesses. Instead, our health care system, unlike systems in many other nations, is skewed toward much more costly specialist care. As important as it is to control costs, another reason to change this pattern is even more potent: it is harmful to patients. People living in geographic areas served by larger numbers of primary care providers have better health outcomes (Starfield et al., 2005b). Conversely, research shows a "weak link" between the number of physicians per capita and health outcomes, except for studies of the supply of primary care physicians. Further, "health systems with primary care as the foundation of care provide the best outcomes at the lowest costs" (Goodman and Grumbach, 2008).

Ironically, several Centers for Medicare and Medicaid Services' (CMS's) policies discourage physicians-in-training from pursuing primary care careers. First, Medicare is the largest source of funding for graduate medical education (physicians' residency programs) (HRSA, 2007). Medicare rules limit support for residencies that take place in "nontraditional" and ambulatory sites, where generalists tend to train and practice; instead, the rules favor hospital-based residencies where specialists traditionally receive their training. The result, according to the Council on Graduate Medical Education, is that "current training models are not preparing physicians for the demands of future practice."

Once primary and specialist physicians complete their residencies—generally with substantial educational debt—Medicare payments are much higher for specialists, which means that those who choose a generalist career will have a much greater financial struggle (Tu and O'Malley, 2007). A variety of strategies have been employed in an attempt to encourage young physicians to choose generalist careers with little long-term success. More effective strategies, involving CMS's reimbursement system, should be attempted (Colwill et al., 2008). This is an example of how different parts of HHS could be brought into greater alignment.

Advanced practice nurses (clinical nurse specialists, nurse practitioners, nurse midwives, and nurse anesthetists) and physician assistants can fill part of the gap in primary care access, and the country had

240,000 advanced practice nurses and 66,000 physician assistants in 2004–2006. Over the years, these midlevel practitioners have increasingly gained the ability to obtain reimbursement for their services, but they still face considerable state-to-state variation in scope-of-practice laws, particularly in the amount of physician oversight they must have and whether they are allowed to write prescriptions. Many of these practitioners have found a congenial home in managed care or in large physician practices where they can perform triage, initial and simple treatment, referral, and patient education roles that improve physician productivity. A disadvantage of substituting these "midlevel" practitioners for physicians is that they may lack physicians' wide range of diagnostic and therapeutic knowledge.

Another longstanding problem is the lack of racial and ethnic diversity in the nation's health professional workforce. The lack of minorities in the professions is important for several reasons. Minority professionals are more likely to serve minority patients, increasing access to care for some underserved groups; in turn, many minority patients prefer being cared for by professionals of their own ethnicity and generally are more satisfied with the care received (IOM, 2004). Health care professionals who share their patients' background and language are more likely to provide culturally competent services, which is especially important for patients who are recent immigrants or lack English proficiency.

African Americans, Hispanic Americans, and Native Americans constitute more than a quarter of the U.S. population, but are only nine percent of the nation's nurses, six percent of physicians, and five percent of dentists (Sullivan Commission on Diversity in the Healthcare Workforce, 2004). Shortages of Asian-American health professionals are often ignored, because the number of Asian-American (or Asian international graduates) health professionals appears relatively high, compared to the size of the Asian-American population. This is misleading, because the Asian-American demographic category covers more than a dozen ethnic groups with starkly different cultures and languages—from Pakistan to Taiwan and Mongolia to Malaysia. Simply having an "Asian" health care provider does not necessarily meet the needs of individual Asian-American patients for culturally competent care.

At a time of workforce shortages, minority groups may represent a large, relatively untapped pool of potential health professionals. A 2004 IOM report recommended assessment of the effectiveness of the Health Resources and Services Administration (HRSA) workforce educational programs in increasing the number of minority graduates and additional support for educational programs working well (IOM, 2004). Certainly this makes sense in light of how essential these programs could be to assuring a workforce that can better meet patients' needs, enhance quality care, and practice in a manner that manages costs.

The Public Health Workforce

The workforce needs of the public health sector often take a back seat, though it is worth remembering that 25 of the 30 years of improvement in longevity in the United States in the twentieth century are attributed to public health improvements (Turnock, 2004).

The inadequate number and training of the nation's public health workforce was brought vividly to national attention following September 11, the anthrax attacks of autumn 2001, and Hurricanes Katrina and Rita (Gebbie and Turnock, 2006; Lister, 2008).

Unfortunately, HRSA's workforce training programs may at present be an undervalued asset. Public health workforce training, in particular, has dramatically declined since 2002. That year, Title VII support for public health, preventive medicine, and dental public health stood at $10.5 million, declining to under $8 million in 2006, and zeroed out in the President's 2009 budget request. A recent IOM committee justly concluded, "the future of Title VII remains unclear" (IOM, 2007b).

In 2005, only 6 percent of local health departments were large—serving populations over 500,000—whereas 41 percent served fewer than 25,000 people. On average (median), these small departments had four professional staff (NACCHO, 2006). Of necessity these individuals must wear many hats, and not all of them fit. They inspect restaurants and other food service establishments as well as environmental health problems; track diseases and intervene in disease outbreaks; improve emergency preparedness through complicated drills and exercises; maintain vital statistics; provide health education; and even, in some cases, provide mental health care, immunizations, school health services, home health services, maternal and child health services, migrant health screenings, and many other functions for vulnerable populations and community residents at large. Finally, in rural areas they spend remarkable amounts of time driving to outlying areas of their jurisdictions. Despite federal expectations, their capacity to respond in a major emergency ("surge capacity") is limited (GAO, 2008b).

Data differ considerably regarding the number of people employed in the nation's 57 state and territorial health departments and nearly 2,900 local health departments. According to a 2007 survey by the Association of State and Territorial Health Officials (ASTHO, 2008), more than 100,000 individuals work in state public health agencies, 34 percent of whom are administrative and clerical personnel. According to a 2005 survey, local health departments employ approximately 160,000 public health workers, again approximately 34 percent of whom are administrative and clerical personnel (NACCHO, 2006).[4]

State and local health department workers are "graying" (Tilson and Berkowitz, 2006), and replacements—if they can be found—too often lack public health training and adequate science backgrounds. Public health careers are unattractive to new recruits because of "low salaries, poor benefits, adverse working conditions, and low status" (Tilson and Berkowitz, 2006). Severely constrained state budgets and rigid hiring practices pose additional barriers to recruitment (Gebbie and Turnock, 2006).

Having a sufficient number of employees is not enough; they also need the right education and skills to carry out their vital functions (Salinsky and Gursky, 2006). The public health workforce—federal, state, and local—continues to be widely criticized for lacking basic science preparation and appropriate public health knowledge and skills, prompting a previous IOM committee to recommend that public health workers should "demonstrate mastery of the core public health competencies appropriate to their jobs" (IOM, 2002). In local public health agencies, "Skill deficits are less apparent than worker shortages but may be more consequential in adversely affecting the quantity and quality of public health services" (Draper et al., 2008). Aware of these problems, public health schools are moving toward credentialing their graduates through the new National Board of Public Health Examiners, which may help public health agencies identify more qualified job candidates. (The two national organizations representing public health departments—ASTHO and National Association of County and City Health Officials [NACCHO]—hope to launch accreditation programs for public health agencies, as well.)

State and local health departments, like the health care system generally, lack racial and ethnic diversity among their employees. The

[4]These survey results report data from, in the former instance, 43 states and the District of Columbia, and, in the latter case, 80 percent of local departments, so the figures do not represent a complete accounting.

NACCHO reports that some 70 percent of local health department workforces are less diverse than the population they serve (Draper et al., 2008).

Telemedicine and Telehealth in a Comprehensive Workforce Strategy

A potentially important mechanism for meeting the health workforce needs of the future could be the extensive application of telemedicine and telehealth[5] services. Such systems have already been deployed in rural, urban, multistate, and international settings to meet the need for specialist and primary care services and for education, training, and supervision of clinical and related health workers. Telehealth systems also can help patients self-manage chronic diseases and conditions.

Leading provider organizations have demonstrated the potential of carefully designed telemedicine programs to improve the productivity of the professional workforce, reduce costs, and improve access to needed services. The success of these efforts led to a recent Federal Communications Commission (FCC) program to fund telemedicine projects, but in scale and ambition it is far short of the potential and the need for such investment. A strong collaboration among HHS, the Veterans Health Administration, the Department of Defense, the FCC, and private-sector organizations around a focused, well-funded initiative could expand telehealth systems as a component of strategies to address health workforce shortages.

Related Recommendations

d. The secretary, in concert with other public and private partners, should *develop a comprehensive national strategy to assess and address current and projected gaps* in the number, professional mix,

---

[5]The terms *telehealth* and *telemedicine* overlap and are often used interchangeably. In this report, *telehealth* refers to the delivery of health-related services and information via telecommunications technologies, while *telemedicine* generally focuses on the use of remote electronic communication and transmission of images and documents between clinicians.

geographic distribution, and diversity of the U.S. public health and health care workforces.

e. **To help close projected gaps, the department should evaluate existing *health care professional training programs*, continued education programs, and graduate medical education funding and encourage Congress to invest in programs with proven effectiveness.**

THE SCIENCE-BASED PROFESSIONS

American bioscientists and bioengineers have made innumerable contributions to the prevention, treatment, and cure of many diseases and to mitigating disability by developing advanced prosthetics and other supportive technologies. A strong, well-educated scientific workforce is critical to maintaining America's economic leadership in the high-tech, knowledge-intensive industries of the twenty-first century.[6]

The number of U.S. workers in science and engineering overall has steadily grown over the past 50 years, with between 4.5 and 5 million working in the "life sciences" in 2000. Our homegrown workforce has been substantially augmented by foreign-born scientists and engineers. However, the Bureau of Labor Statistics projects that the increase in demand for scientists and engineers will be nearly double that for other occupations by 2014. Workforce analysts worry that the country will not be able to meet that rate of growth in demand, given large numbers of impending retirements, a need for greater and greater knowledge and skills among young scientists, and unstable funding for many programs. Women, Latinos, and African Americans remain underrepresented in these fields (National Science Board, 2008b). Another barrier to building our science and engineering workforce are restrictions and administrative complexities facing international students and scholars who want to immigrate to the United States (NRC, 2007).

To address the nation's current health problems, we need not only bench scientists working on new ideas, but a new generation of health

---

[6]The American public professes interest in scientific discoveries, especially medical ones, and a 2006 survey said they support government funding of basic research (87 percent) and are confident in the nation's scientific leaders. In a 2005 survey, 71 percent of Americans supported development of biotechnology, specifically (National Science Board, 2008b).

economists, biostatisticians, epidemiologists, and health care researchers geared to tracking disease trends, assessing programs and payment strategies, and finding the best ways to deliver the fruits of our nation's enormous investment in knowledge.

The problem of workforce shortfalls actually begins at the earliest grade levels. By the time American students reach their teen years, their math and science skills compare poorly to those of students from other developed countries. Meanwhile, students' interest in advanced education in the natural sciences and engineering has declined steadily in recent decades. While other countries are increasing the numbers and skills of their young scientists, America is not (National Science Board, 2006).

Recent real-dollar cutbacks in federal and private-sector support for scientific research, including biomedical research (National Science Board, 2008a), send a signal "to international and American students who may be deterred from pursuing science and engineering careers in this country," warned National Science Board Chairman Dr. Steven Beering in February 2008 (Beering, 2008).

Related Recommendation

f. Congress should give the secretary authority to create new programs that invest in the *future generation of biomedical and health services researchers*, enabling the continued discovery of new, more effective methods of preventing, treating, and curing disease, promoting health, improving health care delivery and organization, and controlling health system costs.

REFERENCES

AcademyHealth. 2006. *2006 HSR impact awardee: The business case for nurse staffing.* Washington, DC: AcademyHealth.

ASTHO (Association of State and Territorial Health Officials). 2008. *2007 state public health workforce survey results.* Washington, DC: ASTHO.

Beering, S. 2008. *Testimony before the Research and Science Education Subcommittee, House Committee on Science and Technology.* Arlington, VA: National Science Foundation.

Buerhaus, P., D. Staiger, and D. Auerbach. 2009. *The future of the nursing workforce in the United States: Data, trends, and implications*. Sudbury, MA: Jones and Bartlett Publishers.

Bush, G. 2003. *Executive order: Presidential management fellows program.* http://www.whitehouse.gov/news/releases/2003/11/print/20031121-7.html (accessed September 8, 2008).

Collins, J. 2001. *Good to great: Why some companies make the leap—and others don't.* New York: HarperBusiness.

Colwill, J. M., J. M. Cultice, and R. L. Kruse. 2008. Will generalist physician supply meet demands of an increasing and aging population? *Health Affairs* 27(3):w232-w241.

Draper, D., R. Hurley, and J. Lauer. 2008. *Public health workforce shortages imperil nation's health.* Washington, DC: Center for Studying Health System Change.

GAO (Government Accountability Office). 2004. *Centers for Disease Control and Prevention: Agency leadership taking steps to improve management and planning, but challenges remain.* Washington, DC: GAO.

GAO. 2008a. *Centers for Disease Control and Prevention: Human capital planning has improved, but strategic view of contractor workforce is needed.* Washington, DC: GAO.

GAO. 2008b. *States are planning for medical surge, but could benefit from shared guidance for allocating scarce resources.* Washington, DC: GAO.

Gebbie, K., and B. Turnock. 2006. The public health workforce, 2006: New challenges. *Health Affairs* 25(4):923-933.

Goodman, D., and K. Grumbach. 2008. Does having more physicians lead to better health system performance? *Journal of the American Medical Association* 299(3):335-337.

Hauer, K. E., S. J. Durning, W. N. Kernan, M. J. Fagan, M. Mintz, P. S. O'Sullivan, M. Battistone, T. DeFer, M. Elnicki, H. Harrell, S. Reddy, C. K. Boscardin, and M. D. Schwartz. 2008. Factors associated with medical students' career choices regarding internal medicine. *Journal of the American Medical Association* 300(10):1154-1164.

HHS (Department of Health and Human Services). 2007. *HHS human capital survey—2007.* Washington, DC: HHS.

HHS Office of Human Resources and ASMB (Assistant Secretary for Management and Budget). 1999. *Building successful organizations: Workforce planning in HHS.* http://www.hhs.gov/ohr/workforce/wfpguide.html (accessed August 19, 2008).

HRSA (Health Resources and Services Administration). 2007. *Nineteenth report: Enhancing flexibility in graduate medical education.* Rockville, MD: Bureau of Health Professions Council on Graduate Medical Education.

HRSA. 2008. *Shortage designation: HPSAs, MUAs, & MUPs*. http://bhpr.hrsa.gov/shortage/ (accessed October 9, 2008).

IOM (Institute of Medicine). 2002. *The future of the public's health in the 21st century.* Washington, DC: The National Academies Press.

IOM. 2004. *In the nation's compelling interest: Ensuring diversity in the health-care workforce.* Washington, DC: The National Academies Press.

IOM. 2007a. *The future of drug safety: Promoting and protecting the health of the public.* Washington, DC: The National Academies Press.

IOM. 2007b. *Training physicians for public health careers.* Washington, DC: The National Academies Press.

IOM. 2008. *Retooling for an aging America: Building the health care workforce.* Washington, DC: The National Academies Press.

Kovner, A. R., and J. R. Knickman, eds. 2008. *Health care delivery in the U.S., 9th edition instructor's guide.* New York: Springer Publishing Company.

Light, P. 2007. *A government ill executed: The depletion of the federal service.* Paper presented at the 2007 Elmer Staats Lecture, Washington, DC.

Lister, S. 2008. *Public health and medical preparedness and response: Issues in the 110th Congress.* Washington, DC: Congressional Research Service.

McKinsey & Company. 2005. Designing better employee benefits. *McKinsey on Health Care* (June).

NACCHO (National Association of County and City Health Officials). 2006. *2005 national profile of local health departments.* Washington, DC: NACCHO.

NACHC (National Association of Community Health Centers). 2007. *The struggle to build a strong workforce at health centers.* Bethesda, MD: NACHC.

National Science Board. 2006. *America's pressing challenge—building a stronger foundation.* Arlington, VA: National Science Board.

National Science Board. 2008a. *Research and development: Essential foundation for U.S. competitiveness in a global economy.* Arlington, VA: National Science Board.

National Science Board. 2008b. *Science and engineering indicators 2008.* Arlington, VA: National Science Board.

NRC (National Research Council). 2007. *Rising above the gathering storm: Energizing and employing America for a brighter economic future.* Washington, DC: The National Academies Press.

OPM (Office of Personnel Management). 2008. *Senior Executive Service: Survey results.* Washington, DC: OPM.

Partnership for Public Service. 2008. *A golden opportunity: Recruiting baby boomers into government.* http://www.ourpublicservice.org/OPS/publications/viewcontentdetails.php?id=122 (accessed September 8, 2008).

Salinsky, E., and E. Gursky. 2006. The case for transforming governmental public health. *Health Affairs* 25(4):1017-1028.

Starfield, B., L. Shi, A. Grover, and J. Macinko. 2005a. The effects of specialist supply on populations' health: Assessing the evidence. *Health Affairs Web Exclusive* w5-97–w95-107.

Starfield, B., L. Shi, and J. Macinko. 2005b. Contribution of primary care to health systems and health. *Milbank Quarterly* 83(3):457-502.

Sullivan Commission on Diversity in the Healthcare Workforce. 2004. *Missing persons: Minorities in the health professions.* Washington, DC: Sullivan Commission on Diversity in the Healthcare Workforce.

Tilson, H., and B. Berkowitz. 2006. The public health enterprise: Examining our twenty-first-century policy challenges. *Health Affairs* 25(4):900-910.

Tu, H., and A. O'Malley. 2007. *Exodus of male physicians from primary care drives shift to specialty practice.* Washington, DC: Center for Studying Health System Change.

Turnock, B. J. 2004. *Public health: What it is and how it works,* 3rd ed. Sudbury, MA: Jones and Bartlett Publishers.

6

Improve Accountability and Decision Making

I repeat ... that all power is a trust; that we are accountable for its exercise; that from the people and for the people all springs, and all must exist.

Benjamin Disraeli

RECOMMENDATION 5

Improve Accountability and Decision Making

A "new compact" between Congress and the department is essential as HHS works toward achieving its vision for a healthy nation, departmental mission, and key health goals. Under this compact, the secretary would provide Congress and the nation regular, rigorous reports about departmental activities and assume greater accountability for improving performance and obtaining results; in return, Congress should allow the department greater flexibility in its internal operations and decision making.

a. **To enable greater accountability, the secretary should oversee development and implementation of a *department-wide data, evaluation, and information system.* The system should be based on a broad analytic framework designed to aid in managing departmental operations, learning from program experience, evaluating the costs and impact of programs, and determining whether they provide sufficient value for the investment of public funds.**
b. **Congress should authorize the secretary to direct funding from the budgets of all departmental units to support the development of an HHS-wide information system. Funding for such a system would benefit all department units.**
c. **The department should use the data, evaluation, and information system to**

- **enable the secretary to *provide Congress with regular reports* on progress toward achieving departmental goals,**
- ***inform policy development*,**
- ***facilitate cross-department activities*,**
- **provide *operational information to program management* for quality improvement and midcourse corrections, and**
- **support effective *long-range planning*.**

d. **For those outside the department, the system should**
   - ***be accessible, transparent, timely, and reliable*, and**
   - **provide *useful, privacy-protected information* regarding department activities.**

e. **The department should *demonstrate accountability* through continuous critical assessment of program efficiency, equity, impact on health, and cost-effectiveness, and through corrective action for underperforming programs.**

f. **The secretary, in collaboration with the surgeon general, should present Congress and the public with an annual "State of the Nation's Health" report that describes progress toward achieving the vision for the nation's health and the department's key health goals.**

g. **Congress should establish *a new, strategic initiative fund* to enable the secretary to support cross-agency and cross-departmental activities that exhibit innovation in responding to twenty-first century challenges, and to respond quickly to new, unforeseen, or expanding public health threats.**

The committee believes that improved accountability and more rigorous decision making will be fundamental to the department's success in creating more value from its activities, in responding to the key health and cost challenges of the twenty-first century, and in earning congressional support for increased flexibility in executing its responsibilities.

To the committee, a strong system of *accountability* provides the information needed to continuously improve program performance in ways that result in better health for Americans. As used in this chapter, the term *accountability* involves a systematic approach that

- establishes a small number of critical, measurable goals,
- provides clearly delineated lines of responsibility,
- sets quantifiable targets and time-specific milestones,
- describes potential barriers and develops strategies to address them,
- projects the investments to be made,
- defines a process for regular reporting and assessment,
- includes a reward and recognition system for staff that promotes achieving goals,
- provides a clear understanding of whether progress is being made, and
- implements corrective action, as needed.

A key question is, "To whom is the department accountable?" The committee believes HHS is primarily accountable to the White House, Congress, and the tax-paying public.

CURRENT DEPARTMENTAL EFFORTS

The current administration and HHS have undertaken major initiatives aimed at increasing performance measurement, which is an important aspect of accountability. The department currently operates under a complex web of internally and externally generated goal-setting and reporting requirements. These requirements include exercises that relate to *Healthy People 2010,* the Government Performance and Results Act of 1993 (GPRA), the Program Assessment Rating Tool (PART), and the President's Management Agenda (PMA), described below. Box 6-1 defines these requirements and illustrates their relationship to the department and each other.

The trend toward greater HHS accountability may have begun with the first version of *Healthy People*, published in 1979, which set a series of 10 health goals for different age groups and described the actions the department would take to reach them. In subsequent iterations, *Healthy People 2000* and *Healthy People 2010*, the number of health issues enumerated has grown considerably. *Healthy People 2010* includes 28 focus

BOX 6-1
Selected Goal-Setting and Reporting Systems

Systems Originating Within the Department:

Department-wide objectives–This annual document lists 20 objectives that are "cascaded down throughout the entire department." While these objectives incorporate major themes from other goal-setting systems, no report is dedicated exclusively to them (HHS, 2008b).

Government Performance Results Act (GPRA) of 1993–GPRA requires agencies to develop five-year strategic plans, updated every three years, as well as annual plans or annual performance budgets, and annual program performance reports. The **strategic plan** defines broad, long-term goals and describes broad strategies for their implementation. The **annual plan** sets specific annual objectives related to the strategic plan's goals and tracks progress toward them. **Annual performance budgets** track a broader set of performance indicators, measuring progress on all department activities. While mainly a mechanism for reporting, performance budgets also state goals that will be achieved with available funding. At the close of each fiscal year, the **annual performance and accountability report** combines performance results with audited financial statements (HHS, 2007).

Secretary's 500-day plan–Implemented by Secretary Michael Leavitt, the secretary's 500-day plan provides the department with steps to take over the course of 500 days that will produce results in 5,000 days. The 500-day plan, which builds on the **secretary's principles** and **priorities,** is updated every 200 days. Progress is charted in the **250-day update** and the report of **major accomplishments** (HHS, 2008a).

Systems Originating Outside the Department:

Healthy People–A set of national health objectives focused on prevention, *Healthy People* was first published in 1979, and subsequent iterations set goals for the years 2000 and 2010. Progress is reported twice each decade as well as in the midcourse review (http://www.healthypeople.gov/).

President's Management Agenda (PMA)–The PMA, announced in 2001, identifies five critical management areas designed to produce better program results. Selected federal programs are assessed each quarter with the **PMA scorecard,** which uses a color-coded evaluation system–"green" indicates full achievement, "yellow" intermediate advancement, and "red" one or more deficiencies (OMB, 2008b).

Program Assessment Rating Tool (PART)–The Office of Management and Budget (OMB) introduced PART in 2002 to examine federal programs in four areas: program purpose and design, strategic planning, program management, and program results. Based on the sum of numerical scores, with "program results" heavily weighted, programs are rated effective, adequate, ineffective, or results not demonstrated. PART is designed to strengthen and reinforce GPRA reporting (OMB, 2008a).

areas, including one on the Public Health Infrastructure, and 467 objectives for the nation's health (HHS, 2000). The welter of objectives of varying importance makes it difficult to perceive how much overall progress has been achieved. Recognizing this dilemma, the department has identified 10 high-priority "leading health indicators" that include selected objectives that are being tracked. These leading indicators are physical activity, overweight and obesity, tobacco use, substance abuse, responsible sexual behavior, mental health, injury and violence, environmental quality, immunization, and access to health care.[1]

All of these indicators represent important health problems, but they are predominantly affected by actions outside the department's control. The problems either result from individual behavior choices or, as in the case of environmental quality, actions of other federal departments and agencies. The department's work in these areas may be helpful at the margins, but they are not meaningful indicators of departmental performance.

Additional health goals for the department are identified in its five-year strategic plan, required by GPRA and updated every three years. The 2007–2012 strategic plan, HHS's most recent, identifies the following four *goals*, derived from its operational responsibilities in health care, public health, human services, and scientific research and development[2]:

- Improve the safety, quality, affordability, and accessibility of health care, including behavioral health care and long-term care.

[1]The State of the USA, Inc., in partnership with the National Academies, is developing a web-based system of tracking trends to inform public policy decision making and research, and an IOM committee is participating in that effort by attempting to identify appropriate health indicators to track.

[2]Note that the "public health promotion and protection, disease prevention, and emergency preparedness" goal accounts for 1 percent of the President's proposed 2009 HHS budget, while the "health care" goal accounts for 93 percent.

- Prevent and control disease, injury, illness, and disability across the lifespan, and protect the public from infectious, occupational, environmental, and terrorist threats.
- Promote the economic and social well-being of individuals, families, and communities.
- Advance the scientific and biomedical research and development related to health and human services.

Because these goals cover every current departmental program and activity, they are too broad to encourage focus. (The current secretary has established 10 other, somewhat narrower *priorities*[3] that are not formally tracked and a 500-day *plan* for the department based on his core principles,[4] both entirely separate from the department's strategic plan.)

Under each of the four strategic plan goals, in turn, are four broad objectives. Progress toward these objectives is measured by *benchmarks* (called "performance indicators") that have established targets and are reported in the annual plan and the annual performance and accountability report, additional requirements of GPRA. What is not clear from the strategic plan is the strategy for reaching the four goals (other than continuing to do what is already being done) and, consequently, whether or how the performance measures relate to strategy. The goals are essentially an endorsement of the *status quo*, not a recipe for meaningful change.

In a separate effort, the administration introduced the PART initiative in 2002,[5] managed by the Office of Management and Budget, with results available on the Internet since 2006 (see http://www.ExpectMore.gov). Staff members of individual programs, in collaboration with Office of Management and Budget (OMB) staff, assess their program's

---

[3]These priorities are: every American insured, insurance for children in need, value-driven health care, information technology, personalized health care, health diplomacy, prevention, Louisiana health care system, pandemic preparedness, and emergency response.

[4]These principles are: care for the truly needy, foster self-reliance; national standards, neighborhood solutions; collaboration, not polarization; solutions transcend political boundaries; markets before mandates; protect privacy; science for facts, progress for priorities; reward results, not programs; change a heart, change a nation; and value life.

[5]In 2005, the PART program received an "Innovations in American Government Award," from the Kennedy School of Government (Harvard University), an award program administered in partnership with the Council for Excellence in Government. In April 2006, it received the Government Performance Management Excellence Award from the Performance Institute, a leading adviser to government on performance issues.

performance (see Box 6-1). The following are the collective PART ratings for the 115 department programs assessed to date:

- Effective (scores of 85–100): 16% of HHS programs
- Moderately effective (70–84): 32%
- Adequate (50–69): 25%
- Ineffective (1–49): 5%
- Results not demonstrated: 22% (OMB, 2008c)

According to OMB, while higher scores are desirable, the more important results of the process are the agencies' *performance improvement plans*, which, with occasional resetting of targets, are intended to produce "continuous improvement of program performance" (OMB, 2008a). The hope is that, by making the ratings database public and by increasing its use by Congress and others, programs will work more aggressively to improve their ratings. However, OMB acknowledges that ratings will not necessarily be reflected in increases or decreases in program budgets, depending on circumstances.

The White House, too, has an initiative to improve governmental operations, called the President's Management Agenda. The following were the PMA's government-wide goals and HHS scores (in italic), as of June 30, 2008:

- Strategic management of human capital—*Mixed results, but worsening since March 2008.*
- Competitive sourcing (now "commercial services management")—*HHS is successfully implementing its plans.*
- Improved financial performance—*Initiative in serious jeopardy. Unlikely to realize objectives absent significant management intervention* (OMB, 2008b).
- Expanded electronic government—*Mixed results, but improving since March 2008.*
- Budget and performance integration—*Mixed results.*

Although these scores appear to be low, OMB concluded that HHS was in fact making progress in all five areas against agreed-upon deliverables and time lines.

The IOM committee, in calling for greater accountability within HHS, recognizes that these efforts are already under way, but believes their very complexity may limit their usefulness to key audiences—

especially Congress and the public. The two principal accountability systems, one mandated under GPRA and devolving from the department's strategic plan, the other OMB's PART system, would probably benefit from consolidation, coordination, and some rethinking, so that they produce more actionable results and the evaluation process becomes more efficient and less burdensome.

However accurate the department becomes at documenting the hundreds of data points in the several required reporting systems described, these systems are not sufficient to establish true accountability.

GREATER ACCOUNTABILITY

As discussed in Chapter 2, a clearly aligned vision and mission and a small set of measurable, time-specific goals are essential for the department to establish meaningful accountability. Without an accountability system keyed to these most important issues, the department will be unable to provide a *cohesive, integrated picture* of the nation's health or its own performance. Current performance assessment systems, described above, do not support true accountability, as defined by the committee. In its view, true accountability requires a dual focus on program implementation (process) and results (outcomes) and should have four components:

1. development of supporting information systems,
2. regular feedback and progress reports to Congress on what these information systems reveal about program management and results,
3. a commitment to make the changes necessary to increase program effectiveness, and
4. a broad assessment—beyond the piecemeal approach of monitoring individual programs—of how well programs *collectively* are working to achieve departmental goals.

Challenges to Creating Effective Accountability Systems[6]

Accountability systems are, in large part, a means of achieving better long-term performance. However, the desire for higher performance can be thwarted if program managers feel threatened by the accountability process. "Few … officials want to publicly commit to hard-to-reach performance targets," says Robert Kaplan, an originator of the Balanced Scorecard. The movement for increased transparency in government (well illustrated by http://www.ExpectMore.gov) increases the number of potential governmental critics and therefore may encourage agencies to set conservative goals and targets. "[L]ower-level department heads become reluctant to commit to any kind of performance target, much less one involving some degree of stretch" (Kaplan, 2000).

As noted previously, HHS already receives considerable oversight from multiple organizations—the White House and the Office of Management and Budget, various congressional committees, and even the public- and private-sector stakeholders involved in the delivery of medical care or committed to the health of the public. These groups each have their own agendas and interests and rarely coordinate—and sometimes compete—with each other. The burden of meeting all these demands can make agencies reluctant to engage in a new process, even if it is better, unless it reduces other reporting requirements.

A collateral benefit of the IOM committee's recommendation that the secretary attempt to build broad consensus around a strong set of longer-term goals would be to counter the tendency of some outside stakeholders to focus on immediate or narrow issues. Shifting this perspective will be difficult, but stakeholders' understanding and buy-in for at least some longer-term goals could go a long way toward preventing the constant pull of short-term concerns that distract from long-term priorities.

Long-term goals and explicit strategies for meeting them are essential to high performance, as is an appropriate framework for measuring progress. Strategy, one of the "essential management elements" the committee considered, requires government officials to thoroughly consider alternatives, make explicit choices, then marshal resources—time, money, and people—to implement them, whether the goal is to improve department operations and managing costs, or the more ambitious "value creation" discussed in Chapter 4. Measurable goals and time-specific

[6]The committee owes a debt to Kaplan (2000) for the organization of this section.

milestones are particularly important in the department's work, since most of the major issues the department faces are inevitably long-term, and its strategies may take a number of years to unfold.

Development of solid strategies may be more feasible as HHS secretaries' tenures are becoming longer. People who expect to hold appointed positions for only a year or two are unlikely to launch laborious strategic development and implementation processes that will play out long after their departure. This holds equally true within agencies whose leaders are appointed. The laborious federal appointment process that frequently keeps key positions vacant or with acting directors for months at a time not only hinders HHS performance, but also militates against accountability.[7]

Finally, for the accountability system to be effective, it needs to include incentives for good performance (and penalties for poor results), for both programs and people. OMB says that the program assessments—good or bad—in the current PART system, for example, are not linked to funding decisions. Until recently, federal agencies generally have not been allowed meaningfully to link employee performance and total compensation. "Pay-for-performance" policies now coming into play, at least for Senior Executive Service members and some other senior-level positions (see Chapter 5), may enable the department to use financial incentives—a powerful motivator in the private sector—to improve program accountability.

IMPROVE CAPABILITY TO MEASURE AND EVALUATE VALUE

The IOM committee takes a broad perspective on the accountability issue, one that distinguishes between "data" and "information." Data are discrete facts; when data are organized, combined, and presented in ways that enables response and action, they become "information." PART and the HHS strategic plan provide data. The committee, by contrast, endorses a higher-level, department-wide *information system*, described below.

The robust data, evaluation, and information system the committee envisions would be akin to an executive information system (EIS) in the

[7]The length of time it takes to fill an administration's top 500 jobs has steadily risen. In the Kennedy administration (1960), it took 2.4 months; in the Bush administration (2000), it took 8.7 months (NRC, 2008).

private sector. Such systems collect and integrate selected data from across their enterprises in a timely way (monthly, weekly, or even daily). These carefully selected data provide the information needed to support a range of management decisions about

- current performance,
- needed changes in strategy,
- potential new programs or discontinuation of underperforming ones,
- improved processes and program operations,
- alignment of efforts across agencies,
- resource allocation, and
- measuring and reporting results.

Developing such a system would be a large undertaking. A good starting point would be to *assemble data around the department's goals and the key health challenges*, described in Chapter 2. These are—by definition—the issues of most national concern, the issues about which Americans need to know most. Over a period of years, other necessary components of the data system could be added and existing data collection efforts updated and improved, through redirection, greater standardization, elimination of redundancies, and so on (NRC, 2001).

Starting with what is useful and available, much of the data for the information system could be drawn from *existing public and private sources* and assembled in creative, multidimensional ways. Although the amount of data already available is vast, it is scattered across agencies throughout government and in many private-sector databases and doesn't necessarily produce actionable information for management.

> An example of creatively combining data from different sources is a surveillance system called the Sentinel Initiative that captures information about Americans' experience with drugs and medical devices.[8] This system enables closer monitoring of product performance and gives rapid indication of any problems that arise, through analysis of existing national electronic claims

---

[8]Creation of such a system was recommended in the 2006 IOM report, *The Future of Drug Safety*, and it was later codified in the Food and Drug Administration Amendments Act of 2007.

> and medical records data maintained by participating private-sector organizations and government entities, including VA [Department of Veterans Affairs], DoD [Department of Defense], and CMS [Centers for Medicare and Medicaid Services]. Thus the information the system produces is of high value for decision making (actionable) and is sharply focused on protecting the health of the public.
>
> Some of the accountability data the department needs will undoubtedly come from the state and local levels. A relatively new branch of health services research called "public health systems research"—which examines the organization, financing, delivery, and impact of public health services (Ix, 2007)—may be especially helpful. Since HHS is the major funder of many of the activities and programs public health systems research evaluates, results of these studies would provide actionable insights regarding program design, funding, and implementation.

Some new data collection efforts may be necessary to fill holes, but the committee is wary of large new efforts and more supportive of *greater coordination among existing data resources*, establishing interoperability among them, and eliminating duplicative resources or ones that are no longer useful.

Current data collection approaches used in the department are too infrequent, too late, and insufficiently detailed for these management purposes; further, they document specific program activities rather than cross-departmental, coordinated achievement of broader goals. (Insofar as these specific program data remain useful to the program managers, they could continue to be collected. However, over time managers may find some of these efforts are unnecessary to assessing the impact of their work and their cross-agency collaborations.)

The secretary should provide strong leadership to make sure the information system becomes a meaningful part of the department's operations, by maintaining oversight of the system as it is developed and implemented, and by ensuring that key officials rely on it when making programmatic decisions. This will reinforce to all HHS staff the importance of program performance.

Related Recommendations

a. **To enable greater accountability, the secretary should oversee development and implementation of a *department-wide data, evaluation, and information system.* The system should be based on a broad analytic framework designed to aid in managing departmental operations, learning from program experience, evaluating the costs and impact of programs, and determining whether they provide sufficient value for the investment of public funds.**

b. **Congress should authorize the secretary to direct funding from the budgets of all departmental units to support the development of an HHS-wide information system. Funding for such a system would benefit all department units.**

Uses of the New Information System

As indicated, the kind of system envisioned by the IOM committee would generate actionable feedback about how health and human services programs are working, whether they need midcourse corrections, or whether they are performing poorly—in ways that cannot be corrected or are too costly for the benefit achieved—and should be terminated. The secretary must make clear that the purpose of the reporting system is to stimulate improvements in the performance of the department and its constituent units, and that system results will guide decisions about current programs and plans for new investments. As each HHS unit works toward its own integrated vision, mission, and goals, the system will be helpful in program management and tracking.

This system could be described as a "neural network" for the department and is a key component of value creation. It would enable a panoramic view across all health and human services programs and inform the secretary how the department's programs are coordinating their efforts to achieve departmental—as well as individual program—goals. It would enable the integration of data on costs and benefits to show the value received by program beneficiaries and the public. And it should allow the secretary and Congress "to periodically reexamine whether current programs and activities remain relevant, appropriate, and effective in delivering the government that Americans want, need, and can afford" (GAO, 2003).

The new system would not be solely an information resource for the federal government, but also could serve health care organizations in the public and private sectors at the national, state, and local levels. Just like the other performance data available today, the system also should be available to Congress and the public in an electronic, easily accessible, and readily understood form.

The secretary, in collaboration with the surgeon general, could draw on this system to create a brief, annual "State of the Nation's Health" report to Congress (perhaps in a joint session involving members of the multiple committees that oversee department activities), framed around the vision for the nation, departmental mission, and key goals. Referring back to the set of established goals in successive years would provide continuity over time and help policy makers and the public better understand progress made and what is needed in order to achieve further improvements. Involving the surgeon general—"America's doctor"—in the preparation, presentation, and dissemination of the report would further strengthen the surgeon general's role as an authoritative voice on health issues and chief advocate for Americans' health, and would demonstrate that the report is scientifically valid rather than politically motivated.

The committee explicitly does not want such a report to stimulate another massive, micro-level data collection effort and lengthy printed document; instead it suggests that this be an orally presented report that utilizes the recommended information system and draws insofar as possible on existing data and analyses.

Related Recommendations

c. **The department should use the data, evaluation, and information system to**
    - **enable the secretary to *provide Congress with regular reports* on progress toward achieving departmental goals,**
    - ***inform policy development*,**
    - ***facilitate cross-department activities*,**

- **provide *operational information to program management* for quality improvement and midcourse corrections, and**
- **support effective *long-range planning*.**

d. For those outside the department, the system should
- ***be accessible, transparent, timely, and reliable*, and**
- **provide *useful, privacy-protected information* regarding department activities.**

e. The department should *demonstrate accountability* through continuous critical assessment of program efficiency, equity, impact on health, and cost-effectiveness, and through corrective action for underperforming programs.

f. The secretary, in collaboration with the surgeon general, should present Congress and the public with an annual "State of the Nation's Health" report that describes progress toward achieving the vision for the nation's health and the department's key health goals.

GREATER DEPARTMENTAL FLEXIBILITY: A NEW COMPACT WITH CONGRESS

The IOM committee strongly believes the secretary needs greater flexibility in program management and department operations, if *flexibility is balanced with greater accountability*, as described above. The IOM committee sees greater departmental accountability *to* Congress in exchange for greater flexibility *from* Congress as an opportunity to create a "new compact" between these two governmental authorities. What the committee is seeking in proposing the "new compact" is a more productive, working relationship between these two arms of government. Striving for greater accountability and greater flexibility undergird the committee's recommendations and can be achieved through a number of mechanisms, described in this report:

1. *Meaningful engagement in priority-setting:* The committee recommends involving Congress (and others) from the outset in establishing agreement on national priorities and HHS's overall direction. Having to weigh future needs against the many current

demands on the department—many of them congressionally mandated—may improve alignment between program needs, mandates, and the budgets to support them.

2. *A responsible appointment process:* The committee recommends that the appointment process for key HHS officials not only ensure that its executives have the administrative, leadership, and technical or scientific expertise to manage their respective areas, but also that vacancies are promptly filled, so that agencies do not experience gaps in leadership.
3. *Improved accountability and reporting:* The committee strongly believes that the department must be held strictly accountable for its performance. To enable this, the committee recommends a robust data collection and analytic system, building on current efforts, that will provide meaningful information about the state of the nation's health and departmental activities. HHS must use this system to inform decision making about future programs and to improve ongoing operations.
4. *A staff commensurate with the needs:* The work of the department demands a high-performing staff, but the committee recognizes that the current HHS workforce is threatened by impending retirements and, at times, inadequate scientific or public health expertise. The secretary can work with the Office of Personnel Management (OPM) to foster flexibility in the hiring process for people who are outside government, in the structuring of benefits and work schedules to retain employees who would otherwise retire, and in supporting the education of a new generation of public health professionals and health scientists.
5. *Support for the department's role in national health issues:* For many reasons outlined in this report, the department must participate actively in any national health reform effort. Over time, Congress will need help in monitoring the impact of reform. It would be greatly aided by the committee's recommendation that the department support (a) increased knowledge about the comparative effectiveness of various preventive and treatment methods and about the organization and delivery of care, as a basis for policy, (b) strengthened public information efforts, and (c) widespread adoption of health information technology.
6. *Increased flexibility:* Were the committee's recommendations adopted, the department would be held to a higher standard of accountability; it would have improved capacity to document

> and improve its own and the health system's performance; and it would have a strong workforce, led by competent, credible executives, working toward widely agreed-upon priorities. In acknowledgement of those strengths, Congress should provide flexibility and opportunities for collaboration, and it should provide the department with adequate funding for its vital work.

Many factors would make this a complex set of negotiations between legislators and the administration. However, it is a worthy goal to try to rationalize this relationship, in light of the kind of responsible and nimble department the country needs today.

The Need for a New Compact

Increasingly stringent limits on the HHS secretary's flexibility are hampering departmental leadership. A secretary's role is to focus on broad goals and strategies and gather the resources to meet them, as well as respond quickly and effectively to emergencies or emerging threats. But this role has become increasingly difficult to carry out, because secretarial authority has eroded to the point that in some areas it is no longer commensurate with the responsibilities of the position.

Most of these limits on authority have come about because of Congress's increased attention to the details of departmental management and operations. Some of the former secretaries interviewed for this report described the degree to which Congress "has become much more directive in specifying the functions of each unit of the department," including crafting job descriptions and the "fine details" of program operations and delivery, such as, "including floors and ceilings on spending and service, as well as a rising tide of earmarks, or what Congress now calls 'congressionally directed funding'," that reflect particular interests (Appendix G).

As a result, the secretary and the department now are in danger of being hamstrung by these externally imposed restrictions. For example, until recently,[9] Medicare could not add prevention benefits without a change in statute. In other cases, Congress has taken away HHS's flexi-

[9]The Medicare Improvement for Patients and Providers Act of 2008, passed in July 2008, allows the Centers for Medicare and Medicaid Services to make national coverage decisions regarding prevention policies and authorizes the secretary of HHS to extend coverage to additional preventive services through the national coverage determination process.

bility to test new approaches. For example, it did not allow CMS to test either competitive pricing of managed care plans in areas with good plan penetration or competitive bidding of clinical laboratory services.

Congress frequently adds new responsibilities to agencies unaccompanied by the resources needed to carry out the new tasks. In a particularly troubling example, over the past two decades, Congress has enacted 125 statutes that directly affect FDA's regulatory responsibilities—requiring new regulations, regulatory programs, or policy. In most cases these new requirements need scientific knowledge or expertise to develop and administer; in some cases they require laboratory research; but *in no case* has Congress provided an appropriation for staff or other resources to implement the new program (FDA Subcommittee on Science and Technology, 2008).

Amid positive comments on the value of congressional engagement and "the salutary benefits of a close and positive working relationship with their authorizing and appropriating committees and subcommittees," the former secretaries who were interviewed had some significant complaints (see Appendix G). One had to do with the sheer number of these committees, each having various requests (see Chapter 2, Box 2-2). There is a burden to having so many sources of congressional inquiry and meeting the ongoing clearance requirements for responding to congressional requests for testimony, reports, and constituent services. For example, between January 2006 and September 2008, 22 high-level FDA staff were called on to testify before Congress on 68 occasions—averaging over two testimonies each month (FDA, 2008).

The IOM committee believes that additional and reinstated decision-making authority is needed in order to give the secretary the flexibility to create value in departmental activities. This authority must come from Congress, with continued appropriate oversight. Examples where greater flexibility has the potential to increase value include the following:

- Rationalize health care provider payment policies, which could not only improve health outcomes and promote better integration of care, but potentially would generate substantial short- and long-term monetary savings.
- Strengthen methods to combat fraud and abuse (not only is this an essential component of program oversight, but it may be a

way to recoup funds that can be used to support other department efforts and recommendations in this report).[10]

- Achieve greater administrative efficiency through, for example, standardizing and improving electronic claims processing or making certain information technology investments (Kleinke, 2005; Taylor et al., 2005).
- Allow Medicare payments to be made to midlevel health care professionals under the direction of physicians, when appropriate and cost effective.
- Simplify program management and oversight rules and reduce unnecessary variability—including in coverage decisions—across programs and HHS regions, not to stifle innovation, but to make working with government more equitable and transparent for program beneficiaries, the public, health care providers, researchers, and other key constituencies.

To facilitate the increased flexibility in authority that the IOM committee recommends, it also believes the secretary needs flexibility to use a modest proportion of program budgets to create a "strategic initiative fund," that would be used to enhance cross-agency and cross-departmental activities that exhibit innovation in responding to twenty-first century challenges, such as those involving the Department of Homeland Security and the protection of the public against risks. The fund could also be used to respond to new, unforeseen, or expanding public health threats that require quick departmental response. The secretary would, of course, be accountable to Congress for the use of this fund, which could—if the added flexibility proves useful—grow over time.

The health sector challenges today are of such magnitude that the department needs the capacity to work flexibly, creatively, and quickly in response to changing situations, and outside the confines of individual agency parameters. Many private-sector businesses have established independent research units—"innovation funds"—to tackle thorny problems, take advantage of new opportunities, or work across established organizational units. In the past, Congress, too, has recognized the need

[10]As an indicator of the potential size of the return, the Department of Justice successfully recovered $9.3 billion between 1996 and 2005 in 379 health care fraud and abuse cases initiated by whistleblowers (Kesselheim and Studdert, 2008).

for this kind of capacity—notably in creation of the Defense Advanced Research Projects Agency.[11]

Such flexibility exists within NIH. A previous IOM committee concluded that emerging biomedical challenges are such that a single NIH institute or center cannot respond adequately and that cross-NIH collaborations are needed. In a 2003 report, it recommended that 5 percent of the overall NIH budget be set aside to allow institute and center directors to fund trans-NIH initiatives of their choosing. A common fund of about 1 percent (1.6 percent in 2007) of total NIH funding—was established in 2004 and is now a statutory requirement, with its own line-item funding. The earlier IOM committee also recommended that the NIH director have a Special Projects Program, independent of the budgets of the individual NIH institutes and centers, to support initiation of high-risk, innovative research. NIH has now established a Director's Pioneer Award Program and a Director's New Innovator Award for purposes similar to those the committee envisioned (IOM, 2003; NIH, 2008a, 2008b).

Related Recommendation

g. **Congress should establish *a new, strategic initiative fund* to enable the secretary to support cross-agency and cross-departmental activities that exhibit innovation in responding to twenty-first century challenges, and to respond quickly to new, unforeseen, or expanding public health threats.**

---

[11]DARPA is the Department of Defense's (DoD's) central research and development organization, established in 1958 in order to prevent military surprises, such as the 1957 launch of *Sputnik* by the Soviet Union. DARPA's impact outside the military may be best exemplified by its role as funder of projects that led to computer networking, hypertext, and other now-ubiquitous technologies that enabled development of the Internet and World Wide Web.

REFERENCES

FDA (Food and Drug Administration). 2008. *Congressional testimony.* http://www.fda.gov/ola/listing.html (accessed October 8, 2008).

FDA Subcommittee on Science and Technology. 2008. *FDA science and mission at risk.* Washington, DC: FDA Science Board.

GAO (Government Accountability Office). 2003. *Executive reorganization authority: Balancing executive and congressional roles in shaping the federal government's structure.* Washington, DC: GAO.

HHS (Department of Health and Human Services). 2000. *Healthy people 2010.* Washington, DC: HHS.

HHS. 2007. *Strategic plan, 2007-2012.* Washington, DC: HHS.

HHS. 2008a. *500-day plan information.* http://www.hhs.gov/500DayPlan/ (accessed October 27, 2008).

HHS. 2008b. *President's management agenda (PMA).* http://www.hhs.gov/pma/ (accessed November 12, 2008).

IOM (Institute of Medicine). 2003. *Enhancing the vitality of the National Institutes of Health: Organizational change to meet new challenges.* Washington, DC: The National Academies Press.

Ix, M. 2007. *Advancing public health systems research: Research priorities and gaps.* Washington, DC: AcademyHealth.

Kaplan, R. 2000. Overcoming the barriers to balanced scorecard use in the public sector. *Balanced Scorecard Report: Harvard Business School* (November 15).

Kesselheim, A., and D. Studdert. 2008. Whistleblower-initiated enforcement actions against health care fraud and abuse in the United States, 1996-2005. *Annals of Internal Medicine* 149:342-349.

Kleinke, J. 2005. Dot-gov: Market failure and the creation of a national health information technology system. *Health Affairs* 24:1246-1262.

NIH (National Institutes of Health). 2008a. *Former Director, Elias A. Zerhouni, M.D.* http://www.nih.gov/about/director/zerhouni_archive.htm (accessed November 17, 2008).

NIH. 2008b. *NIH roadmap for medical research.* http://nihroadmap.nih.gov/ (accessed November 17, 2008).

NRC (National Research Council). 2001. *Toward a health statistics system for the 21st century: Workshop summary.* Washington, DC: National Academy Press.

NRC. 2008. *Science and technology for America's progress: Ensuring the best presidential appointments in the new administration.* Washington, DC: The National Academies Press.

OMB (Office of Management and Budget). 2008a. *Expectmore.Gov: Frequently asked questions.* http://www.whitehouse.gov/omb/expectmore/faq.html (accessed October 8, 2008).

OMB. 2008b. *The President's management agenda: The scorecard.* http://www.whitehouse.gov/results/agenda/scorecard.html (accessed October 27, 2008).

OMB. 2008c. *Dept of Health & Human Service Programs.* http://www.whitehouse.gov/omb/expectmore/agency/009.html (accessed October 27, 2008).

Taylor, R., A. Bower, F. Girosi, J. Bigelow, K. Fonkych, and R. Hillestad. 2005. Promoting health information technology: Is there a case for more-aggressive government action? *Health Affairs* 24:1234-1245.

7

The Transition

Once you get the ear of a politician, you get something real. The highbrows can talk forever and nothing happens. People smile benignly on them and let it go. But once the politician gets an idea, he deals in getting things done. Many are extraordinarily able in devising political plans that hold water, not only in the matter of votes but administratively.

Frances Perkins[1]

Discussions about the role of the secretary in leading a department as large, diverse, and complex as HHS—and preparing it to meet twenty-first century challenges—vividly illustrated for committee members the difficulty of the position. Yet, every few years, a new individual must take up the task, expeditiously learning from predecessors and stakeholders in a process that might unfold like the scenario presented in Box 7-1.

The recommendations in the preceding chapters of this report present a secretary with a long agenda, and no clear indication of what should be done today, next week, next month, or next year. This chapter is not meant to be a rigid blueprint and was not part of the committee's statement of task. But, understanding how important the transition period for new secretaries is, and how much they must do in a short time to "hit the ground running," the committee believed it necessary to translate some of its general thinking—about creating value, about vision and goals, about alignment and accountability, about workforce, and about the other topics that were subjects of its recommendations—into tangible suggestions for action.

---

[1]Frances Perkins, "The Roots of Social Security," address delivered at the Social Security Administration, Baltimore, Maryland (October 23, 1962). Perkins, the first female Cabinet member, was secretary of labor during the entirety of Franklin Roosevelt's presidency and a chief architect of Social Security.

BOX 7-1
The Secretary-Designate–A Scenario

The phone rings, and a senior leader in U.S. domestic or health policy, relaxing at home on the Saturday evening after Thanksgiving, answers. The President-elect is calling to ask this widely respected individual to serve as the twenty-first secretary of the U.S. Department of Health and Human Services. The request elicits an enthusiastic, "I will be honored to serve."

Even though this call was not a surprise, the new secretary-designate feels a mix of excitement and trepidation. The excitement comes from having the opportunity to bring direction and transformative ideas to the $2 trillion health sector. The trepidation lies in the challenge of bringing order to a department with a $737 billion budget and 300 programs.

Soon the briefing process is under way. The appointee must simultaneously prepare to lead the department and for confirmation hearings:

- The appointee listens carefully to current agency heads and many others, learning innumerable details about the current organization and leadership of the 65,000-person department.
- Courtesy visits to Capitol Hill are arranged, and it feels as if the political aspects of the job are building to hurricane force. The appointee hears from many interest groups voicing suggestions about changing programs and operations and warnings against creating new levels of bureaucracy and splitting up or combining agencies.
- Mounds of reports, memoranda, budgets, organizational charts, and academic papers shape the topography of the secretary-designate's temporary Washington office.
- The appointee focuses on developing the department's budget for the next fiscal year–the largest budget of any agency in the history of the United States or, for that matter, any other country.
- The appointee interviews candidates for the team that will run the department. Some current executives want to stay–not always the most effective ones; interest groups recommend various candidates; congressional committee chairs propose their top aides; and the President-elect's transition team and others put forward individuals, some with little familiarity with the substance of health policy or the health sciences.

By January 19, the next secretary has barely had time to think. But that day, the Senate recognizes the appointee's round-the-clock preparations with a vote in favor of confirmation–a signal of confidence in the nominee's ability to make a positive difference.

The next day, as the new chief architect of U.S. health policy, the appointee attends the inaugural ceremony, and somberly takes the oath of office in the presence of immediate family. Then the real work begins.

TRANSITION STEPS

Table 7-1 presents informal advice for achieving a successful transition to a new secretary's tenure. Most of the steps correspond to recommendations contained in this report or originated in discussions of the committee or the summary of interviews with former secretaries, included as Appendix G.

TABLE 7-1 Transition Steps

Step	*Initial Steps: The First 90 Days*	*Remarks*
1	Build the team (Chapters 3 and 5).	Organize and staff the Office of the Secretary and make key appointments. Set a standard of excellence, ensuring scientific and administrative integrity; include career officials to build trust and use knowledge; hold regular meetings to jointly review budget and operations; promote long fixed terms for key science heads.
2	Determine early policy priorities (Chapter 2).	These will drive "first 100 days" decisions and first-year budget, which is likely the best opportunity for initiating major program reforms and will set the standard for future budgets. Priorities should reflect a consensus of top HHS officials, the White House, and Office of Management and Budget, and should include strategies for health reform.
3	Engage with Congress (Chapter 6).	Begin dialog with Congress around the "new compact." What is desired and feasible in terms of accountability for key goals, including making progress on health reform, in exchange for greater flexibility? Encourage the Senate to expedite confirmation hearing for agency heads.
4	Initiate assessment of key challenges and process to define vision, mission, and goals (Chapter 2).	Too many interests will be involved to complete this strategic planning work quickly, but it should be conducted expeditiously—officials should treat this as a priority. Reach out to an array of key individuals within and outside government. Use a variety of communications media to build support around challenges and priorities.
5	Align the team with the initial policy priorities and, when developed, the vision, mission, and goals (Chapter 3).	Practice effective internal communications about challenges and priorities. All agency heads and program directors should be accountable for ensuring alignment. Identify gaps and overlap among programs.

6	Establish a process for making policy and operational decisions (Chapter 3).	Put into place a decision-making process that is rigorous, clear, efficient, and establishes accountability for results.
7	Commission work on the analytic framework for department-wide data, evaluation, and information system (Chapter 6).	Start teams on specific tasks—e.g., assessing utility and overlap of data already collected across agencies, eliminate duplicative or underused data; develop feedback loops so that agencies that can use data from another departmental unit can receive it; initiate discussions with other public- and private-sector entities that collect related information on data sharing. Involve privacy experts from the beginning.
8	Commission development of an HHS workforce development strategy (Chapter 5).	The department is only as good as its people, and an adequate pipeline for recruiting highly qualified staff must be ensured.
Step	***Intermediate Steps: The First Year in Office***	***Remarks***
1	Complete assessment of key challenges and process to define and promulgate vision, mission, and goals (Chapter 2).	Be as inclusive as possible in order to secure buy-in and increase the likelihood that the vision, mission, and goals will be lasting; set the stage for building coalitions.
2	Reorganize HHS structure if necessary (Chapter 3).	The presumption in this report is against major reorganization, but some change may be needed to meet goals and align operations. Reorganization efforts suggested include reducing the number of positions reporting directly to the secretary, and unifying FDA and USDA food safety activities within HHS.

continued

3	Work with the White House and Congress from the outset of health reform efforts (Chapter 2).	Health reform cannot be successfully achieved without the cooperation of the White House, Congress, and the department. The department should play a major role in national health reform efforts because it will ultimately inherit the responsibility of implementing any health reform legislation that is enacted.
4	Review plans and obtain funding for an improved information system (Chapter 6).	Commission rapid review of the current information system; identify reporting capacity needed and gaps in capabilities; develop a plan for investments and staging, with attention to security, simplified access, and usability, among other priorities.
5	Seek to secure predictable funding of the science agencies (Chapter 3).	The NIH, CDC, FDA, and AHRQ must be able to underwrite multiyear investigations and campaigns.
6	Evaluate the state of public health, and ensure its vitality and strength (Chapters 3 and 5).	Conduct a review of the adequacy of the public health workforce, and charge agency heads to review how public health principles, including health promotion and disease prevention, can be more fully integrated into their activities.
7	Evaluate the state of science in HHS, and ensure its vitality and strength (Chapters 3 and 5).	Constant threats are that the scientific workforce will lack the resources and credibility necessary to engage private-sector scientists authoritatively, that agency decisions will reflect politically preferred social values rather than valid and reliable findings, and that programs will calcify rather than adjust to new findings and demonstrated best practices.
8	Develop a strategy for assessing value in health services (Chapter 4).	Establish a plan to review current public and private efforts assessing the costs, effectiveness, and impacts of different preventive and treatment methods and ways of organizing care as a first step in identifying opportunities

Step		Remarks
		for integrating data and gaps in information. Develop a plan for moving forward on highest priority topics.
9	Develop or review the national strategy on the HHS and health workforce (Chapter 5).	Assess problems in numbers, geographic location, specialty mix, and diversity of health professionals and researchers, including the performance of health professions training programs in resolving these imbalances. Within the department, make it easier for private-sector experts to spend time in HHS and for HHS senior staff to gain private-sector experience and other means to maintain the vigor of the department's senior workforce.
10	Simplify operations (Chapter 6).	Examine HHS programs from the perspective of individuals who use them—health care providers, state and local health departments, researchers, patients and families, manufacturers and distributors of regulated products, and so on.
11	Prepare first "Health of the Nation" report (Chapter 6).	This year and thereafter, a concise report to Congress provides an opportunity to talk about progress toward the vision for the nation's health, resolving key health challenges and barriers to further improvements.

Step	***Steps Toward Continuity: Throughout These Secretary's Tenure***	***Remarks***
1	Continuously insist on alignment (Chapters 2 and 3).	The tendency will be for programs to fall out of alignment.
2	Maintain policy and operational decision-making processes throughout all programs (Chapter 3).	Clear consistent decision-making processes will be required throughout the secretary's tenure so that decisions are responsive, timely, and contribute to the department's accountability for results.

continued

3	Promote coordination between public health and health care (Chapter 3).	Medicare and Medicaid reimbursement should not conflict with evidence-based public health strategies.
4	Work closely with Congress and the White House as national health reform options are developed (Chapter 2).	The department should provide leadership by making departmental data available to inform reform options, facilitating the assessment of options, providing departmental resources to help resolve problems, communicating to the public, and implementing enacted reform legislation.
5	Treat state and local health departments as partners (Chapters 3 and 4).	Technical assistance sometimes will be needed to help state and local agencies meet HHS expectations, and two-way communication will help ensure that HHS programs are practical and implemented.
6	Launch the new data system (Chapter 6).	Phase in access by user categories. Include data from other public and private sources, and continue to seek feedback on usability and usefulness.
7	Use plain language in documents and communications (Chapter 4).	Department communications should be culturally competent, jargon free, and avoid legalistic language; strategic communications should be part of the secretary's planning and policy process at all times.
8	Promote electronic information capabilities, including electronic health records (Chapters 4 and 5).	Help the health care system move into the twenty-first century; this can be done through public-private partnerships, incentives or, if necessary, federal mandates.
9	Reward staff performance and innovation (Chapter 5).	This will require a systematic approach and constant negotiations with the Office of Personnel Management and other authorities.
10	Invest in the training of biomedical and health researchers of all disciplines (Chapter 5).	In large measure, this is the future of the nation.

11	Continue emphasis on "value" in health care (Chapter 4).	As new study findings emerge, ensure that they are presented to providers and the public in easily usable form; continue work with public- and private-sector entities to encourage ongoing research in key areas.
12	Continue reporting to Congress on the health of the nation (Chapter 6).	This opportunity to engage Congress in the progress made in reaching departmental goals is important in achieving greater accountability for the department, a cornerstone of the new compact with Congress.

Throughout this report, the committee has acknowledged the tremendous challenges facing the men and women who agree to serve as secretary of HHS. Yet, the importance of these challenges offers strong motivation to accept such a difficult role. The committee's goal was to make the secretary's work easier and to ensure that incumbents could be successful, through adoption of some general principles woven into—and throughout—the foregoing recommendations.

- *Simplify competing priorities*—The department has so many current and potential responsibilities that the secretary's ability to lead a high-performance department is in jeopardy. A compelling and widely agreed-upon vision for the nation's health, mission, and goals will help the secretary and the department focus on the most important work.
- *Build consensus on goals*—Broad agreement about goals—and greater accountability for achieving them—should reduce external pressure, including from Congress, to take on "one more responsibility"—especially without the resources necessary to meet it. With current budgets, only so much can be realistically accomplished.
- *Rely heavily on "best evidence"*—Another way to focus efforts is by looking to science and research for guidance. Policy decisions should be made, insofar as possible, based on evidence of what works. Decisions about program design, implementation, and continuation similarly should be based on evidence of what works—thus the importance of the proposed accountability system. Where scientific opinions differ, the department must have a credible, transparent mechanism for resolving disputes.
- *Use department leverage to improve the health care system*—The department has unequalled influence over the nation's entire health care system and needs to use that leverage to encourage (a) systemwide use of the most effective and efficient prevention and treatment modalities and mechanisms for delivery of care ("building value into the system"), (b) implementation of health information technology, and (c) an emphasis on health promotion, disease prevention, and primary care.
- *Seek meaningful, broad-reaching health reform*—Inevitably the department will be drawn into planning for health reform. Its data and expertise will make essential contributions. A primary focus of health reform discussions will be ways to control costs,

and the secretary must ensure that reform ideas are comprehensive and address how to improve care, not just pay for it. At the same time, the secretary must ensure that the system that results continues to serve Americans who are elderly, disabled, and poor.

- *Look for partners everywhere*—Today's health challenges require new, more effective collaborations—with Congress, with the White House and other federal departments, with state and local government and public health agencies, with health care professionals and providers, with health care leaders worldwide, with the private sector, and with the public.

A

Acronyms and Abbreviations

ACF	Administration for Children and Families
AHRQ	Agency for Healthcare Research and Quality
AoA	Administration on Aging
ASH	assistant secretary for health
ASMB	Assistant Secretary for Management and Budget
ASPE	Assistant Secretary for Planning and Evaluation
ASTHO	Association of State and Territorial Health Officials
ATSDR	Agency for Toxic Substances and Disease Registry
CBO	Congressional Budget Office
CDC	Centers for Disease Control and Prevention
CMS	Centers for Medicare and Medicaid Services
DARPA	Defense Advanced Research Projects Agency
DHS	U.S. Department of Homeland Security
DoD	U.S. Department of Defense
EIS	Executive Information System
EPA	Environmental Protection Agency
ERISA	Employee Retirement Income Security Act
FCC	Federal Communications Commission
FDA	Food and Drug Administration
FEMA	Federal Emergency Management Agency
FSIS	Food Safety and Inspection Service (USDA)
FY	fiscal year

GAO	Government Accountability Office
GPRA	Government Performance and Results Act
GS	General Schedule
HEW	U.S. Department of Health, Education, and Welfare
HHS	U.S. Department of Health and Human Services
HIV/AIDS	human immunodeficiency virus/acquired immunodeficiency syndrome
HRSA	Health Resources and Services Administration
HTA	Health Technology Assessment
HUD	U.S. Department of Housing and Urban Development
IHS	Indian Health Service
IOM	Institute of Medicine
MIPPA	Medicare Improvements for Patients and Providers Act
NACCHO	National Association of County and City Health Officials
NACHC	National Association of Community Health Centers
NASA	National Aeronautics and Space Administration
NHLBI	National Heart, Lung, and Blood Institute
NICE	National Institute for Clinical Excellence
NIH	National Institutes of Health
NRC	National Research Council
NSF	National Science Foundation
OCR	Office for Civil Rights
OIG	Office of the Inspector General
OMB	Office of Management and Budget
ONCHIT	Office of the National Coordinator for Health Information Technology
OPDIV	operating division (HHS)
OPM	Office of Personnel Management
P4P	pay for performance
PART	Program Assessment and Rating Tool
PHSSEF	Public Health and Social Services Emergency Fund
PHS	Public Health Service
PMA	President's Management Agenda

QALY	quality-adjusted life-year
RN	registered nurse
SAMHSA	Substance Abuse and Mental Health Services Administration
SCHIP	State Children's Health Program
SES	Senior Executive Service
SSA	Social Security Administration
USDA	U.S. Department of Agriculture
VA	U.S. Department of Veterans Affairs

B

Letter from Congressmen Waxman and Davis

ONE HUNDRED TENTH CONGRESS

Congress of the United States

House of Representatives

COMMITTEE ON OVERSIGHT AND GOVERNMENT REFORM

2157 RAYBURN HOUSE OFFICE BUILDING

WASHINGTON, DC 20515–6143

MAJORITY (202) 225-5051
FACSIMILE (202) 225-4784
MINORITY (202) 225-5074

www.oversight.house.gov

June 20, 2007

Harvey V. Fineberg, M.D., Ph.D.
President
Institute of Medicine
500 Fifth Street, NW
Washington, DC 20001

Dear Dr. Fineberg:

Our nation faces a dual challenge of growing public health threats and soaring health care costs. A number of pressing public health problems, including the growing burden of chronic disease driven in part by an epidemic of obesity, and the threat of pandemic flu and other emerging infectious diseases, require a focused national response. Meanwhile, the capacity of the federal government, American businesses, and the ability of individual citizens to purchase health care is threatened by rampant growth in health care costs. The steadily rising cost of health care is already eroding employer-sponsored health insurance and placing enormous pressure on public coverage through Medicare and Medicaid. These challenges are interrelated: for example, the burden of chronic disease has major implications for health care spending.

These challenges are not confined to particular states or regions of the country, and for that reason, they cannot effectively be addressed by individual states or private employers. The federal government must be involved.

We are concerned, however, that the key federal department in this effort, the Department of Health and Human Services (HHS), may be hindered in meeting this challenge by its organizational structure. The existing mix of HHS agencies and missions evolved over several Administrations in a largely ad hoc manner. For this reason, HHS may not be optimally configured to achieve the twin goals of advancing health and controlling health care costs.

Harvey V. Fineberg, M.D., Ph.D.
June 20, 2007
Page 2

We are therefore writing to request that the Institute of Medicine undertake a study of whether HHS is ideally organized to meet the public health and health care cost challenges that our nation faces. What are the missions of the Department and its individual agencies, and how do those missions relate to the challenges confronting us? How effectively are the agencies organized to achieve their missions? Could the missions of individual HHS agencies be consolidated or realigned to make them more effective? What recommendations would the IOM make to the Congress and HHS to improve the focus of individual agencies, enhance their accountability, and improve their efficiency? What recommendations would IOM make to more effectively integrate promotion of public health and control of health care costs across the Department?

To be of the most benefit, this study should be concluded within the next year and a half and should produce recommendations that are administratively feasible, can be implemented in a relatively short time frame, and will not require substantial new resources. Thank you for your consideration of this request.

Sincerely,

Henry A. Waxman
Chairman

Tom Davis
Ranking Minority Member

C

HHS Organizational Chart and Missions

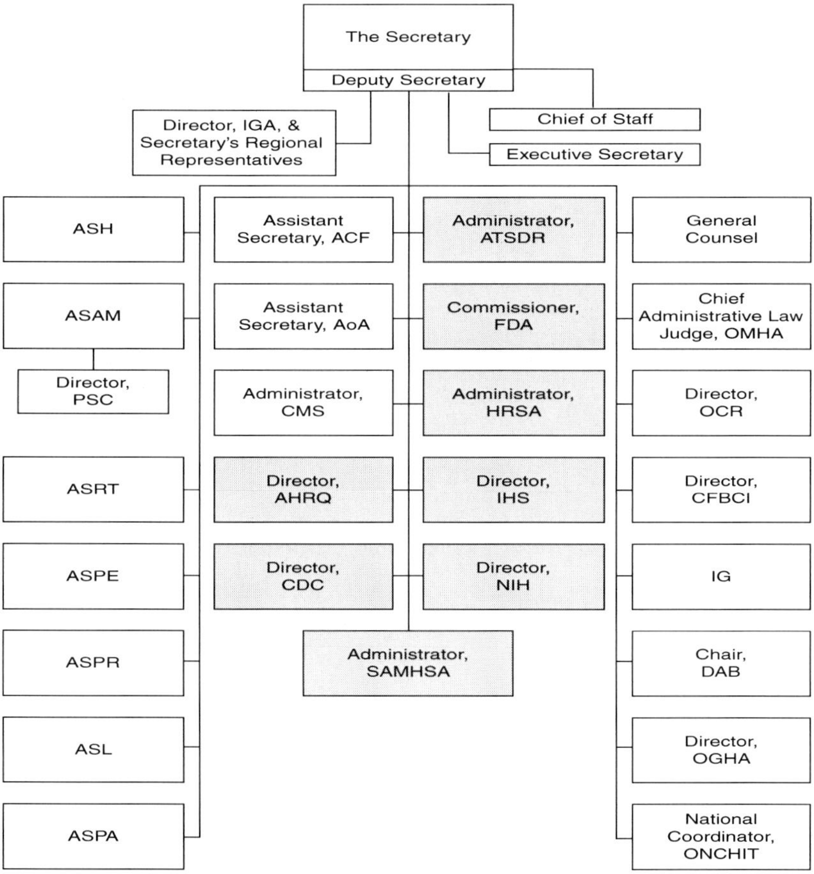

FIGURE C-1 HHS organizational chart.
NOTE: The shaded boxes in the chart indicate agencies included under the Public Health Service (PHS). The PHS also includes the Office of Public Health and Science and the 10 regional health administrators, which are administered under the Assistant Secretary for Health (ASH).
SOURCE: HHS. 2008. *Department of Health and Human Services Organizational Chart.* http://www.hhs.gov/about/orgchart.html (accessed October 8, 2008).

Department of Health and Human Services (HHS)
http://www.hhs.gov
To enhance the health and well-being of Americans by providing for effective health and human services and by fostering sound, sustained advances in the sciences underlying medicine, public health, and social services

Administration for Children and Families (ACF)
http://www.acf.hhs.gov
To promote the economic and social well-being of families, children, individuals, and communities

Agency for Healthcare Research and Quality (AHRQ)
http://www.ahrq.gov
To support, conduct, and disseminate research that improves access to care and the outcomes, quality, cost, and utilization of health care services

Administration on Aging (AoA)
http://www.aoa.gov
To promote the dignity and independence of older people, and to help society prepare for an aging population

Agency for Toxic Substances and Disease Registry (ATSDR)
http://www.atsdr.cdc.gov
To serve the public by using the best science, taking responsive public health actions, and providing trusted health information to prevent harmful exposures and diseases related to toxic substances

Centers for Disease Control and Prevention (CDC)
http://www.cdc.gov
To promote health and quality of life by preventing and controlling disease, injury, and disability

Centers for Medicare and Medicaid Services (CMS)
http://www.cms.hhs.gov
To ensure effective, up-to-date health care coverage and to promote quality care for beneficiaries

Food and Drug Administration (FDA)
http://www.fda.gov
To rigorously assure the safety, efficacy, and security of human and veterinary drugs, biological products, and medical devices, and assure the safety and security of the nation's food supply, cosmetics, and products that emit radiation

Health Resources and Services Administration (HRSA)
http://www.hrsa.gov
To provide the national leadership, program resources, and services needed to improve access to culturally competent, quality health care

Indian Health Service (IHS)
http://www.ihs.gov
To raise the physical, mental, social, and spiritual health of American Indians and Alaska Natives to the highest level

National Institutes of Health (NIH)
http://www.nih.gov
To employ science in pursuit of fundamental knowledge about the nature and behavior of living systems and the application of that knowledge to extend healthy life and reduce the burdens of illness and disability

Substance Abuse and Mental Health Services Administration (SAMHSA)
http://www.samhsa.gov
To build resilience and facilitate recovery for people with or at risk for substance abuse and mental illness

SOURCE: HHS. 2007. *Strategic plan, 2007-2012.* Washington, DC: HHS.

D

U.S. Secretaries of Health, Education, and Welfare (1953–1979) and HHS (1980–Present)

	Secretary	Tenure	President
1.	Oveta Culp **Hobby**	1953–1955	Eisenhower
2.	Marion B. **Folsom**	1955–1958	Eisenhower
3.	Arthur S. **Flemming**	1958–1961	Eisenhower
4.	Abraham I. **Ribicoff**	1961–1962	Kennedy
5.	Anthony J. **Celebrezze**	1962–1965	Kennedy–Johnson
6.	John W. **Gardner**	1965–1968	Johnson
7.	Wilbur J. **Cohen**	1968–1969	Johnson
8.	Robert H. **Finch**	1969–1970	Nixon
9.	Elliot L. **Richardson**	1970–1973	Nixon
10.	Caspar **Weinberger**	1973–1975	Nixon–Ford
11.	F. David **Mathews**	1975–1977	Ford
12.	Joseph A. **Califano, Jr.**	1977–1979	Carter
13.	Patricia Roberts **Harris**	1979–1981	Carter
14.	Richard S. **Schweiker**	1981–1983	Reagan
15.	Margaret O. **Heckler**	1983–1985	Reagan
16.	Otis R. **Bowen**	1985–1989	Reagan
17.	Louis W. **Sullivan**	1989–1993	G. H. W. Bush
18.	Donna E. **Shalala**	1993–2001	Clinton
19.	Tommy G. **Thompson**	2001–2005	G. W. Bush
20.	Michael O. **Leavitt**	2005–present	G. W. Bush

NOTE: The dark line in the table represents the point at which the department's name changed from the Department of Health, Education, and Welfare to the Department of Health and Human Services, and the Department of Education was established as a separate entity.

E

Recommendations Directed to Congress

All of the committee's recommendations for improving the organization and operations of the Department of Health and Human Services (HHS) will benefit from congressional endorsement. Certain recommendations cannot be accomplished effectively, if at all, without corresponding legislative action related to authority and budgetary support.

Below are recommendations directed specifically to Congress. recommendations 2 and 4 relate to the funding and oversight of the department, recommendation 3 relates to the effectiveness and efficiency of the health care system, and recommendation 5 relates to the need for greater flexibility in its internal operations and decision making.

Recommendation 2:
Foster Adaptability and Alignment

2c. The secretary should ensure *a more prominent and powerful role* for the surgeon general, who, in addition to leading the Commissioned Corps, should be a *strong advocate for the health of the American people* and work actively to *educate Americans on important health issues*. The secretary should work with the President and Congress to *establish a process for identifying surgeon general candidates* for Presidential appointment *that gives high priority to qualifications and leadership*, and Congress is strongly urged to consider a *longer term* for this office.

2d. The secretary should work with the President and Congress to establish an appointment process for the department's senior-level officials that *protects the scientific and administrative integrity of major departmental units, promotes progress toward departmental goals*, and is *based primarily on the candidates' qualifications and experience.* Congress again is strongly urged to consider *longer terms* for some of these officials–especially the directors of the National Institutes of Health (NIH) and the Centers for Disease Control and Prevention (CDC), and the commissioner of the Food and Drug Administration (FDA)–which would provide critical continuity in the nation's public health and scientific endeavors.

2e. The President should make timely appointments and Congress should expedite the confirmation process for key HHS officials, including the secretary, deputy secretary, surgeon general, and the heads of FDA and NIH. Secretarial appointments, such as the director of CDC, should also be expedited.

2h. Congress should allocate *sufficient, predictable funding for NIH, CDC, FDA, and AHRQ* in order to preserve and enhance these agencies' scientific missions. Congress should also establish a *specific budget line for AHRQ* that is *independent* of appropriations to other HHS agencies.

2i. To address the growing threat of food-borne illnesses, Congress should *unify the USDA's Food Safety and Inspection Service and the food safety activities of FDA within HHS* and ensure provision of adequate resources for high-quality inspection, enforcement, and research.

Recommendation 3:
Increase Effectiveness and Efficiency of the U.S. Health Care System

3a. The secretary should work with Congress to establish a capability for *assessing the comparative value–including clinical and cost-effectiveness–*of medical interventions and procedures, preventive and treatment technologies, and methods of organizing and delivering care. The assessment of comparative value should begin by leveraging department-wide data sources in conjunction with supportive evidence from providers, payers, and health researchers.[a]

3b. The secretary should work with Congress to ensure that the department's *programs and reimbursement policies are outcomes based,* reflecting best available evidence of value and creating incentives for adoption of best practices, including integration of care, in order to improve quality and efficiency.

[a]The committee did not reach consensus on recommendation 3a. Although the majority of the committee supports the language of the recommendation, David Beier, J.D., Senior Vice President of Global Government and Corporate Affairs, Amgen; Kathleen Buto, M.P.A., Vice President, Health Policy, Johnson & Johnson; and Myrl Weinberg, C.A.E., President, National Health Council, did not agree with the majority's view and provided dissenting opinions, which can be found in Appendix F. They were not able to agree on a common statement.

Recommendation 4:
Strengthen the HHS and
U.S. Public Health and Health Care Workforces

4b. Congress should authorize the department, in cooperation with the Office of Personnel Management, to assemble a package of current and innovative programs and benefits designed to *encourage talented, experienced individuals to transition back and forth between government and private-sector service*, thereby identifying ways to leverage the best of both.

4c. Congress should provide the secretary with additional authority to *reward performance, innovation, and the achievement of results*, through bonuses, merit-based pay, recognition awards, or other mechanisms of proven effectiveness.

4f. Congress should give the secretary authority to create new programs that invest in the *future generation of biomedical and health services researchers*, enabling the continued discovery of new, more effective methods of preventing, treating, and curing disease; promoting health; improving health care delivery and organization; and controlling health system costs.

Recommendation 5:
Improve Accountability and Decision Making

5. A "new compact" between Congress and the department is essential as HHS works toward achieving its vision for a healthy nation, departmental mission, and key health goals. Under this compact, the secretary would provide Congress and the nation regular, rigorous reports about departmental activities and assume greater accountability for improving performance and obtaining results; in return, Congress should allow the department greater flexibility in its internal operations and decision making.

5b. Congress should authorize the secretary to direct funding from the budgets of all departmental units to support the development of an HHS-wide information system. Funding for such a system would benefit all department units.

5g. Congress should establish *a new, strategic initiative fund* to enable the secretary to support cross-agency and cross-departmental activities that exhibit innovation in responding to twenty-first century challenges, and to respond quickly to new, unforeseen, or expanding public health threats.

F

Dissenting Opinions on Recommendation 3a

Deliberations of the committee resulted in consensus on all but one of the recommendations presented in this report. As noted in the report, unanimous agreement could not be reached on recommendation 3a, which is included in Box F-1.

The majority of the committee fully supports the language of this recommendation. However, three members of the committee disagreed with the views of the majority.

The dissenting opinions of David Beier, J.D., Senior Vice President of Global Government and Corporate Affairs, Amgen; Kathleen Buto, M.P.A., Vice President, Health Policy, Johnson & Johnson; and Myrl Weinberg, C.A.E., President, National Health Council, are presented in this appendix.

BOX F-1
Recommendation 3a

The secretary should work with Congress to establish a capability for *assessing the comparative value–including clinical and cost-effectiveness–*of medical interventions and procedures, preventive and treatment technologies, and methods of organizing and delivering care. The assessment of comparative value should begin by leveraging department-wide data sources in conjunction with supportive evidence from providers, payers, and health researchers.

Dissenting Opinion of David Beier, J.D., Senior Vice President of Global Government and Corporate Affairs, Amgen

The committee's report recommends that the secretary of the Department of Health and Human Services (HHS) undertake the sensible step of evaluating the methods of organizing and delivering care (including important concepts such as the use of "medical homes"). Specifically, tasking HHS with a thorough analysis of the benefits and risks of implementing significant health system changes is a prudent and reasonable measure to inform potential future action by the U.S. Congress and the administration. However, the report moves immediately beyond the needed analytic assessment phase and issues specific and detailed recommendations on the topics of comparative effectiveness and cost-effectiveness assessments.

These majority recommendations are controversial, as recognized by the dissenting views expressed by committee members. Further, the fact that the report, at one point, calls for further analysis and then issues a recommendation to mandate the use of new methods for coverage and reimbursement under Medicare, Medicaid, and other federal health care programs suggests that any recommendations made at this juncture are not fully informed by the necessary research identified by the committee.

The report does not explicitly or implicitly endorse any particular health technology assessment (HTA) model. That said, the current policy debate in Washington has been informed by frequent references to the adoption of HTA models from jurisdictions outside the United States, including most prominently the National Institute for Clinical Excellence (NICE) in the United Kingdom.[1] This dissent is a commentary about the risks of adopting those systems. Without acknowledging how comparative effectiveness and cost-effectiveness could be misused, there is substantial risk that the terms of the real policy debate could become obscured.

Below, I discuss three primary areas of concern with the majority's recommendations.

---

[1]Other nations have over time also used HTA authorities, including—most notably—Australia and Canada. In addition, Wales and Scotland in the United Kingdom have their own HTA authorities. Other nations in Europe, including Germany, are moving toward full adoption and application of HTA authority to limit access or to make coverage or price determinations.

1. Foreign models of centralized government decision making should not be applied to the U.S. health care system without full consideration of the implications and associated risks.

Much of the policy debate in Washington has focused on the adoption of some of the most controversial aspects of foreign models for HTA.[2] Foreign models for HTA are generally premised on a basic fact that the government must ration care to a budgetary level rather than to the level determined by a physician to be appropriate for an individual patient. In these systems, lower-cost treatment options are promoted, even though they may be less effective than other available, more advanced therapies. In doing so, severe restrictions on access to the fruits of innovative medicine and medical technology are the natural result. It is inappropriate to endorse the broad application of budget-guided rationing in the U.S. health care system without a thoughtful analysis and evaluation of the implications for those Americans who would be subject to the government decision-making authority's actions.[3] I note that, although the report does not recommend rationing based on cost-effectiveness explicitly, no recommendations against such an approach are included.

In its discussion of these issues, the report also fails to recognize that there are potentially serious consequences to patients and Amer-

[2]A frequently noted example of a foreign government's model for HTA is the United Kingdom and NICE. If the NICE system were applied in the United States, American cancer patients could be required to experience one of the worst levels of cancer care in the developed world. For example, in 2006, the United Kingdom ranked ninth out of 28 European countries for male cancer mortality (where the first has the lowest mortality) and twenty-second out of 28 for female mortality. The mortality figures could be attributable to the slow uptake of new cancer drugs. See U.K. Department of Health. 2007. *U.K. cancer reform strategy*; Karolinska Institute. 2007. *A pan-European comparison regarding patient access to cancer drug*; Reuters. 2008. U.K.'s NICE says "no" to four kidney cancer drugs.

[3]The connection to health budgets is prominent in the report. Specifically, in the discussion of practice patterns, the report relies on an assumption that up to 30 percent of health care spending in the United States could be eliminated if geographic variations in the care intensity were changed to the least intensive levels. This approach, as outlined in a preliminary analysis by the Congressional Budget Office (CBO), assumes that the increased costs in more intensive geographic locations are attributable to the use of more costly technology. However, this point has not been proven since important factors were not accounted for by the CBO. Importantly, the issue of regional variation needs to be addressed by assessing population and sociodemographic issues, facility and specialist access differences (e.g., access to specialized providers), and differences in payment systems employed by health care payers. It is an illusory perspective to assume that comparative effectiveness and cost-effectiveness research will address these issues.

ica's cutting-edge health technology industry. If systemwide decisions are made to limit access to care that is beneficial for patients, those patients who rely on the developments of innovative health care companies will be left without the most effective treatments for grievous illness, and those companies would cease as an economic engine for the American economy.[4]

2. **Any recommendation about specific changes to the health care system is premature before the analysis recommended by the committee is complete.**

As noted above, one of the fundamental concerns with this report is that it calls for changes to the health care system in the absence of a thorough analysis and assessment of potential solutions. In particular, conducting a full assessment of the issues before implementing changes to the health care system is necessary because the fields of comparative effectiveness and cost-effectiveness are not uniformly understood, even among recognized experts in the fields.[5] For this

[4]Centralized government decision making that relies on comparative effectiveness and cost-effectiveness may not provide an appropriate environment and necessary incentives to foster innovation. Developers of innovative products could easily predict an unfavorable cost assessment in areas where competitors are old and inexpensive despite the fact that physicians and patients recognize the need for new solutions and treatments. Similarly, product developers might prefer to focus in areas where existing therapies are expensive, since that provides a better chance of recovering investment, even if the unmet need is less than in other therapy areas. Under such a system, patients may not get access to medicines that society would, on balance, regard as sensible uses of resources.

[5]We note that the report itself blends the use of comparative effectiveness and cost-effectiveness, although experts in the field recognize them as separate and distinct areas of research. There is no standard, shared definition of *comparative effectiveness*, owing to the fact that comparative effectiveness is not yet a mature science. In *Learning what works best: The nation's need for evidence on comparative effectiveness in health care*, a background paper prepared for the IOM's Roundtable on Evidence-Based Medicine, the roundtable staff noted that primary comparative effectiveness research involves the direct generation of clinical information on the relative merits or outcomes of one intervention in comparison to one or more others and that secondary comparative effectiveness research involves the synthesis of primary studies (usually multiple) to allow conclusions to be drawn. Numerous other definitions have been posited. The nascent nature of comparative effectiveness assessments is demonstrated by the fact that, earlier this year, the U.S. Congress mandated a review of comparative effectiveness techniques by the IOM. *Cost-effectiveness* is generally considered a method for measuring the incremental benefits and incremental costs of competing technologies, resulting in a cost-effectiveness ratio. Cost-effectiveness analysis generally produces a number (i.e., an incremental cost-effectiveness ratio or an incremental quality-adjusted life-year). Therefore, any system based on cost-effectiveness will gravitate toward the use of a numerical value in isolation

reason, the committee notes the need for greater evaluation and analysis on the best methods to promote efficiency and to determine "comparative value." In doing so, the committee recognizes that there is distinct merit in analyzing health care delivery systems to determine efficiencies.[6] The committee recommends that the approach to this analysis should be holistic in nature and encompass all available interventions, treatments, and delivery systems (i.e., diagnostics, surgeries, medical treatments, drugs, devices, plan benefit designs, and settings of care). Further, the committee recognizes that any assessment should focus on all available treatment types in a given clinical area, not just new therapies or interventions.

3. **Complex methodological and policy issues surrounding comparative effectiveness and cost-effectiveness, as used by centralized government decision-making entities in foreign countries, should be carefully reviewed to determine whether they are reasonable, given the social values and the acceptance level of rationing in the United States.**

Before new mechanisms for comparative effectiveness and cost-effectiveness in the U.S. health care system are implemented and government-sponsored studies are conducted, it is important that an evaluative framework be developed and vetted by leading experts in the field. The framework must include parameters for assessing the societal value of treatments and interventions (e.g., productivity, quality of life) instead of crude cost assessments.[7]

as opposed to a comprehensive or holistic qualitative assessment of the best treatment for an individual patient.

[6]An analysis by the McKinsey Global Institute found that the additional spending seen in the United States compared to other Western economies is due primarily to operational and intermediation process, not the cost of inputs (e.g., drugs). See McKinsey & Company. 2007. *Accounting for the cost of health care in the United States.*

[7]In fact, there is no consensus regarding the appropriate dollar value per quality-adjusted life-year (QALY) gained upon which to base resource allocation decisions. In the United States, $50,000 per QALY is a frequently cited reference point; however, many investigators have questioned the scientific basis for this reference point and note that it has not been updated (inflationary updates alone would bring the figure closer to $120,000).

This careful approach is advised because the use of cost-effectiveness to inform health care coverage and reimbursement determinations has not been adopted in the United States and has been controversial in other countries for several reasons, including the following:

- *Arbitrary thresholds:* Cost-effectiveness requires the use of thresholds that determine whether there is enough value to justify coverage and reimbursement. There is empiric evidence that current thresholds used to determine coverage and reimbursement in other countries, and even the implicit value of $50,000 to $100,000 QALYs (quality-adjusted life-years), in the United States are too low and are arbitrary. Other well-accepted methods suggest the thresholds should be two to three times higher.[8] This variability raises serious questions about a method that has such an important impact on patients and innovators. Further, while properly performed economic analyses can contribute one element to a multidimensional assessment of a particular technology, cost-effectiveness analysis in particular relies on arbitrary threshold levels (e.g., incremental cost-effectiveness ratio < £30,000) to establish whether any particular technology is "worth it." Experience with other countries suggests that when cost-effectiveness analysis is part of comparative effectiveness assessments, the strong tendency is to rely on these cost-effectiveness ratios and thresholds to make determinations about comparative "value," which in turn are applied to make coverage and reimbursement decisions at the population rather than the individual patient level.
- *Timing:* Cost-effectiveness analyses conducted using standard methods based on questions (and comparisons) posed by payers are filled with large degrees of clinical and economic uncertainty. This is because the evidence base at the time of the evaluation (often at the time of market authorization for one of the products) may not be sufficiently mature to address the relevant questions and the different evidence demands from both regulatory bodies (e.g., the U.S. Food and Drug Administration

---

[8]See R. S. Braithwaite et al. 2008. What does the value of modern medicine say about the $50,000 per quality-adjusted life-year decision rule? *Medical Care* 46(4):349-356; C. Evans. 2004. Use of quality adjusted life years and life years gained as benchmarks in economic evaluations: A critical appraisal. *Health Care Management Science* 1:43-49.

[FDA]) and payers. In other words, large evidence gaps are generally present when these analyses are conducted. Even though uncertainty can be explored in these economic analyses, making national determinations of cost-effectiveness that influence both public and private coverage in the face of such uncertainty, impacting millions of lives, is highly problematic.

- *QALY limitations:* The common metric used in cost-effectiveness (i.e., the QALY) is an imperfect metric with imperfect measurement tools that fails to capture important elements of value. Additionally, the QALY as a measure itself treats the value of each additional year of life equally regardless of age or level of disability, which may not be consistent with social values in the United States.[9] For example, the cost-effectiveness of providing expensive cancer treatment for a 35-year-old working mother could be very different from that of a 75-year-old retiree. Basing the assessment on a single average QALY value or a single threshold could provide payers with justification to limit coverage for all.
- *Rapidly changing prices and technology:* Cost-effectiveness is not well suited to assessing the efficiency of products and markets with dynamic competition involving rapidly changing prices and technological obsolescence.[10] At best, it is a static, point-in-

[9]The use of QALYs as a metric in cost-effectiveness analysis has several limitations. First, how to measure quality-adjusted life-years is quite controversial, because there are methodological challenges and suboptimal measurement instruments available. QALYs simply cannot capture many important aspects of value to an individual (e.g., the reassurance of a test or treatment option or the benefits of preventing bacterial resistance) and patient preferences. The QALY metric also treats the value of each additional year of life equally regardless of age. Social values may be different and apply greater weight to additional life-years in the younger age groups. Additionally, QALYs may also discriminate against the disabled because they will generate fewer QALYs gained from lifesaving treatments than do the young or healthy since they will not have a full recovery. Cost-effectiveness analysis attempts to maximize QALYs, but this may not be consistent with social values. QALYs may fail to capture actual public preferences for spending health resources. People want to pursue goals in health other than maximizing QALYs. They may want to prioritize patient groups in most need, those without treatment options, or vulnerable populations such as Medicare beneficiaries regardless of whether doing so represents a QALY-maximizing strategy. See P. Ubel and M. Chernew. 2000. Willingness to pay for a QALY. *Medical Decision Making* 3:332-342.

[10]There are several aspects of cost-effectiveness analysis that frequently bias the assessment against the innovative or new product. One large bias against innovators is that the assessments are performed at a point in time with a single price, generally a high initial price relative to the products "average" lifetime price over the "on-patent" and "off-patent" periods. This creates a large bias when compared against an older product at

time assessment of average costs for many technologies subject to rapid or substantial change. If cost-effectiveness is used to limit access to some products, it may actually keep costs higher for other, covered products. For medical devices, the rapid iteration of technology and the potential for increased effectiveness when measured over a longer term make cost-effectiveness assessments difficult to perform.

- *Different cost perspectives:* The perspective of an economic analysis is not always a societal perspective. For example, cost-effectiveness may differ depending on the kind of insurance or public program providing the financing. A fully integrated, prepaid health plan with a stable enrollee base might treat a costly prescription drug treatment as cost-effective in avoiding potentially more expensive care, while a Medicare stand-alone prescription drug plan or an insurer facing rapid turnover in enrollees might view the cost-effectiveness very differently. This can lead to the denial of good treatments for those patients who have a clinical need for them, simply because they may appear less cost-effective for the "average" patient.
- *Evolving field:* The fields of comparative effectiveness and cost-effectiveness are not uniformly understood, even among recognized experts in the fields. The committee appropriately notes the need for greater evaluation and analysis of the best methods to promote efficiency and to determine "comparative value." This analysis should be holistic and multidimensional in nature and should encompass all available interventions, treatments, and delivery systems (i.e., diagnostics, surgeries, medical treat-

---

its "commodity" or generic price or the lowest price over its lifetime. In fact, society accrues great value from the new technology in the off-patent period, but because only the initial high price is used in the assessment, the technology may not be seen as cost-effective relative to the threshold set when compared to a generic drug. If the average cost were assumed (based on benchmarks or projections), a very different conclusion might be reached about the value of the innovation. Sometimes generic comparators are (understandably) chosen, with commodity prices, making it unlikely that an incremental innovation proves cost-effective at a price that will ensure an adequate return on investment for the manufacturer. If a return on investment is unlikely, incentives for investment in research and development in that area may disappear and manufacturers will not focus on that disease area, or will focus on small modifications despite the presence of an unmet medical need. See also T. J. Philipson and A. B. Jena. 2006. Who benefits from new medical technologies? Estimates of consumer and producer surpluses for HIV/AIDS drugs. *Forum for Health Economics & Policy* 9(2); A. B. Jena and T. J. Philipson. 2007. Cost-effectiveness as a price control. *Health Affairs* 26(3):696-703.

ments, drugs, devices, plan benefit designs, settings of care). The fact that the committee calls for further analysis suggests an understanding that comparative effectiveness and cost-effectiveness methods are not ready for broad application, especially for coverage and reimbursement under federal health care programs.

- *Separation of costs from comparative effectiveness:* Aware of the tendency to rely on a simplistic numeric threshold to make determinations about comparative "value," some U.S. policy makers advocating for a comparative effectiveness center have urged that comparative effectiveness assessment be kept entirely separate from economic analysis.[11]
- *Rationing:* In the United States, health care rationing based purely on economic analyses, as is done in other countries, does not appear to be consistent with prevalent social values and, thus, is unlikely to be supported.[12] The report lacks any recommendations against such an approach.

Dissenting Opinion of Kathleen Buto, M.P.A., Vice President, Health Policy, Johnson & Johnson

In the chapter "Increase Efficiency and Effectiveness of the U.S. Health Care System," the committee recommends:

> *3a. The secretary should work with Congress to establish a capability for assessing the comparative value—including clinical and* ***cost-effectiveness****—of preventive and treatment technologies, procedures, and methods of organizing and delivering care. The assessment of comparative value should begin by leveraging department-wide data sources in conjunction with supportive evidence from providers, payers, and health researchers.* [bold added for emphasis]

I support having the secretary work with Congress to establish a capability to assess comparative effectiveness on the range of preventive and treatment approaches as described but strongly disagree that the ca-

---

[11]See G. R. Wilensky. 2008. Cost-effectiveness information: Yes, it's important, but keep it separate, please! *Annals of Internal Medicine* 148(12):967-968.

[12]See P. J. Neumann. 2004. Why don't Americans use cost-effectiveness analysis? *American Journal of Managed Care* 10(5):308-312.

pability should include cost-effectiveness. **The crux of the disagreement is whether a federally established capability (or potential entity) should conduct cost-effectiveness assessments that will have an impact nationwide on benefits and coverage.** I acknowledge that patients, physicians, and payers will use the outcomes research to make their own assessments of value. I disagree with having this done at a nationwide level for the following reasons:

- *Cost-effectiveness differs depending on both the type of patient and the kind of insurance or public program providing the financing:* For example, the cost-effectiveness of providing expensive cancer treatment for a 35-year-old working mother could be very different from that of a 75-year-old retiree. Basing the assessment on averages could provide payers with justification to limit coverage for all. A fully integrated, prepaid health plan with a stable enrollee base might treat costly prescription drug treatment as cost-effective in avoiding potentially more expensive care, while a Medicare stand-alone prescription plan or an insurer facing rapid turnover in enrollees might view the cost-effectiveness very differently. This can lead to the denial of good treatments for those patients who have a clinical need for them, simply because they may appear less cost-effective for the "average" patient.
- *Cost-effectiveness analysis will not address underlying drivers of costs:* Comparative effectiveness research will undoubtedly improve the evidence base and lead to better use of health resources, but it will not have a major impact on costs, as the Congressional Budget Office (CBO), RAND, and others have found.[13] One misconception is that pharmaceuticals and medical devices, one focus of interest in applying cost-effectiveness,

[13]P. Orszag. September 5, 2007. Letter to the Honorable Pete Stark. Washington, DC. In the letter to Chairman Stark estimating the impact of enacting a comparative effectiveness entity, Orszag states, "CBO estimates that the information produced by enacting section 904 would reduce total spending for health care services. Specifically total spending—by public and private purchasers—would be reduced by about $.5 billion over the 2008–2012 period and by about $6 billion over the 2008–2017 period. Direct spending by the federal government—mostly for Medicare, Medicaid, and the Federal Employees Health Benefits program—would be reduced by $.1 billion over the 2008–2012 period and $1.3 billion over the 2008–2017 period." A RAND COMPARE analysis reaches a similar conclusion, that comparative effectiveness research will not result in significant savings in the near term. See http://www.randcompare.org.

make up a relatively large percentage of health care costs, when in fact the percentages are quite small.[14] In focusing on including cost-effectiveness as part of comparative effectiveness, the committee's recommendations do not address some of the major drivers of cost including the fact that 75 percent of costs are driven by chronic disease and the role of the fee-for-service payment system in Medicare, where doing more generates more reimbursement. The committee does recommend outcomes-based reimbursement, which is a good thing—but this alone will not significantly change either the management of chronic disease or the incentives that reward doing more.

- *Although the committee does not require payers to adopt coverage or reimbursement based on these assessments, they will do so:* My concern is that cost-effectiveness based on averages will trump consideration of individual clinical value, despite the differences in patients noted above. Insurers are looking for ways to limit high-cost treatments and are more likely to limit access to treatments that do not meet preset, arbitrary cost-effectiveness thresholds, regardless of clinical value to some patients if there is a national assessment to fall back on. In other countries, cost-effectiveness analysis has been a basis for approving or denying access to a treatment for everyone. If cost-effectiveness analysis is used to limit coverage of certain treatments, patients will have to pay the full costs of these treatments if they need them.
- *Methods for assessing cost-effectiveness are imperfect and controversial:* In other countries—the United Kingdom, Australia, Germany, and Canada, cost-effectiveness is assessed using different methods; however, the challenges in all are how to define a comprehensive assessment of effectiveness and how to ensure

[14]For prescription drugs, the Centers for Medicare and Medicaid Services estimates spending in 2006 was about 11 percent of total health care spending. A. Caitlin, C. Cowan, M. Hartman, S. Heffler, and the National Health Expenditure Accounts Team. January/February 2008. National health spending in 2006: A year of change for prescription drugs. *Health Affairs* 27:14-29. Recently, CBO issued a report on the impact of technological change on the growth in health care spending, attributing about half the growth to "changes in medical care made possible by advances in technology." CBO is able to "count" as contributors to growth in costs such factors as growth in personal income, aging of the population, and rising personal income. Everything else is counted as "technological change," including changes in physicians' practices, price increases in technologies and treatments, and other hard-to-quantify cost increases. Congressional Budget Office. January 2008. *Technological change and the growth of health care spending.* Washington, DC: CBO.

that the decision includes all relevant factors, not just the cost-effectiveness ratio. The quality-adjusted life-year (QALY) is the most often used metric of effectiveness, which includes both survival and quality of life on the same measurement plane. This can have the effect of emphasizing life-years added, when some treatments may be more focused on reducing side effects, improving quality of life, or increasing productivity, as examples. Recently, recommendations of the National Institute for Health and Clinical Evidence (NICE), which some cite as a model for comparative effectiveness in the United States, to prevent access to medical technologies that are standards of care outside the United Kingdom—have been criticized by patient groups as denying access to treatments for which there are limited or no alternatives and failing to consider the full impact of treatments on patients, caregivers, and society in general.

- *Cost-effectiveness is not well suited to assessing the efficiency of products or markets with dynamic competition involving rapidly changing prices and technological obsolescence:* At best, it is a static assessment of average costs for many technologies subject to rapid change. If cost-effectiveness is used to limit access to some products, it may actually keep costs higher for covered products. For medical devices, the rapid iteration of technology, and the potential for increased effectiveness when measured over a longer term, make cost-effectiveness assessments difficult to do.
- *Having cost-effectiveness analysis done at a national level will reduce incentives for innovation:* If the result of comparative effectiveness analysis is to limit benefits to "the most effective, lowest-cost option," this may become "the effective-enough, lowest-cost option." This is likely to shift industry investment to less risky, incremental innovation, rather than encourage companies to take the considerable financial risk of producing breakthrough treatments. In the United States, we have the potential to develop a comparative effectiveness capability that increases incentives for breakthrough innovation and is better targeted to individuals, while making it less attractive to develop incremental innovation. Cost-effectiveness assessments provided at a national level may signal the opposite.

In closing, I believe that additional recommendations focused on key drivers of costs, such as improved management of chronic disease and changes in the current fee-for-service reimbursement system, would put in better perspective the role of comparative effectiveness research in improving the effectiveness and efficiency of the health care system.

The charge to the Institute of Medicine (IOM) from Congressmen Waxman and Davis was to undertake a study of "whether HHS is ideally organized to meet the public health and health care cost challenges that the nation faces" and to focus on the missions and organization of the individual agencies. I believe a more appropriate recommendation for improving HHS's leadership in advancing comparative effectiveness research might be to focus first on what HHS can do almost immediately:

> **The secretary should drive improvements in health care in the United States by leveraging the comprehensive data collected by the Centers for Medicare and Medicaid Services, the Food and Drug Administration, the National Institutes of Health, the Agency for Healthcare Research and Quality, and the Centers for Disease Control and Prevention to assess real-world comparative effectiveness of medical interventions and procedures, preventive and treatment technologies, and methods of organizing and delivering care.**

This HHS initiative would complement consideration of legislation to establish a comparative effectiveness entity. The current recommendation to pair cost-effectiveness with a national comparative effectiveness capability is a polarizing issue that could undermine broad consensus in favor of a concerted national effort to support this research.

Dissenting Opinion of Myrl Weinberg, C.A.E., President, National Health Council

In the chapter "Increase Efficiency and Effectiveness of the U.S. Health Care System," the committee recommends:

> *3a. The secretary should work with Congress to establish a capability for assessing the comparative value—including clinical and* ***cost-effectiveness****—of preventive and treatment*

> *technologies, procedures, and methods of organizing and delivering care. The assessment of comparative value should begin by leveraging department-wide data sources in conjunction with supportive evidence from providers, payers, and health researchers.* [bold added for emphasis]

I support having the secretary work with Congress to establish a capability to assess comparative effectiveness of the range of preventive and treatment approaches as described. However, I do not agree with including cost-effectiveness in the recommendation. **The crux of my disagreement is that cost-effectiveness, which addresses the issue of collective health care costs, does not adequately protect the needs of individual patients to enhance their physical and mental health status.** While cost-effectiveness studies have a societal value, equally important is how this information is used to benefit the individual. According to the IOM's Roundtable on Evidence-Based Medicine, "Value in health care is expressed as the physical health and sense of well-being achieved relative to the cost. This means getting the right care at the right time to the right patient for the right price." Such value cannot be accomplished if the social gain of managing health care costs is achieved at the expense of individual physical and mental health.

I am concerned that cost-effectiveness data based on averages will trump consideration of individual clinical value. Used this way, clinical effectiveness analyses could be used to limit coverage of treatments vital to particular individuals' "physical health and sense of well-being." In support of my dissenting opinion I offer the following observations.

- *Cost-effectiveness differs depending on both the type of patient and the kind of insurance or public program providing the financing:* For example, the cost-effectiveness of providing expensive cancer treatment for a 35-year-old working mother could be very different from that of a 75-year-old retiree. Basing the assessment on averages could provide payers with justification to limit coverage for all. A fully integrated, prepaid health plan with a stable enrollee base might treat costly prescription drug treatment as cost-effective in avoiding potentially more expensive care, while a Medicare stand-alone prescription plan or an insurer facing rapid turnover in enrollees might view the cost-effectiveness very differently. This can lead to the denial of good treatments for those patients who have a clinical need for them, simply because they may appear less cost-effective for the "average" patient.

- *Cost-effectiveness analysis will not address underlying drivers of costs:* Comparative effectiveness research will undoubtedly improve the evidence base and lead to better use of health resources, but it will not have a major impact on costs, as the Congressional Budget Office (CBO), RAND, and others have found.[15] One misconception is that pharmaceuticals and medical devices, one focus of interest in applying cost-effectiveness, make up a relatively large percentage of health care costs, when in fact the percentages are quite small.[16] In focusing on including cost-effectiveness as part of comparative effectiveness, the committee's recommendations do not address some of the major drivers of cost including the fact that 75 percent of costs are driven by chronic disease and the role of the fee-for-service payment system in Medicare, where doing more generates more reimbursement. The committee does recommend outcomes-based reimbursement, which is a good thing—but this alone will not significantly change either the management of chronic disease or the incentives that reward doing more.

---

[15]P. Orszag, September 5, 2007. Letter to the Honorable Pete Stark. Washington, DC. In the letter to Chairman Stark estimating the impact of enacting a comparative effectiveness entity, Orszag states, "CBO estimates that the information produced by enacting section 904 would reduce total spending for health care services. Specifically total spending—by public and private purchasers—would be reduced by about $.5 billion over the 2008–2012 period and by about $6 billion over the 2008–2017 period. Direct spending by the federal government—mostly for Medicare, Medicaid, and the Federal Employees Health Benefits program—would be reduced by $.1 billion over the 2008–2012 period and $1.3 billion over the 2008–2017 period." A RAND COMPARE analysis reaches a similar conclusion, that comparative effectiveness research will not result in significant savings in the near term. See www.randcompare.org.

[16]For prescription drugs, the Centers for Medicare and Medicaid Services estimates spending in 2006 was about 11 percent of total health care spending. A. Caitlin, C. Cowan, M. Hartman, S. Heffler, and the National Health Expenditure Accounts Team. January/February 2008. National health spending in 2006: A year of change for prescription drugs. *Health Affairs* 27:14-29. Recently, CBO issued a report on the impact of technological change on the growth in health care spending, attributing about half the growth to "changes in medical care made possible by advances in technology." CBO is able to "count" as contributors to growth in costs such factors as growth in personal income, aging of the population, and rising personal income. Everything else is counted as "technological change," including changes in physicians' practices, price increases in technologies and treatments, and other hard-to-quantify cost increases. Congressional Budget Office. January 2008. *Technological change and the growth of health care spending.* Washington, DC: CBO.

In closing, the charge to the committee from Congressmen Waxman and Davis was to undertake a study of "whether HHS is ideally organized to meet the public health and health care cost challenges that the nation faces" and to focus on the missions and organization of the individual agencies. Kathy Buto (see dissenting opinion of K. Buto) and I believe that a more appropriate recommendation on improving comparative effectiveness capability might be the following:

> **The secretary should drive improvements in health care in the United States by leveraging the comprehensive data collected by Centers for Medicare and Medicaid Services, the Food and Drug Administration, the National Institutes of Health, the Agency for Healthcare Research and Quality, and the Centers for Disease Control and Prevention to assess real-world comparative effectiveness of medical interventions and procedures, preventive and treatment technologies, and methods of organizing and delivering care.**

G

The Reorganization Option: Views from Former Secretaries of the U.S. Department of Health and Human Services

Paul C. Light, Ph.D.
Robert F. Wagner School of Public Service
New York University

INTRODUCTION

Structure is a central contributor to the overall performance of any organization. It affects the movement of information up and down the chain of command, the level of cooperation between divisions, the development and implementation of policy, and workforce morale. Whether measured by centralization, job specialization, height and width, complexity, implied autonomy, professionalization, or administrative red tape, structure has been repeatedly shown to affect the profitability, innovativeness, customer satisfaction, and flexibility of organizations.

This relationship between structure and performance is so powerful and easily designed relative to policy change that it has often prompted calls for reorganization—dozens of bills are introduced in each Congress to create new departments and reshuffle existing agencies. In government, restructuring has been a particularly popular response to national crisis and the desire for greater administrative accountability, even though it is rarely accompanied by reorganizations of basic oversight structures such as the congressional committee system. Built on the foundations of scientific management—that is, the notion that there is one right way to organize a given activity such as homeland security—the federal government has generally been constructed around a common architecture of hoped-for centralization, specialization, and professionalism.

This paper analyzes the need for structural reform at the Department of Health and Human Services (HHS). Drawing upon interviews with the six former secretaries who began their tenures at the start of the past six presidential administrations (Gerald Ford, Jimmy Carter, Ronald Reagan, George H. W. Bush, Bill Clinton, and George W. Bush), this paper focuses on their views of reorganization as a palliative for achieving and maintaining high levels of performance in the future.[1] The paper begins with a brief overview of the rationale for reorganization and then turns to the general conclusions that emerged from the interviews.

THE ALLURE OF REORGANIZATION

There are many perfectly legitimate reasons to reorganize, but one of them is not immediacy. History suggests that reorganizations of any size are rarely complete upon signing. Congress often goes back into reorganizations to fine-tune, reconsider, and rearrange its work long after passage. This is certainly the case with the Departments of Defense and of Health, Education, and Welfare, for example.

Congress has returned to Defense Department reorganization at least five times over the past 50 years, for example, starting with (1) the 1958 Department of Defense Reorganization Act (P.L. 85-599), which strengthened coordination among the armed services; (2) the 1980 Defense Officer Personnel Management Act (P.L. 96-513), which revised military promotion and retirement practices; (3) the 1985 Defense Procurement Improvement Act (P.L. 99-0145), which was a direct response to the procurement scandals of the early 1980s; (4) the 1985 Goldwater-Nichols Department of Defense Reorganization Act (P.L. 99-433), which once again sought to strengthen coordination; and (5) the 1989 Base Closure and Realignment Act (P.L. 100-526).

Congress has returned to health, education, and welfare reorganization even more frequently, most notably the Department of Education Organization Act in 1979 (P.L. 96-88), which set asunder what President Eisenhower had joined together, and the 1994 Social Security Independence and Improvement Act (P.L. 103-296), which separated the Social Security Administration from what had been renamed the Department of Health and Human Services in 1979.

---

[1]The six secretaries interviewed for this project were promised anonymity. Therefore, all quotes in this paper are on a not-for-attribution basis.

History suggests that government reorganizations are usually a work in progress. Indeed, this author cannot find a single reorganization over the past 70 years that has *not* been changed in some material way at a later time. Indeed, the *U.S. Government Manual* (http://www.gpo access.gov/gmanual/) provides more than 50 pages of executive organizations that have been terminated, transferred, or changed in name since March 4, 1933, the date of Franklin Roosevelt's inauguration. Congress and the President create new agencies, then rearrange, downsize, coordinate, and rearrange them again.

For example, Congress and the President began thinking about how to reorganize the new Department of Homeland Security on the day they created it. In all, there have been at least two internal reorganizations since the department opened for business in March 2003 and a legislative reorganization that involved the Federal Emergency Management Agency in 2006. Indeed, the President anticipated the need for reorganization in Section 733 of his original proposal, which gave the new secretary authority to "establish, consolidate, alter, or discontinue such organization units within the Department, as he may deem necessary or appropriate." Although the White House rightly notes that this is the same authority granted to the secretary of education under the 1979 statute, one must remember that the Department of Education consisted of less than 5,000 employees, while the new department started with 170,000 employees and has grown since.

The decision to create a new federal entity or reorganize existing agencies is not bound by a hard calculus, however. Rather, it involves a balancing test in which one must ask whether the nation would be better served by a new sorting of responsibilities. Simply asked, if a cabinet-level department or agency is the answer, what is the question? At least five possibilities come to mind.

- Reorganization can give a particular issue such as homeland security or veterans affairs a higher priority inside the federal establishment. That is certainly what Congress intended when it elevated the Veterans Administration to cabinet status in 1988. Although the bill was delayed in the Senate due to concerns regarding veterans appeals of benefits decisions, Congress eventually concluded that veterans policy merited the heightened visibility and importance that would come with a statutory seat at the cabinet table, and the perquisites that come with it.

- Reorganization can help integrate, coordinate, or otherwise rationalize existing policy by bringing lower-level organizations together under a single head. That is clearly what Congress intended in creating the Department of Energy in 1977. Congress and the President both agreed that the nation would be better served with a single entity in charge of energy policy than a tangled web of diffuse, often competing agencies. That is also what Congress tried to accomplish in establishing the Department of Defense in 1947 and the National Aeronautics and Space Administration in 1958. It is useful to note that all three of these examples were in response to perceived threats: the Cold War and communism in 1947, fears of losing the space race in 1958, and the moral equivalent of war for energy independence in 1977.
- Reorganization can provide a platform for a new or rapidly expanding governmental activity. That is what drove Congress to create the Department of Housing and Urban Development (HUD) in 1965. Although the federal government was involved in housing long before HUD, the new department was built as a base for what was anticipated to be a rapid rise in federal involvement. However, Congress did not place all housing programs within the new department.
- Reorganization can help forge a strategic vision for governing. This is what Congress expected in creating the Department of Transportation in 1966. The federal government had been involved in building roads and bridges for almost 200 years when Congress created the department, but needed to coordinate its highway programs with its airports, airways, rail, and coastal programs. By pulling all modes of transportation under the same organization, Congress improved the odds that national transportation planning would be better served. Congress expected the same in not disapproving the reorganization plan that created the Environmental Protection Agency in 1970.
- Reorganization can increase accountability to Congress, the President, and the public by making a department's budget and personnel clearer to all, its presidential appointees subject to Senate confirmation, its spending subject to integrated oversight by Congress and its Office of Inspector General, and its vision plain to see. Although it is tempting to believe that such accountability is only a spreadsheet away, cabinet status conveys a megaphone that little else in Washington does. One should never

> discount the impact of perquisites in the political island called Washington, DC. This is certainly what Congress intended to convey in not disapproving the reorganization plan that created the Department of Health, Education, and Welfare in 1953. It is also what it intended 25 years later when it split the Department of Education from that entity.

Even if one can find ample history to support reorganization, it is important to note that creating or redesigning departments or agencies is not a panacea for all that ails a given function. Merely combining similar units will not produce coherent policy, for example, nor will it yield better performance, increase morale, or raise budgets. It most certainly will not make broken agencies whole. If an agency is not working in another department, there is no reason to believe that it will work well in the new department. Conversely, if an agency is working well in another department or as an independent agency, there is no reason to believe that it will continue to work as well in the new department. Bluntly put, "If it's broke, don't move it; if it ain't broke, leave it alone."

The elevation of an existing agency to cabinet status is no guarantee of success either, a point well illustrated by the elevation of the Veterans Administration to cabinet status in 1988. Congress and the President felt that the department would use its newly granted status to provide better, faster health care and benefit processing. Yet neither came to pass. From this author's perspective in studying the reorganization, veterans won a seat at the cabinet table, but no guarantee of stronger leadership, more funding to replace antiquated systems, or a greater commitment to veterans care.

HOW THE SECRETARIES VIEW REORGANIZATION

Department secretaries bring an important perspective to the analysis of reorganization and its costs and benefits. Some secretaries enter office at the beginning of the implementation process, while others are in office when the reorganization takes effect. Some recommend reorganizations, whereas others oppose them. However, all of the secretaries interviewed for this paper understood that reorganization is a difficult task—simply put, it should only be undertaken with a clear rationale and reasonable expectations.

The Costs of Reorganization

Much of the concern involved the size of the reorganization. Two of the six secretaries interviewed for this project had been through large-scale reorganizations—Donna Shalala was secretary when the Social Security Administration (SSA) was removed from the department, while Tommy Thompson was secretary when the Department of Homeland Security absorbed several high-profile units from HHS. A third spent his first months in office rationalizing a host of programs in one "fell swoop"—Joseph Califano moved quickly to implement the most significant organizational reforms since the department was created. The rest of the secretaries had been through smaller-scale reorganizations—general tightening of authority, the statutory creation of the Office of Inspector General in 1975, streamlining of the drug approval process, and so forth.

Whether pushed from outside the department by Congress or inside by the secretary, the secretaries interviewed for this project emphasized the costs of large-scale versus smaller-scale reorganizations. First, large-scale reorganizations absorb much greater political capital even when compared to major policy reforms such as the back-to-back Social Security crises in the late Carter and early Reagan administrations. At a minimum, large-scale reorganizations create enormous turmoil within the department as pieces break off rather like icebergs from an ice shelf. "Reorganization is not a lever for changing culture," said one former secretary. "Confidence does not improve by reorganizing chaos—greater efficiency, yes, but no effect on positive motivation to serve the customer." Nevertheless, given greater legislative freedom and White House support, several argued that the department was due for a major overhaul—once every 50 years is not overkill.

Reorganizations also tend to create temporary, but significant, short-term declines in productivity as staffs try to untangle shared systems. Even reorganizations that involve clean breaks such as the creation of the Department of Education create significant effects as they back out of what was then the HEW hierarchy. "The last thing we should focus on is structure—too many jurisdictions to deal with in any reasonable time," said another secretary. "It is a huge commitment of energy with much less yield than policy change or more aggressive leadership."

Reorganization does not always involve structure. All of the secretaries interviewed for this project had been through some kind of management reform—management by objectives under President Ford; zero-base budgeting under President Carter; the war on waste, fraud, and abuse under President Reagan; the quality movement under President George H. W. Bush; reinventing government under President Clinton; and the President's Management Agenda under George W. Bush. Many secretaries had also instituted their own internal reforms, most of which were designed to strengthen secretarial oversight of the budgeting and policy process or to create a greater sense of collective endeavor such as Thompson's "One HHS" campaign. "Don't move boxes," said a secretary about the first days in office. "Work with the Senior Executive Service until your political help arrives, adopt a 4-year agenda, and get the budget together quickly."

Like structural reorganizations, these process changes vary in size and complexity. Large-scale reforms such as Reagan's war on waste or Clinton's reinventing government create significant obligations for the secretary, while smaller reforms that originate either outside or inside the department can be more easily delegated to the deputy secretary or an assistant secretary.

According to the secretaries, the most successful process changes have involved efforts to create synergies between the operating units within the department, which sometimes act as quasi-independent states. "The Food and Drug Administration and Centers for Disease Control acted like independent agencies," one secretary said. "The secretary had little impact on their agenda; Congress did. So the key is to get them to stop going around the secretary to Capitol Hill, not merge or reorganize them."

The Impact of Change

Some reorganizations are doomed to failure from the very beginning. All of the secretaries interviewed opined that some reorganizations may not be immediately "implementable" given the systems and structure that currently exists. Although all acknowledged the inertia that resides within any government organization, they also pointed to the deleterious effects of "moving boxes" as a fad that has less than ideal effects.

Thus, just as the reasons for reorganization vary, so do the impacts. Some are better designed to deal with a particular problem such as welfare fraud, while others bear little connection to bureaucratic reality. As one secretary noted, "The organizational challenges were the size of the department, but department reorganization was not at the top of the list of fixes—[the] major problem was creating a unified identity in the minds of advocacy groups and Congress, not split things off or add new functions. You have to address the independence instincts by vision, regional offices, hammering the message, opening channels directly to you."

As a result, the secretaries were clearly in favor of deep consultation with the White House and Congress *before,* not after, a major reorganization occurs—consultation that was perhaps less robust than warranted in the Department of Education, SSA, and homeland security reorganizations. Whether well designed or not, the department needs to have its say, particularly given the potential effects of large-scale reorganizations. Surprise is not well tolerated within any organization, let alone one with such significant responsibilities.

The secretaries also listed a number of caveats connected to reorganizations, large scale or small scale.

- Reorganizations may do little to alter organizational culture. Several secretaries noted that the department's primary problems involved organization culture, not structure. Yet whether culture was the problem or not, all of the secretaries were hesitant to embrace large- or small-scale reorganization as a particularly effective method for changing culture. In this regard, their views fit well with research in public administration, which views structural reorganization as a very inefficient tool for creating a new culture: Well designed and implemented, structural reorganization can produce economies of scale and integrated policy, but it is far down the list of interventions that shape culture, except perhaps to the detriment of a shared commitment to values such as customer service, collaboration, and a shared sense of mission. "Symbolic change is more important than organization. You've got to find good people and trust them, create an environment in which people feel comfortable investing in shared ideas. It is better to be a respected manager by walking around, rather than a good box mover."

  This does not mean that the secretaries were unalterably opposed to reorganization as a tool for creating synergies surrounding a particular mission. Several were quite willing to endorse small-scale reorganizations such as merging the food inspection function at the Food and Drug Administration with elements of the food inspection function at the Department of Agriculture. "That makes sense to me," said a recent secretary. "There's no reason to have the responsibilities divided. No benefit for the public." At least one secretary was quite concerned about the continued disputes over the department's role in homeland security. However, synergies and pass-backs are not guarantees of a greater sense of shared mission or ways to create a common culture. "The department is a confederacy," said a secretary. "You've got all these semiautonomous agencies. My transition into office involved a White House plan to add an entirely new layer of political appointees to corral the agencies, but that would have weakened my role as secretary. I was used to a different style as a university president—appoint very talented people, coordinate them through the secretary's office."

- Reorganizations can eclipse major policy concerns. The next HHS secretary will face a long list of major policy challenges, most notably the rapidly approaching Medicare crisis. All of the secretaries agreed that even a small reorganization could create a significant distraction from such issues. Again, the literature on public administration reinforces the worry. It is safe to suggest that reorganizations of any kind will force the secretary to deal with a host of unanticipated issues, not the least of which is recruiting or merging the leadership of the new or reorganized agency. "You lose two years of other opportunities," said a secretary. "[You] can get to the same place by other means, by taking control of the bureaucracy, by putting very smart people in key jobs."

The secretary and his or her team must maintain their focus on key issues, whether operations or new policy initiatives. Developing the testimony, completing studies, outlining new organizational charts, generating the political momentum, and soothing employee concerns—all the efforts needed for a successful reorganization require time and energy that might be better spent on addressing operational problems at agencies such as the Food and Drug Administration and preparing other agencies such as the Centers for Medicare and Medicaid Services for coming policy challenges. The secretary must also prepare for the onslaught of oversight and legal challenges. "I was the most sued person in Washington at the time," said a secretary. "I was the target of 20,000 lawsuits, and had 200 lawyers working full-time to respond. And I was personally liable in many cases because the liability laws were not changed until I left office."

Notwithstanding these costs, reorganizations can improve efficiency and effectiveness. Although the secretaries were generally cautious about the value of reorganization, several did suggest that efficiencies and effectiveness can be found through changes in both structure and process. Indeed, all engaged in at least one or more small-scale reorganizations such as combining the budget and personnel function during the Clinton administration. The combination put the two functions together in an effort to ensure increased accountability among the department's units and appears to have accomplished its goal. "I wanted more decisions made by the secretary," said one secretary of his own small-scale reorganizations. "I wanted a more synchronized budgeting process, not one in which agencies went directly to Congress or the White House. I also wanted to pull information up to the top and coordinate action across the agencies. Anything that Congress couldn't fund somehow found its way to HHS, so I wanted a better sense of common mission."

Such secretary-driven reorganizations are more difficult to design and implement today than they were in the 1970s and 1980s, in large measure because Congress has become much more directive in specifying the functions of each unit of the department in statute. Whereas the department's organic statute gave the secretary significant discretion in determining the job description of Senate-confirmed appointees, recent augmentations in that authority have been more precise, or limiting perhaps. As the secretary's authority to undertake small-scale reorganization has dwindled, so too has the secretary's ability to move quickly to adjust to changing circumstances such as the threat created by biological weapons or potential pandemics.

Reorganization clearly carries costs and benefits, which the secretaries noted in the interviews. Also, there may be equally effective approaches that avoid the greatest costs.

Congress can lower the operating cost of the department without significant reorganization, for example. As the congressional role in limiting executive discretion has grown, so has congressional engagement in the fine details of program delivery, including floors and ceilings on spending and services, as well as a rising tide of earmarks, or what Congress now calls "congressionally directed funding." Some of these earmarks involve what appear to be backdoor requests by the department's own operating units, but others appear to reflect the more traditional dynamics of incumbency advantage and parochial interests. "The Hill was a problem for me," said a secretary. "There was nothing that the committees set as out of bounds. There are so many things the department does that matter back home that Congress really can't stay out of it."

Although all of the secretaries interviewed for this paper recognized the value of congressional engagement, including the salutary benefits of a close and positive working relationship with their authorizing and appropriating committees and subcommittees, there were occasional complaints about the many sources of congressional inquiry and the ongoing clearance requirements for responding to congressional requests for testimony, reports, and constituent services.

Secretary Richard Schweiker may have entered office with the greatest advantages in negotiating with Congress—after all, he had served in both the House and the Senate, had served on the key health authorizing committees in both chambers, and was the ranking member of the Senate health appropriations subcommittee at the time of his appointment. However, other secretaries entered office with good personal relationships as well. "I took advantage of the celebrity of the cabinet post, and always went to the member's office rather than holding court in the secretary's suite," said one secretary. "I also focused on small reorganizations that involved things like technology. The Hill doesn't really know much about running things, so there was room there."

Alternatives to Reorganization

Whatever the reorganization agenda, all of the secretaries were sensitive to the need for close working relationships with the White House. Although all understood the President's stake in overseeing what is one of the flagship departments of government, there were occasional—but intense—concerns about the degree of White House engagement in the department's policy and operational agenda. There was also great concern about the department's participation, or lack thereof, in several high-profile decisions over the past 30 years.

Nevertheless, Congress and the President remain at the center of the HHS universe and have constitutional responsibility for enacting and executing the laws. One device for avoiding the elongated process for securing organizational reform while honoring the separation of powers would be the restoration of the President's reorganization authority as a tool for smaller-scale reorganizations that must now wind their way through a highly complicated congressional structure. This authority once gave the President the freedom to propose reorganization plans to

Congress under a one- or two-house legislative veto. Overturned by the Supreme Court in the early 1980s as an unconstitutional delegation of legislative power, the reorganization authority has never been restored. It could easily pass constitutional muster today under a fast-track process modeled on the approach used in the military base closing act and might be one way to give secretaries of all departments greater leeway in governing their organizations.

Hence, the secretaries tended to focus more on the problems a new secretary might face, rather than the value of a particular reorganization strategy.

- **Connective tissue and shared vision are essential for organizational success.** Again to the issue of process and culture, the former HHS secretaries argued that the biggest organizational problem in the department is not the lack of formal integration of its units, but the effectiveness of the connective tissue through information technology, budgeting, policy development, strategic messaging, and so forth. This connective tissue can be mandated through legislation—note the current emphasis on cybersecurity measures—but it is implemented through secretarial persuasion and employee commitment. Thus, the secretaries generally agreed that Congress and the President should consider the potential cost and benefits of major initiatives, including their own management agendas, on the departments of government.

  Many of the secretaries interviewed for this paper created that connective tissue by holding frequent meetings with their internal "cabinet" of operating officers. Many also spent time reaching out to front-line employees, and several were intimately involved in the civil service recruiting process. One even had an explicit commitment to "capture" as many high-level interns as possible in competition with other departments. Yet whatever their strategy, almost all put an unyielding emphasis on communication through the department. Although this communication involved secretarial messages down through a dense hierarchy, it often involved independent channels from the bottom up, including ad hoc meetings with employees during lunchtime at the department's cafeteria.
- **Appointees matter.** No matter when they served, all of the secretaries interviewed for this project said that the secretary of HHS should have the ability to appoint his or her team to senior

positions in the department. They recognize that they and their staffs operate on behalf of the President in faithfully executing the laws, but also believe that creating a common culture starts at the top with agreement and loyalty from their top lieutenants.

Appointees have different roles at different points of time on the secretarial calendar, however. Each secretary interviewed for this project expressed somewhat different priorities in filling positions, priorities that changed with circumstances, crises, and particular controversies such as stem cell research. All also understood the difference between their personal staff in the secretary's office and the Senate-confirmed staff that ran the operating units such as the Food and Drug Administration (FDA). The secretaries were unanimous in their desire to bring their own team into office as quickly as possible, a commitment that required fast action "before the White House personnel office was able to step in and stop my appointments," as one secretary put it. "I brought 25 people with me," another secretary remembered. "The top operating people were experts, all knew health care, and I had veto authority because of my relationship with the President."

The appointments process has clearly changed dramatically over the past 30 years, of course. There are now more appointees subject to Senate confirmation, including the inspectors general for example, and the White House now plays a much more aggressive role in making the initial decisions about who will occupy the 3,000 or so political positions at the top of the executive hierarchy.

There are ways to circumnavigate this centralization—all of the secretaries recognized the value of entering office at the start of the term with a firm list of candidates for the top jobs. Doing so places the secretary at an advantage in dealing with a relatively young Office of Presidential Personnel. Secretaries can also use their influence with the President and/or Vice President to ensure that their chosen candidates for the top posts end up on the lists of three or four White House recommendations that arrive at the department. "I had my team in place before the White House did," said one secretary, "and I always arranged to have my top choice end up on the interview lists that came from the White House later in the term. I took the White House role as a given, and worked around it." Another secretary did the same.

Frustrated in appointing a trusted aide as deputy secretary, he appointed the aide to a newly created chief of staff post within the secretary's office.

There is little the secretary can do by him- or herself about the sluggish appointments process, however. Secretaries cannot accelerate the vetting process that requires so much time to complete; they cannot require the White House to move more quickly in filling vacancies late in the term; and they cannot force the Senate to hold the requisite hearings that precede confirmation. The secretaries interviewed for this project certainly understand that some appointments such as surgeon general and FDA commissioner are particularly controversial, but controversy need not create long vacancies.

If there is one reform on which the secretaries emphatically agreed, it is a long-overdue reform of the presidential appointments process to (1) give the secretaries more authority to appoint their own teams, especially in the secretary's suite, and (2) accelerate the nomination and confirmation process to fill vacancies as fast as possible. This is no insignificant task, especially in an era when the presidential appointments process has slowed dramatically. As Table G-1 shows, secretaries are always confirmed quickly, but lower-level offices take more time. The next secretary will be lucky to have most of his or her Senate-confirmed officers in place by early summer and will almost certainly wait longer to fill more controversial posts such as surgeon general.

- **The department's people matter most.** Whatever reorganization might emerge through future legislation or executive order, the secretaries believed that the department's people are its most important resource. Without indicting the current civil service for its own sluggish performance per se, several secretaries did emphasize the need for better recruitment, retention, promotion, and training programs to ensure a steady supply of talent as the baby boom generation retires over the next decade. Such reorganization need not be restricted to one department but appears to be a prerequisite for effective performance as one generation of employees arrives and another leaves.

TABLE G-1 Confirmation Dates for Initial Appointees to Key Department Posts

Position	George H. W. Bush	Bill Clinton	George W. Bush
Secretary	3/1/89	1/21/93	1/24/01
Under or deputy secretary	5/10/89	5/24/93	5/26/01
Assistant secretary for health	4/19/89	7/1/93	1/25/02
FDA commissioner	10/27/90	Holdover	1/25/02
Heath Care Financing Administration—Centers for Medicare and Medicaid Services	2/1/90	5/24/94	5/25/01
Assistant secretary for program evaluation	1/30/90	5/28/93	5/25/01
Assistant secretary for management and budget[a]	5/1/89[b]	5/24/93	1/25/02
National Institutes of Health director	3/21/91	11/20/93	5/2/02
Surgeon general	3/1/90	9/7/93	7/23/02

[a]The title and division of responsibilities associated with this position have varied over time.

[b]This position was not subject to Senate confirmation in 1989.

The secretary is the most important person in the department, of course. In leading the flagship domestic policy department, the HHS secretary sets the tone for a long list of other departments and agencies and is easily one of the most visible cabinet secretaries in government.

Each secretary brings a somewhat different style into office, of course. Several of the secretaries interviewed for this paper were former members of Congress; several others were governors; and several others were former university presidents. The experiences could not be more different. Governors tend to have a command-and-control orientation, wanting to centralize authority upward, while university presidents are much more familiar with a collegial approach that involves an acknowledgment of decentralization. Some experiences emphasize informal relationships, while others place the focus on tight direction.

The choice of style depends in part on what the President wants from the department. Indeed, the relationship with the President is by far the most important resource a new secretary can have. Secretaries having close personal relationships with the President have a greater chance to influence everything from appointments to the policy agenda. "I had no surprises," said one. "I knew the President and could play that card at any time. I never did, but the fact that people knew I could mattered most."

Advice to the Next Secretary

These views from the past six secretaries provide valuable advice to the next HHS secretary. Indeed, several of the secretaries interviewed for this project were quite explicit about what the next secretary should do to take hold of the department in the first few months of service. Suffice it to say that large-scale reorganization is not on the list.

All of the secretaries suggested that the next secretary focus first on a unifying vision for the department. Although they recognize that the department has many responsibilities, dozens of which are spelled out in the annual performance report, the secretary needs to identify a very small number of priorities that should preoccupy the operating units (e.g., obesity, evidence-based management). Instead of the 11 priorities currently listed on the HHS website, the secretaries seemed to favor five or fewer.

The past secretaries also put a premium on developing a strong relationship with the White House. Much as they may have bristled at White House involvement in the appointments process, they all understood that they had to forge strong ties to the White House surrounding key policy issues such as welfare and health care reform. Several noted that they had been surprised by White House policy decisions in part because they lacked strong ties to the executive staff.

The secretaries also talked about the value of good metrics for measuring performance. However, they did not uniformly embrace the highly detailed reporting required under the 1994 Government Performance and Results Act. Rather, they focused on the need for evidence-based care, value for the dollar, and a strong scientific rationale for making decisions ranging from Medicare and Medicaid reimbursement to risk-based food inspections.

Finally, the secretaries put their emphasis on building a mission-centered culture within the department. It is easy for HHS to divide into a series of isolated silos that are far from a "family of agencies," as the department's current metaphor describes them. If the department is to restore and maintain public confidence in its programs and priorities, it must articulate a unifying message that reinforces its role as the premier locus for protecting and enhancing the quality of life for all Americans.

CONCLUSION

The secretaries interviewed for this project agreed that reorganization is one of many tools for improving organizational performance. Because this philosophy of reform originates in the scientific management movement spurred forward by operations research and Frederick Taylor, it also carries the hubris perhaps that there is "one best way" for building an efficient bureaucracy.

Scientific management still holds promise for improving organizational efficiency, whether through shared administrative, or "back office" functions or through organizational synergies that might not otherwise exist under a "czar" or other integrative mechanism. However, it is only one of several philosophies for reform and competes against those who believe that increased performance comes from more aggressive oversight against fraud, waste, and abuse; more transparency regarding organizational action; or breaking free of the rules that scientific management creates.

This is not to argue that reorganization is unwarranted in all cases—to the contrary, it provides significant benefits as discussed earlier in this paper. However, the history of reorganization suggests that it may be most effective when used as a tool of last resort—that is, policy makers might be well advised to try other methods for improvement before they use reorganizations. Such methods can be more easily reversed but may solve the problem at lower cost. Being conservative may be just as wise in reorganization as it is in medicine.

Interview Schedule

Tommy Thompson, July 7, 2008
David Matthews, July 8, 2008
Donna Shalala, July 10, 2008
Richard Schweiker, July 11, 2008
Louis Sullivan, July 31, 2008
Joseph Califano, August 19, 2008

H

Statutory Framework for the Organization and Management of the U.S. Department of Health and Human Services

Darrel J. Grinstead, J.D.
Hogan & Hartson, LLP

BACKGROUND AND PURPOSE

The purpose of this paper is to describe and analyze the relevant statutes and other legal authority under which the U.S. Department of Health and Human Service (the department or HHS) was established and is currently organized. This paper has been commissioned by the Institute of Medicine (IOM) of the National Academies to assist an ad hoc committee assembled by the IOM to examine the current mission, governance, and organizational structure of the department. The committee is charged with making recommendations to Congress and HHS to ensure that the department is aligned to meet the public health and health care challenges that our nation faces.

The department was first established as a cabinet-level entity in 1953 as the Department of Health, Education, and Welfare (HEW). The name was changed to the Department of Health and Human Services in 1980 when the education functions were spun off to the Department of Education.[1] From the beginning, the department was charged with administering two major statutes that had been on the books for years prior to that time: the Social Security Act and the Public Health Service Act. These two statutes still comprise the majority of the authorities administered by the department. However, there were many other statutes and programs that completed the mission of the department, and all of this statutory authority continued to grow and change in ways designed to meet the evolving health and human services needs of the nation. This multiplicity of governing laws, and the great variety in the extent to which they con-

[1]P.L. 96-88, October 17, 1979.

strain management's organizational decisions, make it difficult to articulate general principles or rules that will fully describe the statutory landscape of the department's structure and the discretion left to the secretary to reorganize the department.

For that reason, this paper provides (1) an overview of the general and specific organizational authority of the secretary; (2) a discussion of how that authority has been exercised historically; (3) an analysis, based on the current organization of the department, of the specific statutory provisions that may currently constrain that authority and how those constraints vary substantially among the different parts of the department; and (4) suggestions of means by which statutory limits on the secretary's authority to organize the department can be addressed. A more detailed listing of statutory directions and constraints affecting the secretary's organizational authority over the components of the department is contained in the appendix to this paper.

GENERAL AUTHORITY OF THE SECRETARY TO ORGANIZE THE DEPARTMENT

Reorganization Plan No. 1 of 1953

As noted above, the department was created, and the cabinet-level position of the secretary of health, education, and welfare was established, when President Eisenhower submitted Reorganization Plan No. 1 of 1953, which was approved by the Congress on April 1, 1953.[2] The Reorganization Plan essentially elevated the Federal Security Agency (which then contained the Social Security Administration, the Public Health Service, the Office of Education, and several smaller agencies) to cabinet status. The combined agencies were taken whole into the new department, along with the head of those agencies, such as the commissioner of Social Security and the surgeon general, who thereafter reported to the HEW secretary rather than the President.

---

[2]Reorganization Plan No. 1 of 1953 was issued under the authority of the Reorganization Act of 1949, which gave the President broad authority to reorganize the executive branch. To eliminate any doubt over the constitutionality of such broad authority, Congress ratified the Reorganization Plan by passing a statue giving it an effective date. 42 U.S.C.A. § 3501. The broad authority in the Reorganization Act of 1949 has since expired.

Although the original organization of the department reflected the preexisting organization of its constituent agencies, from the very beginning the secretary had broad authority to reorganize the various functions and components of the department. Section 6 of Reorganization Plan No. 1 provides:

> The Secretary may from time to time make such provisions as the Secretary deems appropriate authorizing the performance of any of the functions of the Secretary by any other officer, or by any agency or employee, of the Department.

Under this authority, which is still in place, as well as under a broadly applicable statute that gives similar authority to the heads of all executive departments,[3] the secretary has authority to assign the performance of functions vested in him by law to subordinate officers or organizations within the department as long as such assignments are not inconsistent with law. With this important qualification, which is examined later, the secretary has broad authority to reorganize the department through the redistribution of functions for which he is responsible.[4]

Reorganization Plan No. 3 of 1966

Almost all of the statutory provisions that establish the programs and the mission of the department place the authority to administer those functions in the secretary. Thus, the statutes creating the Social Security Act programs administered by the department, such as Medicare and Medicaid, as well as the Public Health Service Act programs, place the authority to carry out the thousands of program functions, including the making of grants, the payment of program benefits, and the issuance of regulations, in the position of the secretary. This was not always the case. When Reorganization Plan No. 1 was issued, most of the Public Health Service Act (PHSA) authorities were placed in the surgeon general. This remained so until 1966 when Reorganization Plan No. 3 was issued. That

---

[3]5 U.S.C. § 301 reads as follows: The head of an executive department or military department may prescribe regulations for the government of his department, the conduct of its employees, the distribution and performance of its business, and the custody, use, and preservation of its records, papers, and property.

[4]1980 WL 16137 (Comp. Gen.), B-199491.

plan, which was also approved by the Congress, transferred all the functions and authority of the surgeon general to the secretary of health, education, and welfare. With the adoption of Reorganization Plan No. 3, a major statutory impediment to the exercise of the secretary's reorganization authority with respect to Public Health Service (PHS) programs was removed. As seen later, however, in the 40-plus years since the adoption of this plan, organizational requirements imposed by statute have increasingly reemerged.

At the time of Reorganization Plan No. 3, the PHS was composed of four agencies: the National Institutes of Health, the Bureau of Medical Services, the Bureau of State Services, and the Office of the Surgeon General. All the authorities of PHS had to be administered through one of these offices. In submitting the Reorganization Plan, the President stated that this organizational structure was outmoded in light of the many new health problems and issues that had arisen and the many new programs that had been adopted in the 20 years since that organizational structure was created. He pointed out that the secretary also administered other programs not within PHS, such as Medicare, Medicaid, and the regulation of food and drugs through the Food and Drug Administration (FDA), that required the secretary to have the ability to coordinate health activities across program lines. He therefore proposed, and Congress approved, that the secretary should have broad authority to reorganize these programs according to modern principles of organizational design so that all of these programs could be administered in an integrated and efficient manner.[5]

Since that time, most of the statutory authorities administered by the department have been placed in the secretary, and the theory of Reorganization Plan No. 3 was for the secretary to have broad discretion to organize those functions into subunits of the department; to delegate the performance of those functions to the various officers who are in charge of those subunits; and to reorganize those functions, subunits, and officers largely as he sees fit. However, limits on that authority have been enacted by Congress in numerous statutory provisions creating specific offices and officials in the department and in some cases specifying the reporting relationship between those officials and the secretary. These statutory provisions impose the most significant legal constraints on the secretary's ability to reorganize the department, and as we see later, most of these statutory directions as to how functions of the department should

[5]42 U.S.C.A. § 202, note.

be organized apply to the programs authorized by the Public Health Service Act.

HISTORY OF THE SECRETARY'S EXERCISE OF REORGANIZATION AUTHORITY

Over the past 65 years of the department's existence, secretaries have used their authority to reorganize the department in many ways. Initially, the department was organized somewhat along the lines of the combined components. Public Health Service components were originally organized under the surgeon general, who reported to the secretary. The Old-Age, Survivors, and Disability Insurance (OASDI) programs remained with the commissioner of Social Security, but various other programs authorized by the Social Security Act, mainly those providing assistance to state-operated welfare programs, were delegated to a new entity created by the secretary, the commissioner of Social and Rehabilitation Services (SRS). To this new entity, through secretarial delegation, also went such programs as the Older Americans Act and the Rehabilitation Act. When Medicare and Medicaid were enacted in 1965, the secretary delegated Medicare to the commissioner of Social Security, presumably because it was a direct assistance program with eligibility established under Title II of the Social Security Act, like the OASDI program. Medicaid, on the other hand, being a state grant program, was delegated to the commissioner of SRS. These organizational decisions were made by the secretary administratively, under his reorganization authority discussed above, because the Social Security Act and the other authorities affected were vested by statute in the secretary and contained no provisions instructing the secretary how to organize them.

In the ensuing years, the secretary used the reorganization authority discussed above to move programs around and to abolish and create offices and agencies as necessary to reflect mission and program changes, and to implement different theories of organization and management. Thus, in 1977, when a different secretary decided it made more sense to have the two major health care assistance programs, Medicare and Medicaid, administered under a single administrative unit, the secretary used his authority to move both programs into a new component that he created, the Health Care Financing Administration (HCFA), under a newly created administrator. Similarly, he abolished the SRS and its commissioner and assigned all of its programs to a new assistant secretary for human development services. After the enactment of Reorganization Plan No. 3 in 1966, which removed the Public Health Services programs from the authority of the surgeon general and vested them in the secretary, the secretary redelegated those programs to the operational control of the assistant secretary for health. Those programs remained with the assistant secretary for health until 1995 when a different secretary choose to have each of the major public health programs (National Institutes of Health, Centers for Disease Control and Prevention, Substance Abuse and Mental Health Services Administration, Indian Health Service, Agency for Healthcare Research and Quality, etc.) report directly to the secretary.

The secretary has similar broad authority to reorganize and assign functions to his senior staff (i.e., those officials at the assistant secretary level). Reorganization Plan No. 1 initially assigned an undersecretary (executive level 3)[6] and two assistant secretaries to the department. Additional assistant secretaries and a general counsel were subsequently added, but the functions and responsibilities of the assistant secretaries (with the exception of the assistant secretary for aging, the assistant secretary for families and children, and the assistant secretary for administration and management) are not specified in the statute. Thus, the secretary was and remains free to change the title, role, and responsibilities of most of the assistant secretaries. Of the secretary's senior staff, only the general counsel's title and functions are specified in law.[7] The remaining senior staff positions (chief of staff, executive secretary, director of intergovernmental affairs, director of the Office for Civil Rights, etc.) are all positions created under the secretary's general organizational authority and those positions may be abolished or changed at the secretary's discretion.

The purpose of the foregoing discussion has been to demonstrate the extent of the secretary's reorganization authority over a large portion of the department's programs. Virtually all of the programs vested in the secretary under the Social Security Act, and the remaining programs currently administered through the Administration for Families and Children, are not subject to statutory constraints as to their organizational placement within the department. Nor is the secretary limited in his authority to organize and assign functions to his senior staff. For reasons beyond the scope of analysis in this paper, however, the programs au-

---

[6]The position of undersecretary was elevated to deputy secretary (executive level 2) in 1990.

[7]42 U.S.C.A. § 3504.

thorized under the Public Health Service Act and related statutes are subject to considerably more direction from Congress with regard to how they should be organized and to which official they are to be assigned. The extent of those statutory constraints is discussed in the following section.

Statutory Provisions Affecting the Authority to Reorganize the Department

As indicated in the preceding discussion, there is great variety among the statutes authorizing the department's programs in the extent to which they impose organizational limitations. There is also considerable variety in the types of statutory organizational directives that Congress has placed on those programs. Some discussion of the means by which Congress has adopted organizational instructions for the various programs may be useful.

There are numerous examples in which Congress has directed that a specifically named program office be established to administer a specific program or group of programs. For example, section 306 of the PHSA provides: "There is established in the Department of Health and Human Services the National Center for Health Statistics. . . ." The act says nothing more about where the center is to be placed organizationally, thus giving the secretary discretion as to where it is to be located and through what official it is to report to the secretary.

Where the statute creates an office to administer only a single program, this type of provision creates little or no organizational constraint on the secretary because he can place that office where he wants. This paper does not focus on such provisions. However, where Congress has created a major organizational entity that is charged with the administration of a entire subset of the department's programs (e.g., the establishment of the Substance Abuse and Mental Health Services Administration [SAMHSA] by section 501 of the PHSA), compliance with that statute may substantially restrict the secretary's options for organizing his programs. Those are the types of provisions examined in this paper.

Some statutes, particularly the PHSA, specify that the secretary is to perform a particular program function "acting through" a particular program official or "through" a named program office (which may or may not have been created by statute). For example, numerous provisions in the PHSA provide, "The Secretary, acting through the Director of the

Centers for Disease Control and Prevention [or some other PHSA agency], shall carry out a program to [make grants or conduct research in a particular area of concern]." This type of provision is also a major impediment to any attempt by the secretary to reassign functions as he or she deems appropriate; accordingly, we examine the effects of such provisions.

The remainder of this section attempts to analyze the significant statutory provisions that impinge on the secretary's authority to reorganize the major programs of the department. (We do not look at the hundreds of advisory committees and boards created by statute, because those provisions do not affect basic organizational decisions, and in any event the secretary is able to manage and control those entities through the Federal Advisory Committee Act.) For convenience, this analysis has been organized according to the existing operating components of the department. Organizing the paper in this way is not meant to suggest that any such component must be preserved in any reorganization because, as we have seen, some of those components do not have statutory status.

To make this task manageable and the paper useful, we do not list every such statutory provision. Where a type of statutory provision applies to several programs within an operating component, those provisions are discussed generically. However, for the convenience of the committee, we have attached an appendix listing statutory provisions that we believe have to be considered in the context of any reorganization study of the department.[8]

Administration for Children and Families

The Administration for Children and Families (ACF) was created administratively in 1991 as the successor to the Office of Human Development Services. The programs it administers are established under title IV of the Social Security Act (including Temporary Assistance for Needy Families, Child Welfare Services, Adoption Assistance, and Child Support Enforcement) and under a variety of other statutes providing for assistance to disadvantaged and vulnerable populations (refugees, disadvantaged children, Native Americans, and individuals with disabilities).

[8]While we have attempted to be thorough in identifying the relevant statutory provisions, given the time allotted and the size of the task, we cannot guarantee that our listing is exhaustive. Further research may be warranted in light of particular options that are developed by the committee.

ACF is headed by an assistant secretary appointed by the President and confirmed by the Senate. That position was created by section 416 of the Social Security Act as the "Assistant Secretary for Family Support." The only duty of that office specified by law is administration of the Temporary Assistance for Needy Families block grant program and the Child Support and Establishment of Paternity program; however, nothing prevented the secretary from assigning the assistant secretary additional duties, so the title of that position was changed administratively to the "Assistant Secretary for Children and Families." We could find no other statutory provisions limiting the secretary's authority to reorganize or reassign any of these programs or officials to other parts of the department.

Administration on Aging

Of the non-PHS agencies in the department, the Administration on Aging (AoA) is subject to the most limiting statutory provisions dictating its organizational placement and structure. Section 201 of the Older Americans Act[9] establishes the Administration on Aging and creates the position of assistant secretary for aging, appointed by the President with the advice and consent of the Senate. The statute requires that there be a direct reporting relationship between the assistant secretary and the secretary, and in performing his functions under the statute the assistant secretary must be directly responsible to the secretary. None of the functions of AoA (including those carried out in the regional offices) may be delegated to an official who is not directly responsible to the secretary.

The statute also specifies the creation of certain offices within AoA, including an Office for American Indians, Alaskan Natives, and Hawaiian Programs; an Office of Long-Term Ombudsman Program; and an office responsible for elder abuse and prevention services.

Centers for Medicare and Medicaid Services (CMS)

As discussed earlier, programs authorized under the Social Security Act (SSA), such as Medicare and Medicaid, are subject to almost no statutory directions or limitations with respect to how or where they are

---

[9]42 U.S.C.A. § 3011.

organized. The secretary has discretion to assign the administration of those programs to whatever entity within the department he may choose or create and to designate the official he chooses to be in charge of those programs. Likewise, there are no statutory directions or limitations on the internal organization of whatever unit he specifies to administer those programs. As we have seen, no statutory provision directs that Medicare and Medicaid, or any of the components thereof, be administered by the same organizational unit within the department.

The only statutory provisions we have found that appear to affect the organization of CMS are in section 1117 of the SSA. Subsection (a) thereof requires that the administrator of the Health Care Financing Administration (HCFA) shall be appointed by the President with the advice and consent of the Senate. Subsection (b) establishes within the administration the position of chief actuary, requires that he be in direct line authority to the administrator, and specifies that he may be removed only for cause. Interestingly, section 1117 does not create the position of administrator; it merely requires that it be an advice and consent position. That provision did not prevent the secretary from renaming HCFA as the Centers for Medicare and Medicaid Services in 2001, nor would it seem to prevent the secretary from eliminating that position and/or reorganizing the functions thereof.

Agency for Healthcare Research and Quality

Section 901 of the PHSA establishes within PHS the Agency for Healthcare Research and Quality (AHRQ) and specifies that it be headed by a director appointed by the secretary. The statute requires that the functions of the agency specified in title IX of the PHSA shall be carried out through the director.

Title IX contains no other organizational directions or limitations on AHRQ. However, other parts of the PHSA contain a number of provisions directing the secretary to carry out certain functions through AHRQ (e.g., the conduct of studies to support organ donation and organ recovery, preservation, and transportation [sec. 377C]; the conduct of a research, evaluation, and assessment program on the impact and cost-effectiveness of HIV treatments [sec. 2673]). (The appendix to this paper contains a list of the provisions.) There are other provisions requiring or encouraging consultation with AHRQ by the secretary and other officials with respect to certain of their functions, but these do not seem to impinge on organizational decisions.

Centers for Disease Control and Prevention

The Centers for Disease Control and Prevention (CDC) began life as the Communicable Disease Center in 1946. It was transferred to the new Department of Health, Education, and Welfare along with other parts of the Public Health Service in 1953 under Reorganization Plan No. 1. Its name was changed to the Center for Disease Control in 1970 (apparently without statutory direction or ratification) and changed again administratively to the Centers for Disease Control and Prevention in 1980 to reflect a new organization of the agency. So far as we can ascertain, all this was done without explicit statutory authority, because we can find no statute creating or naming the agency, although by this date there were many references in the Public Health Service Act and other statutes to the Center for Disease Control. However, in 1992, P.L. 102-531 amended all statutory references to the Center for Disease Control to the Centers for Disease Control and Prevention.

Since there is no statute establishing CDC or its director, or directing how or through whom it reports to the secretary, the secretary has considerable discretion as to how it is organized, where it should be placed within the department, and what its relationship should be to other components that have related missions. However, the statute is very specific with respect to the programs that are to be administered through CDC. Although there are few directions in law as to the internal organization of CDC,[10] the Public Health Service Act is replete with provisions directing that various programs or activities of the PHS shall be carried out "through" the CDC. While not dictating a particular organizational structure or reporting relationship, these dozens of statutory provisions will have to be taken into account in any restructuring of PHS programs. The functions and activities that the statute requires to be performed through CDC are listed in the appendix.

---

[10]Section 317C of the PHSA establishes within CDC a center to be known as the National Center for Birth Defects and Developmental Disabilities. We are not aware of other organization entities that are made part of CDC by statute. The National Institute of Occupational Safety and Health was established within HHS in 1970 (29 U.S.C.A. § 671), but its organizational placement within CDC was an administrative decision.

Food and Drug Administration

The Food and Drug Administration (FDA), along with the commissioner of food and drugs, was transferred to the department as part of the 1953 Reorganization Plan. Its statutory origins were with the Department of Agriculture, but it had been transferred to the Federal Security Agency in 1940. In 1988, its statutory status was made explicit by section 503 of the Health Omnibus Program Extension Act (21 U.S.C.A. § 393(a)) that "established in the Department of Health and Human Services the Food and Drug Administration" and the position of commissioner of food and drugs, who is appointed by the President with the advice and consent of the Senate. The secretary is to oversee the operation of FDA and to carry out his responsibility to ensure the safety of food and the safety and effectiveness of drugs through FDA.

The Food, Drug, and Cosmetic Act does not specify the internal organization of FDA. The only statutory provisions we could find relating to particular components of FDA are (1) the Best Pharmaceuticals for Children Act, adopted in 2002, which created within FDA an Office of Pediatric Therapeutics, and (2) a provision added to the Food, Drug, and Cosmetic Act in 2007 creating an Office of the Chief Scientist in the Office of the Commissioner.

National Institutes of Health

No component of the department is subject to greater statutory control with respect to its internal organization than the National Institutes of Health (NIH). NIH is established as an agency of the PHS by section 401 of the PHSA, which also specifies that there are 24 statutorily named national research institutes and national centers. As discussed below, the secretary may add new institutes or terminate existing ones, except that the total number of such institutes and centers may not exceed 27. Section 402 establishes the position of the director of NIH, who shall be appointed by the President with the advice and consent of the Senate. The statute does not require that there be a direct reporting relationship between the director and the secretary.[11]

Title IV of the PHSA sets forth in detail the mission, programs, and grant authority of each of the institutes and centers of NIH. It also con-

[11]These sections were substantially revised by the National Institutes of Health Reform Act of 2006, section 101, which became law on January 15, 2007.

tains provisions specifying the organizational structure of each institute. (Special statutory provisions relating to the organization of the institutes are set forth in the appendix.) Section 405 provides that the director of the National Cancer Institute shall be appointed by the President (no advice and consent) and the directors of the remaining institutes shall be appointed by the secretary. That section also requires that the director of each national research institute shall report directly to the director of NIH.

Although the statute contains detailed statutory instructions as to the organization of NIH and its components, it also provides authority for the secretary and the director to change that organizational structure. Section 401(d)(2) permits the secretary to establish additional institutes within NIH (subject to the numerical limit of 27 discussed above) if he determines this necessary to carry out the research, training, and information missions of NIH. That section also permits the secretary to reorganize the functions of any institute or to abolish any institute if he determines that it is no longer required. Such additions, abolishments, or reorganizations may not be put into effect before the expiration of 180 days after the congressional committees having jurisdiction over NIH are provided written notice of such action.[12]

Section 401(c) requires that within the Office of the Director there shall be a Division of Program Coordination, Planning, and Strategic Initiatives, which shall contain six named offices and any other office within the Office of the Director existing on January 14, 2007.[13] Notwithstanding this specificity, section 401(c)(3) permits the director of NIH, after a series of public hearings and with the approval of the secretary, to reorganize, add to, terminate, or transfer the functions of these offices if he or she determines that the management and efficiency of the offices would be improved by such a reorganization. Section 401(c)(4) permits each institute director, after a series of public hearings and with the approval of the director, to reorganize the divisions and other organizational units of the institute as necessary to improve the management and operation of the institute. All of these reorganization authorities may override the specific statutory organizational provisions discussed above.

---

[12]The relevant committees are the Committee on Energy and Commerce of the House of Representatives and the Committee on Health, Education, Labor, and Pensions of the Senate.

[13]The named offices are the Office of AIDS Research, the Office of Research on Women's Health, the Office of Behavioral and Social Sciences Research, the Office of Disease Prevention, the Office of Dietary Supplements, and the Office of Rare Diseases.

A provision was added to section 401 as part of the National Institutes of Health Reform Act of 2006 requiring the secretary to establish a Scientific Management Review Board within NIH for the purpose of advising the secretary and NIH officials on the use of the reorganization authorities discussed above. The board, which is composed of a mix of institute directors and individuals who are not officers or employees of the United States but who have interests in NIH, is to issue a report, not less often than every seven years, providing its recommendations regarding the use of those authorities. Other than board recommendations calling for the establishment, termination, or consolidation of one or more institutes, or a reorganization of the Office of the Director, a recommendation of the board for a reorganization must be implemented within three years, unless the director of NIH submits a report to the congressional committees of jurisdiction containing specific objections to such recommendations.

Health Resources and Services Administration

We could find no provision of law creating the Health Resources and Services Administration (HRSA), which was created administratively in 1982 by combining several offices (including the Health Resources Administration, the Health Services Administration, the Bureau of Health Facilities, and the Bureau of Health Professions) into a single agency. Although HRSA is not a statutory entity, the PHSA contains dozens of references to the agency, principally provisions requiring that the secretary carry out certain functions or programs through HRSA. (See appendix.) Nor does the statute specify any particular organizational structure for HRSA, but it does refer to a number of organizational units with the agency, including the Office of Rural Health Policy (42 U.S.C. 912), the Maternal and Child Health Bureau (sec. 330A(d)), the Office for the Advancement of Telehealth (sec. 330K), the Division of Organ Transplantation (sec. 379), the Division of Nursing (sec. 464X), and the Division of Trauma and Emergency Medical Systems (sec. 1201). Most of the remaining major units within HRSA were created administratively to reflect the wide variety of programs that have been delegated to the agency.

Substance Abuse and Mental Health Services Administration

The Substance Abuse and Mental Health Services Administration (SAMHSA) was created as an agency of the PHS by section 501 of the PHSA. That section also created within SAMHSA the Center for Substance Abuse Treatment, the Center for Substance Abuse Prevention, and the Center for Mental Health Services. The statute establishes an administrator, to be appointed by the President with the advice and consent of the Senate, and it permits the administrator, with the approval of the secretary, to appoint a deputy administrator. The statute permits, but does not require, the appointment within SAMHSA of an associate administrator for alcohol prevention and treatment policy, and it requires the appointment of an associate administrator for women's services. The statute does not require that there be a direct reporting relationship between the administrator and the secretary.

The statute specifies that the directors of each of the three main centers within SAMHSA shall administer a precise set of activities within his or her bailiwick. The statute also places the authority for some programs and activities within SAMHSA in the secretary, In this respect, SAMHSA is similar to NIH in that the statute is inconsistent about program activities in terms of whether those activities are placed in the secretary to be delegated to a particular official or at his discretion, or whether the statute vests the activity directly in a named official. To the extent that the statute names a particular statutorily created official to carry out certain activities, the secretary's discretion to reorganize those activities is limited.

Agency for Toxic Substances and Disease Registry

The Agency for Toxic Substances and Disease Registry (ATSDR) was established in HHS in 1980 by section 104(i) of the Comprehensive Environmental Response, Compensation, and Liability Act (CERCLA; also known as "Superfund"). That section requires that the administrator of the agency shall report directly to the surgeon general, but since all of his functions and authority were transferred to the secretary by the 1966 Reorganization Plan, the direct reporting relationship is to the secretary. Subsequent statutory enactments assigning various functions relating to toxic substances to the secretary (e.g., the requirement in 10 U.S.C.A. § 2704 to develop certain toxicological profiles) have required that the secretary shall carry out those functions through ATSDR. (See appendix for the list of functions so assigned.)

Indian Health Service

The Indian Health Service (IHS) was established by statute as part of the PHS by section 601 of the Indian Health Care Improvement Act of 1988.[14] That section also specifies that IHS shall be administered by a director who shall be appointed by the President with the advice and consent of the Senate. The statute specifies that the director shall report to the secretary of HHS through the assistant secretary for health. The statute requires that IHS "shall be an agency within the Public Health Service of the Department of Health and Human Services, and shall not be an office, component, or unit of any other agency of the Department." The statute goes on to provide that the secretary shall carry out, through the director of IHS, all his authorities with respect to IHS and other programs administered by the secretary through which health care is provided to Indians based on their status as Indians. This statutory provision would seem to preclude the reorganization of any such program under another agency or office within the department.

Regional Offices

There is very little in the statutes about the establishment or role of the regional offices of the department. A few programs (e.g., AoA) refer to regional offices but merely affirm that certain requirements as to organizational responsibilities shall apply to the regional offices as well. The secretary is largely free to establish or revise the role of the regional offices through reorganization.

---

[14] 42 U.S.C.A. § 1661.

Organization of the Health Functions of Other Federal Agencies

Undersecretary for Health in the Department of Veterans Affairs

The health function in the Department of Veterans Affairs (VA) is headed by an undersecretary for health. He or she is appointed by the President, with Senate confirmation, and is directly responsible to the secretary of veterans affairs for the operation of the Veterans Health Administration, including all health functions and facilities of the department. Unlike most other presidential appointees in the executive branch, the undersecretary is required to be appointed without regard to political affiliation or activity, but rather on the basis of professional qualifications as a health care practitioner or administrator and prior experience in connection with veterans health programs (38 U.S.C.A. § 305).

The statute calls for a commission to be established whenever a vacancy occurs in the office of undersecretary for the purpose of nominating at least three qualified individuals for appointment to the position by the President. After those names are submitted to the President, he may ask the commission to submit additional nominations for his consideration. The commission is composed of (1) three persons representing clinical care, medical research, and education activities affected by the Veterans Health Administration; (2) two persons representing veterans served by the Veterans Health Administration; (3) two persons with experience in or similar to the management of veterans health services or research; (4) the deputy secretary of veterans affairs; (5) the chairman of a Special Medical Advisory Group in the department; and (6) at the secretary's discretion, a former undersecretary or chief medical officer of the VA.

The statute formerly established a term of office of four years for this position, but that provision was eliminated in 2006.[15]

The Department of Agriculture's Food Safety Inspection Service

The Office of the Undersecretary for Food Safety was created by section 261 of the Department of Agriculture Reorganization Act of

---

[15]P.L. 109-461, § 210(a)(1), (2).

1994, title II of P.L. 103-354. That section merely states that the undersecretary shall be delegated those functions and duties under the jurisdiction of the Department of Agriculture that are primarily related to food safety. The undersecretary is appointed by the President, with the advice and consent of the Senate, from among individuals with specialized training or significant experience with food safety or public health programs.

The principal responsibility of the undersecretary is overseeing the policies and programs of the Food Safety and Inspection Service (FSIS) of the Department of Agriculture. The FSIS is responsible for the implementation and enforcement of the food safety laws that are the responsibility of the department—the Federal Meat Inspection Act, the Poultry Products Inspection Act, and the Egg Products Inspection Act. Through the administrator of FSIS, the undersecretary supervises a staff of approximately 7,500 persons, including scientists, international food safety experts, field office food inspectors, enforcement officers, and others. The FSIS is the largest category of employees in the Department of Agriculture.

ADDRESSING STATUTORY ORGANIZATIONAL ISSUES IN A REORGANIZATION

As we have seen, statutory provisions that establish or direct organizational features of the department differ in the extent to which they create a serious barrier to administrative reorganization. For example, the mere creation of an office to carry out a given function, does not constrain the ability of the secretary to place that function or office where he or she sees fit. On the other hand, the creation of a particular office within the department or within a component of the department and a statutory assignment to that office of a particular set of programs and functions are requirements that must be given some effect. However, such a provision does not necessarily bar the secretary from accomplishing organizational objectives. For example, in 1978, after Congress had directed that the commissioner on aging should report directly to the Office of the Secretary, the secretary was able to achieve his goal of having the Administration on Aging be part of the Office of Human Development Services (OHDS) by placing OHDS within the Office of the Secretary.

There are a number of major components of the department that were not created by statute but seem to have acquired statutory status over the years by having been statutorily assigned certain functions by name (e.g., HRSA, CDC, CMS). We do not believe that the fact that a statute refers to an agency by a name that was established administratively would prevent the secretary from renaming, abolishing, or consolidating that agency. Some meaning could be given to the statutory assignment of functions or programs to that agency by simply reassigning those functions or program within the reorganization.

There are other ways of dealing with what appear to be hard-and-fast statutory instructions regarding organization. Section 201 of the PHSA states that "[t]he Public Health Service in the Department of Health and Human Services shall be administered by the Assistant Secretary for Health under the supervision and direction of the Secretary." Yet that provision did not prevent the secretary from reorganizing the functions of PHS to create a direct reporting relationship between the secretary and the major components of the PHS. Apparently effect was given to this requirement by having the assistant secretary have some indirect role in the administration of the PHS agencies.

Thus, there are a number of ways to deal with reorganizational proposals that may involve statutory constraints. In the end, it will be necessary to review such proposals against the statutory framework discussed above. The statutes, although an important concern, should not ultimately prevent the adoption of management reforms and organizational changes that are necessary to achieve the most efficient and effective operation of the programs the agency is charged with administering.

APPENDIX: STATUTORY CONSTRAINTS ON HHS ORGANIZATION

Administration on Children and Families

- SSA, sec. 416. The programs under the part [Temporary Assistance to Needy Families] and part D [Child Support Enforcement] shall be administered by an Assistant Secretary for Family Support. . . .

  (42 U.S.C. § 616)

- SSA, sec. 454. "The Secretary shall establish, within the Department of Health and Human Services a separate organizational unit, under the direction of a designee of the Secretary, who shall report directly to the Secretary and who shall—[administered the Office of Child Support Enforcement]. . . ."
  (42 U.S.C. § 652)
- "(a) Grants authorized; (1) In general, [t]he *Secretary of Health and Human Services, acting through the Administration of Children and Families*, in partnership with the Secretary of Housing and Urban Development, *shall* award grants, contracts, or cooperative agreements for a period of not less than 2 years to eligible entities to develop long-term sustainability and self-sufficiency options for adult and youth victims of domestic violence, dating violence, sexual assault, and stalking who are currently homeless or at risk for becoming homeless."
  (42 U.S.C. § 14043e-3. Subchapter on Violence Against Women. Collaborative grants to increase the long-term stability of victims.)

Agency for Healthcare Research and Quality

- "(c) Coordination of activities through units of Department; (1) The Secretary shall coordinate all health services research, evaluations, and demonstrations, all health statistical and epidemiological activities, and all research, evaluations, and demonstrations respecting the assessment of health care technology undertaken and supported through units of the Department of Health and Human Services. *To the maximum extent feasible such coordination shall be carried out through the Agency for Healthcare Research and Quality* and the National Center for Health Statistics."
  (42 U.S.C. § 242b. Subchapter on General Powers and Duties. Research and Investigations. General authority respecting research, evaluations, and demonstrations in health statistics, health services, and health care technology.)
- "(a) Development of supportive information; *The Secretary, acting through the Director of the Agency for Healthcare Research and Quality, shall develop scientific evidence in support of efforts to increase organ donation and improve the recovery, preservation, and transportation of organs*."

"(c) Research and dissemination; *The Secretary, acting through the Director of the Agency for Healthcare Research and Quality, as appropriate, shall provide support for research and dissemination of findings....*"

(42 U.S.C. § 274f-3. Subchapter on General Powers and Duties. Organ Transplants. Studies relating to organ donation and the recovery, preservation, and transportation of organs.)

- "(a) In general; There is established within the Public Health Service an agency to be known as the Agency for Healthcare Research and Quality, which shall be headed by a director appointed by the Secretary. *The Secretary shall carry out this subchapter acting through the Director.*"

  (42 U.S.C. § 299. Subchapter on Agency for Healthcare Research and Quality. Establishment and General Duties. Mission and Duties.)

- "(1) In general; *The Secretary, acting through the Director* and in consultation with the Commissioner of Food and Drugs, *shall establish a program* for the purpose of making one or more grants for the establishment and operation of one or more centers to carry out the activities specified in paragraph (2)."

  (42 U.S.C. § 299b-1. Subchapter on Agency for Healthcare Research and Quality. Health Care Improvement Research. Private-public partnerships to improve organization and delivery.)

- "(2) Annual report; Beginning in fiscal year 2003, the *Secretary, acting through the Director, shall submit to Congress* an annual report on national trends in the quality of health care provided to the American people."

  (42 U.S.C. § 299b-2. Subchapter on Agency for Healthcare Research and Quality. Health Care Improvement Research. Information on quality and cost of care.)

- "(a) Requirement; (1) In general; To avoid duplication and ensure that Federal resources are used efficiently and effectively, the *Secretary, acting through the Director, shall coordinate all research, evaluations, and demonstrations* related to health services research, quality measurement and quality improvement activities undertaken and supported by the Federal Government."

  (42 U.S.C. § 299b-6. Subchapter on Agency for Healthcare Research and Quality. Health Care Improvement Research.

Coordination of Federal Government quality improvement efforts.)

- "(a) Research, demonstrations, and evaluations; (1) Improvement of effectiveness and efficiency; (A) In general; To improve the quality, effectiveness, and efficiency of health care delivered pursuant to the programs established under titles XVIII, XIX, and XXI of the Social Security Act … *the Secretary acting through the Director of the Agency for Healthcare Research and Quality (in this section referred to as the 'Director'), shall conduct and support research* to meet the priorities and requests for scientific evidence and information identified by such programs with respect to—(i) the outcomes, comparative clinical effectiveness, and appropriateness of health care items and services (including prescription drugs); and (ii) strategies for improving the efficiency and effectiveness of such programs, including the ways in which such items and services are organized, managed, and delivered under such programs."

  (42 U.S.C. § 299b-7. Subchapter on Agency for Healthcare Research and Quality. Health Care Improvement Research. Research on outcomes of health care items and services.)

- "(a) Establishment of program; (1) In general; *The Secretary, acting through the Director of the Agency for Healthcare Research and Quality, shall*—(A) conduct and support research with respect to the outcomes, effectiveness, and appropriateness of health care services and procedures in order to identify the manner in which diseases, disorders, and other health conditions can most effectively and appropriately be prevented, diagnosed, treated, and managed clinically; and (B) assure that the needs and priorities of the program under subchapter XVIII of this chapter are appropriately reflected in the development and periodic review and updating (through the process set forth in section 299b-2 of this title) of treatment-specific or condition-specific practice guidelines for clinical treatments and conditions in forms appropriate for use in clinical practice, for use in educational programs, and for use in reviewing quality and appropriateness of medical care."

  (42 U.S.C. § 299b-12. Subchapter on General Provisions, Peer Review, and Administrative Simplification. General Provisions. Research on outcomes of health care services and procedures.)

- (a) Purpose; *The Secretary, acting through the Director of the Centers for Disease Control and Prevention and the Director of the Agency for Healthcare Research and Quality, shall award grants and contracts to fund research* on effective interventions in the health care setting that prevent domestic violence, dating violence, and sexual assault across the lifespan and that prevent the health effects of such violence and improve the safety and health of individuals who are currently being victimized.
  (42 U.S.C. § 13973. Subchapter on Violence Against Women. Safe Homes for Women. Research on Effective Interventions to Address Violence Against Women. Research on effective interventions in the health care setting.)

Centers for Disease Control and Prevention

- "(e) The Secretary, acting through the Director of the Centers for Disease Control and Prevention, shall expand, intensify, and coordinate the activities of the Centers for Disease Control and Prevention with respect to preterm labor and delivery and infant mortality."
  (42 U.S.C. § 241. Subchapter on General Powers and Duties. Research and Investigations. Research and investigations generally.)
- "(a) In general; *The Secretary of Health and Human Services, acting through the Director of the Centers for Disease Control and Prevention and in consultation with the Commissioner of Food and Drugs, shall* improve (including by educating physicians and other health care providers) the collection of, and publish as it becomes available, national data on—(1) the prevalence of food allergies; (2) the incidence of clinically significant or serious adverse events related to food allergies; and (3) the use of different modes of treatment for and prevention of allergic responses to foods."
  (42 U.S.C. § 242r. Subchapter on General Powers and Duties. Research and Investigations. Improvement and publication of data on food-related allergic responses.)
- "(a) Prevention; (1) Public education; *The Secretary, acting through the Director of the Centers for Disease Control and Prevention, shall carry out a program to educate health profes-*

sionals and paraprofessionals and the general public on the prevention of lead poisoning in infants and children. In carrying out the program, the Secretary shall make available information concerning the health effects of low-level lead toxicity, the causes of lead poisoning, and the primary and secondary preventive measures that may be taken to prevent such poisoning."

"(b) Technology assessment and epidemiology; *The Secretary, acting through the Director of the Centers for Disease Control and Prevention, shall, directly or through grants or contracts—* [conduct various activities relation to the detection and treatment of lead toxicity in children]."

(42 U.S.C. § 247b-3. Subchapter on General Powers and Duties. Federal-State Cooperation. Education, technology assessment, and epidemiology regarding lead poisoning.)

- "(d) Technical assistance, data management, and applied research; (1) Centers for Disease Control and Prevention; Under the existing authority of the Public Health Service Act [42 U.S.C.A. § 201 et seq.], *the Secretary, acting through the Director of the Centers for Disease Control and Prevention, shall make awards of grants or cooperative agreements* to provide technical assistance to State agencies to complement an intramural program and to conduct applied research related to newborn and infant hearing screening, evaluation and intervention programs and systems."

  (42 U.S.C. § 247b-4a. Subchapter on General Powers and Duties. Federal-State Cooperation. Early detection, diagnosis, and interventions for newborns and infants with hearing loss.)

- "(b) Studies on relationship between prematurity and birth defects; (1) In general; *The Secretary of Health and Human Services, acting through the Director of the Centers for Disease Control and Prevention, shall,* subject to the availability of appropriations, conduct ongoing epidemiological studies on the relationship between prematurity, birth defects, and developmental disabilities."

  "(c) Pregnancy risk assessment monitoring survey; (1) In general; *The Secretary of Health and Human Services, acting through the Director of the Centers for Disease Control and Prevention, shall establish* systems for the collection of maternal-infant clinical and biomedical information, including electronic health records, electronic databases, and biobanks, to link with the Pregnancy Risk Assessment Monitoring System (PRAMS) and other epidemiological studies of prematurity in order to track pregnancy outcomes and prevent preterm birth."

(42 U.S.C. § 247b-4f. Subchapter on General Powers and Duties. Federal-State Cooperation. Research relating to preterm labor and delivery and the care, treatment, and outcomes of preterm and low birthweight infants.)

- "*The Secretary, acting through the Director of the Centers for Disease Control and Prevention, shall establish fellowship and training programs* to be conducted by such Centers to train individuals to develop skills in epidemiology, surveillance, laboratory analysis, and other disease detection and prevention methods. Such programs shall be designed to enable health professionals and health personnel trained under such programs to work, after receiving such training, in local, State, national, and international efforts toward the prevention and control of diseases, injuries, and disabilities. Such fellowships and training may be administered through the use of either appointment or nonappointment procedures."

  (42 U.S.C. § 247b-8. Subchapter on General Powers and Duties. Federal-State Cooperation. Fellowship and training programs.)

- "(a) Surveillance on juvenile diabetes; *The Secretary, acting through the Director of the Centers for Disease Control and Prevention, shall develop* a sentinel system to collect data on juvenile diabetes, including with respect to incidence and prevalence, and shall establish a national database for such data."

  (42 U.S.C. § 247b-9. Subchapter on General Powers and Duties. Federal-State Cooperation. Diabetes in children and youth.)

- "(a) In general; *The Secretary, acting through the Director of the Centers for Disease Control and Prevention, shall*—(1) conduct local asthma surveillance activities to collect data on the prevalence and severity of asthma and the quality of asthma management; (2) compile and annually publish data on the prevalence of children suffering from asthma in each State; and (3) to the extent practicable, compile and publish data on the childhood mortality rate associated with asthma nationally."

  (42 U.S.C. § 247b-10. Subchapter on General Powers and

Duties. Federal-State Cooperation. Compilation of data on asthma.)

- "(a) In general; *The Secretary, acting through the Director of the Centers for Disease Control and Prevention, shall expand and intensify programs* (directly or through grants or contracts) for the following purposes: [to conduct education and research on the effects of folic acid in the prevention of birth defects]."

  (42 U.S.C. § 247b-11. Subchapter on General Powers and Duties. Federal-State Cooperation. Effects of folic acid in prevention of birth defects.)

- "(a) In general; *The Secretary, acting through the Director of the Centers for Disease Control and Prevention, shall carry out programs*—[to carry out various activities related to the implications and prevention of prenatal smoking, alcohol and illegal drug use]."

  (42 U.S.C. § 247b-13. Subchapter on General Powers and Duties. Federal-State Cooperation. Prenatal and postnatal health.)

- "(b) Community water fluoridation; (1) In general; *The Secretary, acting through the Director of the Centers for Disease Control and Prevention and in collaboration with the Director of the Indian Health Service, shall establish* a demonstration project that is designed to assist rural water systems in successfully implementing the water fluoridation guidelines of the Centers for Disease Control and Prevention that are entitled 'Engineering and Administrative Recommendations for Water Fluoridation, 1995' (referred to in this subsection as the 'EARWF')."

  (42 U.S.C. § 247b-14. Subchapter on General Powers and Duties. Federal-State Cooperation. Oral health promotion and disease prevention.)

- "(a) Surveillance; (1) In general; *The Secretary, acting through the Centers for Disease Control and Prevention, shall*—(A) enter into cooperative agreements with States and other entities to conduct sentinel surveillance or other special studies that would determine the prevalence in various age groups and populations of specific types of human papillomavirus (referred to in this section as 'HPV') in different sites in various regions of the United States, through collection of special specimens for HPV using a variety of laboratory-based testing and diagnostic tools; and (B) develop and analyze data from the HPV sentinel surveillance system described in subparagraph (A)."

"(b) Prevention activities; education program; (1) In general; *The Secretary, acting through the Centers for Disease Control and Prevention, shall* conduct prevention research on HPV...."

(42 U.S.C. § 247b-17. Subchapter on General Powers and Duties. Federal-State Cooperation. Human papillomavirus [Johanna's law].)

- "(a) Agreements for purchases; (1) In general; Not later than 180 days after October 27, 1992, *the Secretary, acting through the Director of the Centers for Disease Control and Prevention* and in consultation with the Administrator of the Health Resources and Services Administration, *shall* enter into negotiations with manufacturers of vaccines for the purpose of establishing and maintaining agreements under which entities described in paragraph (2) may purchase vaccines from the manufacturers at the prices specified in the agreements."

  (42 U.S.C. § 256c. Subchapter on General Powers and Duties. Primary Health Care. Bulk Purchases of Vaccines for Certain Programs. Bulk purchases of vaccines for certain programs.)
- "(a) With respect to activities that are authorized in sections 280b and 280b-1 of this title, *the Secretary, acting through the Director of the Centers for Disease Control and Prevention, shall carry out such activities* with respect to interpersonal violence within families and among acquaintances."

  (42 U.S.C. § 280b-1a. Subchapter on General Powers and Duties. Prevention and Control of Injuries. Interpersonal violence within families and among acquaintances.)
- "(a) Permitted use; *The Secretary, acting through the National Center for Injury Prevention and Control at the Centers for Disease Control and Prevention, shall award targeted grants* to States to be used for rape prevention and education programs conducted by rape crisis centers, State sexual assault coalitions, and other public and private nonprofit entities. . . ."

  (42 U.S.C. § 280b-1b. Subchapter on General Powers and Duties. Prevention and Control of Injuries. Use of allotments for rape prevention education.)
- "(a) Authority to award grants; (1) In general; *The Secretary, acting through the Director of the Centers for Disease Control and Prevention, shall award grants* to eligible State, tribal, terri-

torial, or local entities to strengthen the response of State, tribal, territorial, or local health care systems to domestic violence, dating violence, sexual assault, and stalking."

(42 U.S.C. § 280g-4. Subchapter on General Powers and Duties. Additional Programs. Grants to foster public health responses to domestic violence, dating violence, sexual assault, and stalking.)

- "(a) In general; *The Secretary, acting through the Centers for Disease Control and Prevention and in consultation with the Director of the National Institutes of Health, shall*—[conduct research and education activities relating to physical activity and the prevention of obesity]."

  (42 U.S.C. § 280h-1. Subchapter on General Powers and Duties. Programs to Improve the Health of Children. Applied research program.)
- "(a) In general; *The Secretary, acting through the Director of the Centers for Disease Control and Prevention, and in collaboration with national, State, and local partners, physical activity organizations, nutrition experts, and health professional organizations, shall develop* a national public campaign to promote and educate children and their parents concerning—(1) the health risks associated with obesity, inactivity, and poor nutrition; (2) ways in which to incorporate physical activity into daily living; and (3) the benefits of good nutrition and strategies to improve eating habits."

  (42 U.S.C. § 280h-2. Subchapter on General Powers and Duties. Programs to Improve the Health of Children. Education campaign.)
- "(a) In general; *The Secretary, acting through the Director of the Centers for Disease Control and Prevention*, in collaboration with the Administrator of the Health Resources and Services Administration and the heads of other agencies, and in consultation with appropriate health professional associations, *shall develop and carry out a program* to educate and train health professionals in effective strategies to—(1) better identify and assess patients with obesity or an eating disorder or patients at-risk of becoming obese or developing an eating disorder; (2) counsel, refer, or treat patients with obesity or an eating disorder; and (3) educate patients and their families about effective strategies to improve dietary habits and establish appropriate levels of

physical activity."

(42 U.S.C. § 280h-3. Subchapter on General Powers and Duties. Programs to Improve the Health of Children. Health professional education and training.)

- "(b) Centers of excellence in autism spectrum disorder epidemiology; (1) In general; *The Secretary, acting through the Director of the Centers for Disease Control and Prevention, shall*, subject to the availability of appropriations, award grants or cooperative agreements for the establishment of regional centers of excellence in autism spectrum disorder and other developmental disabilities epidemiology for the purpose of collecting and analyzing information on the number, incidence, correlates, and causes of autism spectrum disorder and other developmental disabilities."

    (42 U.S.C. § 280i. Subchapter on General Powers and Duties. Programs Relating to Autism. Developmental disabilities surveillance and research program.)

- "(a) In general; *The Secretary, acting through the Director of the Centers for Disease Control and Prevention* and in consultation with the Advisory Committee on Heritable Disorders in Newborns and Children established under section 300b-10 of this title, *shall provide for*—(1) quality assurance for laboratories involved in screening newborns and children for heritable disorders, including quality assurance for newborn-screening tests, performance evaluation services, and technical assistance and technology transfer to newborn screening laboratories to ensure analytic validity and utility of screening tests; and (2) appropriate quality control and other performance test materials to evaluate the performance of new screening tools."

    (42 U.S.C. § 300b-12. Subchapter on Genetic Diseases, Hemophilia Programs, and Sudden Infant Death Syndrome. Genetic Diseases. Laboratory quality.)

- "(a) In general; Not later than 180 days after April 24, 2008, *the Secretary, acting through the Director of the Centers for Disease Control and Prevention and in consultation with the Administrator and State departments of health (or related agencies), shall develop* a national contingency plan for newborn screening for use by a State, region, or consortia of States in the event of a public health emergency."

(42 U.S.C. § 300b-14. Subchapter on Genetic Diseases, He-

mophilia Programs, and Sudden Infant Death Syndrome. Genetic Diseases. National contingency plan for newborn screening.)

- "(d) Coordinating committee regarding year 2020 health objectives; *The Secretary, acting through the Director of the Centers for Disease Control and Prevention, shall establish* a committee to coordinate the activities of the agencies of the Public Health Service (and other appropriate Federal agencies) that are carried out toward achieving the objectives established by the Secretary for reductions in the rate of mortality from breast and cervical cancer in the United States by the year 2020."

  (42 U.S.C. § 300k. Subchapter on Preventive Health Measures with Respect to Breast and Cervical Cancers. Establishment of program of grants to States.)

- "(b) Grants and contracts for additional purposes; After consultation with the Administrator of the Agency for International Development, *the Secretary, acting through the Director of the Centers for Disease Control and Prevention, shall under section 2421 of this title make grants to, enter into contracts with, and provide technical assistance to*, international organizations concerned with public health and may provide technical assistance to foreign governments, in order to support—(1) projects for training individuals with respect to developing skills and technical expertise for use in the prevention, diagnosis, and treatment of acquired immune deficiency syndrome; and (2) epidemiological research relating to acquired immune deficiency syndrome."

  (42 U.S.C. § 300cc-15. Subchapter on Research with Respect to Acquired Immune Deficiency Syndrome. Research Authority. Support of international efforts.)

- "(b) Epidemiological and demographic data; (1) *The Secretary, acting through the Director of the Centers for Disease Control and Prevention, shall develop an epidemiological data base and shall provide for long-term studies* for the purposes of—(A) collecting information on the demographic characteristics of the population of individuals infected with the etiologic agent for acquired immune deficiency syndrome and the natural history of such infection; and (B) developing models demonstrating the long-term domestic and international patterns of the transmission of such etiologic agent."

  (42 U.S.C. § 300cc-20. Subchapter on Research with Re-

spect to Acquired Immune Deficiency Syndrome. Research Authority. Additional authority with respect to research.)

- "(a) In general; *The Secretary, acting through the Director of the Centers for Disease Control and Prevention, shall establish fellowship and training programs* to be conducted by the Centers for Disease Control and Prevention to train individuals to develop skills in epidemiology, surveillance, testing, counseling, education, information, and laboratory analysis relating to acquired immune deficiency syndrome."

  "The Secretary of Health and Human Services, acting through the Director of the Centers for Disease Control and Prevention, shall establish an office for the purpose of ensuring that, in carrying out the duties of the Secretary with respect to prevention of acquired immune deficiency syndrome, the Secretary develops and implements prevention programs targeted at minority populations and provides appropriate technical assistance in the implementation of such programs."

  (42 U.S.C. § 300ee-1. Subchapter on Prevention of Acquired Immune Deficiency Syndrome. Establishment of office with respect to minority health and acquired immune deficiency syndrome.)

- "(a) Development and dissemination of guidelines; Not later than 90 days after November 4, 1988, *the Secretary of Health and Human Services* (hereafter in this section referred to as the 'Secretary'), *acting through the Director of the Centers for Disease Control and Prevention, shall develop, issue, and disseminate emergency guidelines* to all health workers and public safety workers (including emergency response employees) in the United States concerning—(1) methods to reduce the risk in the workplace of becoming infected with the etiologic agent for acquired immune deficiency syndrome; and (2) circumstances under which exposure to such etiologic agent may occur."

  "(c) Development and dissemination of model curriculum for emergency response employees; (1) Not later than 90 days after November 4, 1988, *the Secretary, acting through the Director of the Centers for Disease Control and Prevention, shall develop a model curriculum for emergency response employees* with respect to the prevention of exposure to the etiologic agent for acquired immune deficiency syndrome during the process of responding to emergencies."

(42 U.S.C. § 300ee-2. Subchapter on Prevention of Acquired Immune Deficiency Syndrome. Information for health and public safety workers.)

- "(a) Comprehensive information plan; *The Secretary, acting through the Director of the Centers for Disease Control and Prevention, shall annually prepare a comprehensive plan*, including a budget, for a National Acquired Immune Deficiency Syndrome Information Program. The plan shall contain provisions to implement the provisions of this subchapter. The Director shall submit such plan to the Secretary. The authority established in this subsection may not be construed to be the exclusive authority for the Director to carry out information activities with respect to acquired immune deficiency syndrome."

    (42 U.S.C. § 300ee-31. Subchapter on Research with Respect to Acquired Immune Deficiency Syndrome. National Information Programs. Availability of information to general public.)

- "(b) Allocations; (2) After consultation with the Director of the Office of Minority Health and with the Indian Health Service, *the Secretary, acting through the Director of the Centers for Disease Control and Prevention, shall, not later than 90 days after November 4, 1988, publish guidelines* to provide procedures for applications for funding pursuant to paragraph (1) and for public comment."

    (42 U.S.C. § 300cc-34. Subchapter on Prevention of Acquired Immune Deficiency Syndrome. National Information Programs. Authorization of appropriations.)

- "(a) In general; In the case of States whose laws or regulations are in accordance with subsection (b) of this section, the Secretary, acting through the Centers for Disease Control and Prevention, shall make grants to such States for the purposes described in subsection (c) of this section."

    (42 U.S.C. § 300ff-33. Subchapter on HIV Health Care Services Program. Care Grant Program. Provisions Concerning Pregnancy and Perinatal Transmission of HIV.)

Food and Drug Administration

- "(g) Regulation of combination products; (4)(A) Not later than 60 days after October 26, 2002, the Secretary shall establish within the Office of the Commissioner of Food and Drugs an office to ensure the prompt assignment of combination products to agency centers, the timely and effective premarket review of such products, and consistent and appropriate postmarket regulation of like products subject to the same statutory requirements to the extent permitted by law. (F) *The Secretary, acting through the Office, shall review each agreement, guidance, or practice of the Secretary that is specific to the assignment of combination products to agency centers and shall determine* whether the agreement, guidance, or practice is consistent with the requirements of this subsection."

  (21 U.S.C. § 353. Title 21: Food and Drugs. Federal Food, Drug, and Cosmetic Act. Drugs and Devices. Exemptions and consideration for certain drugs, devices, and biological products.)
- "(h) Guidance of documents; (3) *The Secretary, acting through the Commissioner, shall maintain electronically and update and publish periodically* in the Federal Register a list of guidance documents. All such documents shall be made available to the public."

  (21 U.S.C. § 371. Federal Food, Drug, and Cosmetic Act. General Authority. General Administrative Provisions. Regulations and hearings.)
- "(a) In general; *The Secretary, acting through the Commissioner of Food and Drugs, shall automate appropriate activities of the Food and Drug Administration to ensure timely review of activities regulated under this chapter.*"

  (21 U.S.C. § 379d. Title 21: Food and Drugs. Federal Food, Drug, and Cosmetic Act. General Authority. General Administrative Provisions. Automation of Food and Drug Administration.)
- "(2) General powers; *The Secretary, through the Commissioner, shall be responsible for executing this chapter and for*—(A) providing overall direction to the Food and Drug Administration and establishing and implementing general policies respecting the management and operation of programs and activities of the

Food and Drug Administration; (B) coordinating and overseeing the operation of all administrative entities within the Administration; (C) research relating to foods, drugs, cosmetics, and devices in carrying out this chapter; (D) conducting educational and public information programs relating to the responsibilities of the Food and Drug Administration; and (E) performing such other functions as the Secretary may prescribe."

(21 U.S.C. § 393. Title 21: Food and Drugs. Federal Food, Drug, and Cosmetic Act. Miscellaneous. Food and Drug Administration.)

National Institutes of Health

- "(a) Establishment; priorities; Subject to available appropriations, *the Secretary, acting through the National Institute of Mental Health, the National Institutes of Health, and the Administration on Aging, shall promote* the establishment of family support groups to provide, without charge, educational, emotional, and practical support to assist individuals with Alzheimer's disease or a related memory disorder and members of the families of such individuals."

  (42 U.S.C. § 247a. Subchapter on General Powers and Duties. Family support groups for Alzheimer's disease patients.)
- "(a) Appointment; The National Institutes of Health shall be headed by the Director of NIH who shall be appointed by the President with the advice and consent of the Senate. The Director of NIH shall perform functions as provided under subsection (b) of this section and as the Secretary may otherwise prescribe.

  (b) Duties and authority; In carrying out the purposes of section 241 of this title, *the Secretary, acting through the Director of NIH—*

  (1) shall carry out this subchapter, including being responsible for the overall direction of the National Institutes of Health and for the establishment and implementation of general policies respecting the management and operation of programs and activities within the National Institutes of Health;"

> [There follows a list of 22 more general and specific function to be carried out by the Secretary through the Director.]

"(h) Increased participation of women and disadvantaged individuals in biomedical and behavioral research; The *Secretary, acting through the Director of NIH and the Directors of the agencies of the National Institutes of Health, shall*, in conducting and supporting programs for research, research training, recruitment, and other activities, provide for an increase in the number of women and individuals from disadvantaged backgrounds (including racial and ethnic minorities) in the fields of biomedical and behavioral research."

"(i) Data bank of information on clinical trials for drugs for serious or life-threatening diseases and conditions; (1)(A) *The Secretary, acting through the Director of NIH, shall establish, maintain, and operate a data ban*k of information on clinical trials for drugs for serious or life-threatening diseases and conditions (in this subsection referred to as the 'data bank')."

"(j) Expanded clinical trial registry data bank; (2) Expansion of clinical trial registry data bank with respect to clinical trial information; (A) In general; (i) Expansion of data bank; To enhance patient enrollment and provide a mechanism to track subsequent progress of clinical trials, *the Secretary, acting through the Director of NIH, shall expand*, in accordance with this subsection, the clinical trials registry of the data bank described under subsection (i)(1) of this section (referred to in this subsection as the 'registry data bank'). The Director of NIH shall ensure that the registry data bank is made publicly available through the Internet. (B) Inclusion of results; *The Secretary, acting through the Director of NIH, shall*—[expand the registry data bank and ensure its availability to the public]."

"(5) Coordination and compliance; (C) Quality control; (i) Pilot quality control project; Until the effective date of the regulations issued under paragraph (3)(D), the *Secretary, acting through the Director of NIH and the Commissioner of Food and Drugs, shall conduct a pilot project* to determine the optimal method of verification to help to ensure that the clinical trial information submitted under paragraph (3)(C) is non-promotional and is not false or misleading in any particular under subparagraph (D)."

(42 U.S.C. § 282. Subchapter on National Research Institute. National Institutes of Health. Director of the National Institutes of Health.)

- "*The Secretary, acting through the Director of NIH, shall establish an electronic system* to uniformly code research grants and activities of the Office of the Director and of all the national research institutes and national centers. The electronic system shall be searchable by a variety of codes, such as the type of research grant, the research entity managing the grant, and the public health area of interest. When permissible, the Secretary, acting through the Director of NIH, shall provide information on relevant literature and patents that are associated with research activities of the National Institutes of Health."

  (42 U.S.C. § 282b. Subchapter on National Research Institute. National Institutes of Health. Electronic coding of grants and activities.)
- "(b) Duties and authority; grants, contracts, and cooperative agreements; (1) In carrying out the purposes of section 241 of this title with respect to human diseases or disorders or other aspects of human health for which the national research institutes were established, *the Secretary, acting through the Director of each national research institute—(A) shall* encourage and support research, investigations, experiments, demonstrations, and studies in the health sciences related to—[various general health issues]. . . . *The Secretary, acting through the Director of each national research institute—(C) shall*, subject to section 300cc-40b(d)(2) of this title, receive from the President and the Office of Management and Budget directly all funds appropriated by the Congress for obligation and expenditure by the Institute."

  (42 U.S.C. § 284. Subchapter on National Research Institutes. General Provisions Respecting National Research Institutes. Directors of national research institutes.)
- "(a) List of priority issues in pediatric therapeutics; (1) In general; Not later than one year after September 27, 2007, *the Secretary, acting through the Director of the National Institutes of Health and in consultation with the Commissioner of Food* and Drugs and experts in pediatric research, shall develop and publish a priority list of needs in pediatric therapeutics, including drugs or indications that require study. The list shall be revised every three years."

"(b) Pediatric studies and research; *The Secretary, acting through the National Institutes of Health, shall award funds to entities* that have the expertise to conduct pediatric clinical trials or other research (including qualified universities, hospitals, laboratories, contract research organizations, practice groups, federally funded programs such as pediatric pharmacology research units, other public or private institutions, or individuals) to enable the entities to conduct the drug studies or other research on the issues described in subsection (a) of this section. The Secretary may use contracts, grants, or other appropriate funding mechanisms to award funds under this subsection."

"(c) Process for proposed pediatric study requests and labeling changes; (3) Requests for proposals; If the Commissioner of Food and Drugs does not receive a response to a written request issued under paragraph (2) not later than 30 days after the date on which a request was issued, *the Secretary, acting through the Director of the National Institutes of Health and in consultation with the Commissioner of Food and Drugs, shall publish a request for proposals* to conduct the pediatric studies described in the written request in accordance with subsection (b) of this section;"

"(d) Dissemination of pediatric information; Not later than one year after September 27, 2007, *the Secretary, acting through the Director of the National Institutes of Health, shall study* the feasibility of establishing a compilation of information on pediatric drug use and report the findings to Congress."

(42 U.S.C. § 284m. Subchapter on National Research Institutes. General Provisions Respecting national Research Institutes. Program for pediatric studies of drugs.)

- "(c) Report to Congress; Not later than the end of fiscal year 2009, *the Secretary, acting through the Director of NIH, shall conduct an evaluation of the activities under this section and submit a report to the Congress* on the results of such evaluation."

  (42 U.S.C. § 284n. Subchapter on National Research Institutes. General Provisions Respecting National Research Institutes.)

- "(b) Clinical trial infrastructure/innovative treatments for juvenile diabetes; *The Secretary, acting through the Director of the National Institutes of Health, shall support* regional clinical research centers for the prevention, detection, treatment, and cure of juvenile diabetes. (c) Prevention of type 1 diabetes; *The Secretary, acting through the appropriate agencies, shall provide for a national effort to prevent type 1 diabetes*."

(42 U.S.C. § 285c-9. Subchapter on National Research Institutes. Specific Provisions Respecting National Research Institutes. National Institute of Diabetes and Digestive Kidney Diseases. Juvenile diabetes.)

- "(c) Report to Congress; Not later than the end of fiscal year 2009, t*he Secretary, acting through the Director of NIH, shall conduct an evaluation* of the activities under this section and submit a report to the Congress on the results of such evaluation."

  (42 U.S.C. § 284m. Subchapter on National Research Institutes. General Provisions Respecting National Research Institutes. Certain demonstration projects.)

- "*The Secretary, acting through the Director of the National Institutes of Health, shall provide administrative support and support services* to the Director of the Center and *shall ensure* that such support takes maximum advantage of existing administrative structures at the agencies of the National Institutes of Health."

  (42 U.S.C. § 287c-34. Subchapter on National Research Institutes. Other agencies of NIH. Establishment of National Center on Minority Health and Health Disparities. General provisions regarding the center.)

- "(a) In general; *The Secretary, acting through the Director of the National Institutes of Health, shall establish a program* to enter into contracts with qualified health professionals under which such health professionals agree to conduct clinical research, in consideration of the Federal Government agreeing to repay, for each year of service conducting such research, not more than $35,000 of the principal and interest of the educational loans of such health professionals."

  (42 U.S.C. § 288-5a. Subchapter on National Research Institutes. Awards and Training. Loan repayment program regarding clinical researchers.)

- "(a) Applications for biomedical and behavioral research grants, cooperative agreements, and contracts; regulations; (1) *The Secretary, acting through the Director of NIH, shall by regulation require* appropriate technical and scientific peer review of—(A) applications made for grants and cooperative agreements under this chapter for biomedical and behavioral research; and (B) applications made for biomedical and behavioral research and development contracts to be administered through the National Institutes of Health."

(42 U.S.C. § 289a. Subchapter on National Research Institutes. General Provisions. Peer review requirements.)

- "(b) Ethical review of research; (5) Ethics advisory boards; (J) *The Secretary, acting through the Director of the National Institutes of Health, shall provide to each ethics board reasonable staff and assistance* to carry out the duties of the board."

  (42 U.S.C. § 289a-1. Subchapter on National Research Institutes. General Provisions. Certain provisions regarding review and approval of proposals for research.)
- "If the Secretary determines, after consultation with the Director of NIH, the Commissioner of the Food and Drug Administration, or the Director of the Centers for Disease Control and Prevention, that a disease or disorder constitutes a public health emergency, *the Secretary, acting through the Director of NIH*—(1) shall [take various actions to expedite action to address such emergency]."

  (42 U.S.C. § 289c. Subchapter on National Research Institutes. General Provisions. Research on public health emergencies; report to Congressional committees.)
- "(a) Establishment of guidelines; *The Secretary, acting through the Director of NIH, shall establish guidelines for the following:* (1) The proper care of animals to be used in biomedical and behavioral research. (2) The proper treatment of animals while being used in such research. Guidelines under this paragraph shall require—(A) the appropriate use of tranquilizers, analgesics, anesthetics, paralytics, and euthanasia for animals in such research; and (B) appropriate pre-surgical and post-surgical veterinary medical and nursing care for animals in such research. Such guidelines shall not be construed to prescribe methods of research. (3) The organization and operation of animal care committees in accordance with subsection (b) of this section."

  (42 U.S.C. § 289d. Subchapter on National Research Institutes. General Provisions. Animals in research.)

- "(a) In general; *The Secretary shall, acting through the Director of NIH, establish a nonprofit corporation* to be known as the Foundation for the National Institutes of Health (hereafter in this section referred to as the 'Foundation')."
  (42 U.S.C. § 290b. Subchapter on National Research Institutes. Foundation for the National Institutes of Health. Establishment and duties of Foundation.)
- "(a) In general; *The Secretary, acting through the Director of the National Institutes of Health (in this section referred to as the "Director"), shall establish a comprehensive program* of conducting basic and clinical research on trauma (in this section referred to as the "Program"). The Program shall include research regarding the diagnosis, treatment, rehabilitation, and general management of trauma."
  (42 U.S.C. § 300d-61. Subchapter on Trauma Care. Interagency Program for Trauma Research. Establishment of program.)
- "(a) In general; *The Secretary, acting through the Director of the National Cancer Institute and the Director of the National Institute of Allergy and Infectious Diseases, shall for each such Institute establish a clinical evaluation unit at the Clinical Center at the National Institutes of Health....* (b) Personnel and administrative support; (1) For the purposes described in subsection (a) of this section, *the Secretary, acting through the Director of the National Institutes of Health, shall provide each of the clinical evaluation units required in such subsection*—(A)(i) with not less than 50 beds; or (ii) with an outpatient clinical capacity equal to not less than twice the outpatient clinical capacity, with respect to acquired immune deficiency syndrome, possessed by the Clinical Center of the National Institutes of Health on June 1, 1988; and (B) with such personnel, such administrative support, and such other support services as may be necessary."
  (42 U.S.C. § 300cc-11. Subchapter on Research with Respect to Acquired Immune Deficiency Syndrome. Clinical evaluation units at National Institutes of Health.)
- "(a) Grants and contracts for research; (1) Under section 242 of this title, *the Secretary, acting through the Director of the National Institutes of Health—(A) shall*, for the purpose described

in paragraph (2), make grants to, enter into cooperative agreements and contracts with, and provide technical assistance to, international organizations concerned with public health...."

(42 U.S.C. § 300cc-15. Subchapter on Research with Respect to Acquired Immune Deficiency Syndrome. Research Authority. Support of international efforts.)

- "(2) A grant or contract under paragraph (1) shall be provided in accordance with policies established by *the Secretary, acting through the Director of the National Institutes of Health, and after consultation with the advisory council for the National Institute of Allergy and Infectious Diseases*."

  (42 U.S.C. § 300cc-16. Subchapter on Research with Respect to Acquired Immune Deficiency Syndrome. Research Authority. Research centers.)

- "(a) Administrative support for Office; *The Secretary, acting through the Director of the National Institutes of Health, shall provide administrative support and support services* to the Director of the Office and shall ensure that such support takes maximum advantage of existing administrative structures at the agencies of the National Institutes of Health."

  (42 U.S.C. § 300cc-45. Subchapter on Research with Respect to Acquired Immune Deficiency Syndrome. Office of AIDS Research. General Provisions. General provisions regarding Office.)

[NOTE: Title IV of the PHSA vests in the Director of each of the separate institutes within NIH the authority to carry out the functions of the institute. The statute also creates within some of the institutes separate subunits to carry out particular functions. Because of the volume of such provisions (there are at least 19 statutorily created institutes and 5 national centers, plus the Library of Medicine) we have not attempted to list the organizational features of each institute.]

Agency for Toxic Substances and Disease Registry

- "(f) Functions of HHS to be carried out through ATSDR.—The functions of the Secretary of Health and Human Services under this section shall be carried out through the Administrator of the Agency for Toxic Substances and Disease Registry of the Department of Health and Human Services established under section 104(i) of CERCLA (42 U.S.C. 9604(i)).”

(10 U.S.C. § 2704. Title 10: Armed Forces. Subtitle A: General Military Law. Service, Supply, and Procurement. Environmental Restoration. Commonly found unregulated hazardous substances.)

- “(1) *The Secretary of Health and Human Services (hereafter in this subsection referred to as the ‘Secretary’), acting through the Director of the Centers for Disease Control, (CDC), and the Director of the National Institute of Environmental Health Sciences, shall jointly conduct a study* of the sources of lead exposure in children who have elevated blood lead levels (or other indicators of elevated lead body burden), as defined by the Director of the Centers for Disease Control.”

  (15 U.S.C. § 2704. Title 15: Commerce and Trade. Toxic Substances Control. Subchapter on Lead Exposure Reduction. Lead abatement and measurement.)

Indian Health Service

- “(a) Establishment
  . . . there is established within the Public Health Service of the Department of Health and Human Services the Indian Health Service. The Indian Health Service shall be administered by a Director, who shall be appointed by the President, with the advice and consent of the Senate. The Director of the Indian Health Service shall report to the Secretary through the Assistant Secretary for Health of the Department of Health and Human Services.”
  “(b) Agency status
  The Indian Health Service shall be an agency within the Public Health Service of the Department of Health and Human Services, and shall not be an office, component, or unit of any other agency of the Department.”

  (25 U.S.C. § 1661)

The Indian Health Service was created under this provision which is codified in title 25, United States Code—Indians. However it contains many references to the Secretary of Health and Human Services, including the following:

- "$10,000,000 shall remain available until expended, for the establishment of an Indian Catastrophic Health Emergency Fund (hereinafter referred to as the 'Fund'). On and after October 18, 1986, the Fund is to cover the Indian Health Service portion of the medical expenses of catastrophic illness falling within the responsibility of the Service and *shall be administered by the Secretary of Health and Human Services, acting through the central office of the Indian Health Service*."

  (25 U.S.C. § 1683. Title 25: Indians. Chapter 18: Indian Health Care. Subchapter: Miscellaneous. Indian Catastrophic Health Emergency Fund.)
- "(a) Implementation; The Secretary of the Interior, acting through the Bureau of Indian Affairs, *and the Secretary of Health and Human Services, acting through the Indian Health Service, shall bear equal responsibility for the implementation of this chapter in cooperation with Indian tribes*."

  (25 U.S.C. § 2413. Chapter 26: Indian Alcohol and Substance Abuse Prevention and Treatment. Subchapter on Coordination of Resources and Programs. Department of responsibility.)

Also see 42 U.S.C. § 1616a, which requires the Secretary, through the Indian Health Service to establish a program known as the Indian Health Service Loan Repayment Program, and 42 U.S.C. § 1621d, which requires the Secretary, acting through the [Indian Health] Service, to conduct a study of the feasibility and desirability of funding hospice services for Indians.

Substance Abuse and Mental Health Services Administration

- "(d) Authorities; The *Secretary, acting through the Administrator, shall*—

  (1) supervise the functions of the agencies of the Administration in order to assure that the programs carried out through each such agency receive appropriate and equitable support and that there is cooperation among the agencies in the implementation of such programs;"

  [There follows a list of 17 instructions as to the organization and functions of SAMHSA.]

(42 U.S.C. § 290aa. Subchapter on Substance Abuse and Mental Health Services Administration. Organization and General Authorities. Substance Abuse and Mental Health Services Administration.)

- "(a) Requirement of annual collection of data on mental illness and substance abuse; *The Secretary, acting through the Administrator, shall collect data* each year on—(1) the national incidence and prevalence of the various forms of mental illness and substance abuse; and (2) the incidence and prevalence of such various forms in major metropolitan areas selected by the Administrator."

  (42 U.S.C. § 290aa-4. Subchapter on Substance Abuse and Mental Health Services Administration. Organization and General Authorities. Data collection.)

- "(a) Establishment; (1) In general; *The Secretary, acting through the Administrator of the Substance Abuse and Mental Health Services Administration, shall make grants* to public and nonprofit private entities for the purpose of carrying out [various] programs…."

  (42 U.S.C. § 290bb-25. Subchapter on Substance Abuse and Mental Health Services Administration. Center for Substance Abuse Prevention. Grants for services for children of substance abusers.)

- "(a) Program authorized; *The Secretary, acting through the Director of the Prevention Center, may make grants* to public and nonprofit private entities to develop and implement model substance abuse prevention programs to provide early intervention and substance abuse prevention services for individuals of high-risk families and the communities in which such individuals reside."

  (42 U.S.C. § 290bb-25a. Subchapter on Substance Abuse and Mental Health Services Administration. Centers and Programs. Center for Substance Abuse Prevention. Grants for strengthening families.)

- "(a) Program authorized; *The Secretary, acting through the Administrator of the Substance Abuse and Mental Health Services Administration, and in consultation with the Administrator of the Office of Juvenile Justice and Delinquency Prevention, the Director of the Bureau of Justice Assistance and the Director of the*

National Institutes of Health—(1) shall award grants or contracts to public or nonprofit private entities to establish not more than four research, training, and technical assistance centers to carry out the activities described in subsection (c) of this section; and (2) *shall award a competitive grant* to 1 additional research, training, and technical assistance center to carry out the activities described in subsection (d) of this section."

(42 U.S.C. § 290bb-34. Subchapter on Substance Abuse and Mental Health Services Administration. Centers and Programs. Center for Mental Health Services. Youth interagency research, training, and technical assistance centers.)

- "In general; *The Secretary, acting through the Director of the Center for Mental Health Services, and in consultation with the Director of the Center for Substance Abuse Treatment, the Administrator of the Office of Juvenile Justice and Delinquency Prevention, and the Director of the Special Education Programs, shall award grants* on a competitive basis to State or local juvenile justice agencies to enable such agencies to provide aftercare services for youth offenders who have been discharged from facilities in the juvenile or criminal justice system and have serious emotional disturbances or are at risk of developing such disturbances."

  (42 U.S.C. § 290bb-35. Subchapter on Substance Abuse and Mental Health Services Administration. Centers and Programs. Center for Mental Health Services. Services for youth offenders.)

- "(a) In general; *The Secretary, acting through the Administrator of the Substance Abuse and Mental Health Services Administration, shall award grants or cooperative agreements* to eligible entities to—[carry out various activities with respect to youth suicide prevention]."

  (42 U.S.C. § 290bb-36. Subchapter on Substance Abuse and Mental Health Services Administration. Centers and Programs. Center for Mental Health Services. Youth suicide early intervention and prevention strategies.)

- "For the purpose of carrying out section 290cc-22 of this title, *the Secretary, acting through the Director of the Center for Mental Health Services, shall for each of the fiscal years 1991 through 1994 make an allotment* for each State in an amount determined in accordance with section 290cc-24 of this title. The

Secretary shall make payments, as grants, each such fiscal year to each State from the allotment for the State if the Secretary approves for the fiscal year involved an application submitted by the State pursuant to section 290cc-29 of this title."

(42 U.S.C. § 290cc-21. Subchapter on Substance Abuse and Mental Health Services Administration. Projects for Assistance in Transition from Homelessness. Formula grants to States.)

- "(a) Programs and services; (1) Development; *The Secretary, acting through the Administrator of the Substance Abuse and Mental Health Services Administration, shall be responsible for fostering substance abuse prevention and treatment programs and services* in State and local governments and in private industry. (2) Model programs; (A) In general; Consistent with the responsibilities described in paragraph (1), *the Secretary, acting through the Administrator of the Substance Abuse and Mental Health Services Administration, shall develop a variety of model programs* suitable for replication on a cost-effective basis in different types of business concerns and State and local governmental entities. (B) Dissemination of information; *The Secretary, acting through the Administrator of the Substance Abuse and Mental Health Services Administration, shall disseminate information and materials* relative to such model programs to the State agencies responsible for the administration of substance abuse prevention, treatment, and rehabilitation activities and shall, to the extent feasible provide technical assistance to such agencies as requested."

  (42 U.S.C. § 290dd. Subchapter on Substance Abuse and Mental Health Services Administration. Miscellaneous Provisions Relating to Substance Abuse and Mental Health. Substance abuse among government and other employees.)

- "(a) Grants to certain public entities; (1) In general; *The Secretary, acting through the Director of the Center for Mental Health Services, shall make grants to public entities* for the purpose of providing comprehensive community mental health services to children with a serious emotional disturbance."

  (42 U.S.C. § 290ff. Subchapter on Substance Abuse and Mental Health Services Administration. Children with Serious Emotional Disturbances. Comprehensive community mental health services for children with serious emotional

disturbances.)

- "In general; For the purpose described in subsection (b) of this section, *the Secretary, acting through the Director of the Center for Mental Health Services, shall make an allotment* each fiscal year for each State in an amount determined in accordance with section 300x-7 of this title. The Secretary shall make a grant to the State of the allotment made for the State for the fiscal year if the State submits to the Secretary an application in accordance with section 300x-6 of this title."

  (42 U.S.C. § 300x. Subchapter on Block Grants Regarding Mental Health and Substance Abuse. Block Grants for Community Mental Health Services. Formula grants to states.)
- "(a) In general; For the purpose described in subsection (b) of this section, *the Secretary, acting through the Center for Substance Abuse Treatment, shall make an allotment each fiscal year* for each State in an amount determined in accordance with section 300x-33 of this title. The Secretary shall make a grant to the State of the allotment made for the State for the fiscal year if the State submits to the Secretary an application in accordance with section 300x-32 of this title."

  (42 U.S.C. § 300x-21. Subchapter on Block Grants Regarding Mental Health and Substance Abuse. Block Grants for Prevention and Treatment of Substance Abuse. Formula grants to States.)
- "(b) State plan; (3) Authority of center for substance abuse prevention; With respect to plans submitted by the States under subsection (a)(6) of this section, *the Secretary, acting through the Director of the Center for Substance Abuse Prevention, shall review and approve or disapprove the provisions of the plans* that relate to prevention activities."

  (42 U.S.C. § 300x-32. Subchapter on Block Grants Regarding Mental Health and Substance Abuse. Block Grants for Prevention and Treatment of Substance Abuse. Application for grant; approval of State plan.)
- "(b) Allocations for technical assistance, national data base, data collection, and program evaluations; (2) Activities of center for substance abuse prevention; Of the amounts reserved under paragraph (1) for a fiscal year, the Secretary, acting through the Director of the Center for Substance Abuse Prevention, shall ob-

ligate 20 percent for carrying out paragraph (1)(C), section 300x-58(a) of this title with respect to prevention activities, and section 290bb-21(d) of this title."

(42 U.S.C. § 300x-35. Subchapter on Block Grants Regarding Mental Health and Substance Abuse. Block Grants for Prevention and Treatment of Substance Abuse. Funding.)

Health Resources and Services Administration

- "(a) Training; *The Secretary of Health and Human Services, acting through the Administrator of the Health Resources and Services Administration and in collaboration with the Administrator of the Centers for Medicare & Medicaid Services and the Director of the Centers for Disease Control and Prevention, shall conduct education and training programs* for physicians and other health care providers regarding childhood lead poisoning, current screening and treatment recommendations and requirements, and the scientific, medical, and public health basis for those policies."

  (42 U.S.C. § 247b-3a. Subchapter on General Powers and Duties. Federal-State Cooperation. Training and reports by the health resources and services administration.)
- "(c) Statewide newborn and infant hearing screening, evaluation and intervention programs and systems; Under the existing authority of the Public Health Service Act [42 U.S.C.A. § 201 et seq.], *the Secretary of Health and Human Services (in this section referred to as the 'Secretary'), acting through the Administrator of the Health Resources and Services Administration, shall make awards of grants or cooperative agreements* to develop statewide newborn and infant hearing screening, evaluation and intervention programs and systems for the following purposes":

  [To develop and monitor the efficacy of statewide newborn and infant hearing screening, evaluation and intervention programs and systems].

(42 U.S.C. § 247b-4a. Subchapter on General Powers and Duties. Federal-State Cooperation. Early detection, diagno-

sis, and interventions for newborns and infants with hearing loss.)

- "(a) In general; *The Secretary, acting through the Administrator of the Health Resources and Services Administration, shall establish a program* to fund innovative oral health activities that improve the oral health of children under 6 years of age who are eligible for services provided under a Federal health program, to increase the utilization of dental services by such children, and to decrease the incidence of early childhood and baby bottle tooth decay."

  (42 U.S.C. § 247d-8. Subchapter on General Powers and Duties. Federal-State Cooperation. Coordinated program to improve pediatric oral health.)

- "(6) Participation of certain eligible health clinics; (C) Not later than 1 year after October 17, 2000, the Secretary shall submit to the appropriate committees of the Congress a report evaluating the extent to which adoption information and referral, upon request, are provided by eligible health centers. . . . *The reports required by this subparagraph shall be conducted by the Secretary acting through the Administrator of the Health Resources and Services Administration and in collaboration with the Director of the Agency for Healthcare Research and Quality.*"

  (42 U.S.C. § 247b-3a. Subchapter on General Powers and Duties. Federal-State Cooperation. Training and reports by the Health Resources and Services Administration.)

- "(c) Statewide newborn and infant hearing screening, evaluation and intervention programs and systems; Under the existing authority of the Public Health Service Act [42 U.S.C.A. § 201 et seq.], *the Secretary of Health and Human Services (in this section referred to as the 'Secretary'), acting through the Administrator of the Health Resources and Services Administration, shall make awards of grants or cooperative agreements* to develop statewide newborn and infant hearing screening, evaluation and intervention programs and systems for the following purposes…."

  (42 U.S.C. § 247b-4a. Subchapter on General Powers and Duties. Federal-State Cooperation. Early detection, diagnosis, and interventions for newborns and infants with hearing loss.)

- "(a) In general; *The Secretary, acting through the Administrator of the Health Resources and Services Administration, shall establish a program* to fund innovative oral health activities that improve the oral health of children under 6 years of age who are eligible for services provided under a Federal health program, to increase the utilization of dental services by such children, and to decrease the incidence of early childhood and baby bottle tooth decay."

(42 U.S.C. § 247d-8. Subchapter on General Powers and Duties. Federal-State Cooperation. Coordinated program to improve pediatric oral health.)

- "(a) In general; (1) Continuation and expansion of program; *The Secretary, acting through the Administrator of the Health Resources and Services Administration, Maternal and Child Health Bureau, shall under authority of this section continue in effect the Healthy Start Initiative* and may, during fiscal year 2001 and subsequent years, carry out such program on a national basis."

  (42 U.S.C. § 254c-8. Subchapter on General Powers and Duties. Primary Health Care. Health Centers. Healthy Start for infants.)
- "(a) Grants; *The Secretary, acting through the Administrator of the Health Resources and Services Administration (referred to in this section as the 'Secretary') shall award grants to eligible entities* to enable such entities to provide for improved emergency medical services in rural areas."

  (42 U.S.C. § 254c-15. Subchapter on General Powers and Duties. Primary Health Care. Health Centers. Rural emergency medical service training and equipment assistance program.)
- "(3) Annual reporting required; (D) Report to Congress; Not later than the end of fiscal year 2011, *the Secretary, acting through the Administrator of the Health Resources and Services Administration, shall submit a report to the Congress*—(i) summarizing the information submitted in reports to the Secretary under subparagraph (B); (ii) describing the results of the program carried out under this section; and (iii) making recommendations for improvements to the program."

  (42 U.S.C. § 256e. Subchapter on General Powers and Duties. Primary Health Care. Support of Graduate Medical Education Programs in Children's Hospitals. Program of payments to children's hospitals that operate graduate medi-

cal education programs.)

- "(a) Establishment; *The Secretary, acting through the Administrator of the Health Resources and Services Administration, shall by one or more contracts establish and maintain a C.W. Bill Young Cell Transplantation Program* (referred to in this section as the 'Program'), successor to the National Bone Marrow Donor Registry, that has the purpose of increasing the number of transplants for recipients suitably matched to biologically unrelated donors of bone marrow and cord blood, and that meets the requirements of this section."

    (42 U.S.C. § 274k. Subchapter on General Powers and Duties. General Powers and Duties. C.W. Bill Young Cell Transplantation Program. National program.)

- "(a) In general; *The Secretary, acting through the Administrator of the Health Resources and Services Administration, shall make not less than 5, and not more than 20, grants to States* for the purpose of assisting grantees in carrying out demonstration projects—(1) to identify low-income individuals who can avoid institutionalization or prolonged hospitalization if skilled medical services, skilled nursing care services, homemaker or home health aide services, or personal care services are provided in the homes of the individuals; (2) to pay the costs of the provision of such services in the homes of such individuals; and (3) to coordinate the provision by public and private entities of such services, and other long-term care services, in the homes of such individuals."

    (42 U.S.C. § 280c. Subchapter on General Powers and Duties. Health Care Services in the Home. Grants for Demonstration Projects. Establishment of program.)

- "(a) In general; (1) Establishment of program; *The Secretary, acting through the Administrator of the Health Resources and Services Administration, shall make grants to eligible entities* to pay the Federal share of the cost of providing the services specified in subsection (b) of this section to families in which a member is—(A) a pregnant woman at risk of delivering an infant with a health or developmental complication; or (B) a child less than 3 years of age—(i) who is experiencing or is at risk of a health or developmental complication, or of child abuse or neglect; or (ii) who has been prenatally exposed to maternal substance abuse."

    (42 U.S.C. § 280c-6. Subchapter on General Powers and Du-

ties. Health Care Services in the Home. Grants for Home Visiting Services for at-Risk Families. Projects to improve maternal, infant, and child health.)

- "(a) Statewide newborn and infant hearing screening, evaluation and intervention programs and systems; *The Secretary, acting through the Administrator of the Health Resources and Services Administration, shall make awards of grants or cooperative agreements* to develop statewide newborn and infant hearing screening, evaluation and intervention programs and systems for the following purposes":

  (42 U.S.C. § 280g-1. Subchapter on General Powers and Duties. Additional Programs. Early detection, diagnosis, and treatment regarding hearing loss in infants.)

- "Grants; *The Secretary, acting through the Director of the Health Resources and Services Administration, shall award grants* under this section to develop interdisciplinary training and education programs that provide undergraduate, graduate, post-graduate medical, nursing (including advanced practice nursing students), and other health professions students with an understanding of, and clinical skills pertinent to, domestic violence, sexual assault, stalking, and dating violence."

  (42 U.S.C. § 294h. Subchapter on Health Professions Education. Interdisciplinary training and education on domestic violence and other types of violence and abuse.)

- "(f) Peer review regarding certain programs; (3) Administration; *This subsection shall be carried out by the Secretary acting through the Administrator of the Health Resources and Services Administration.*"

  (42 U.S.C. § 295o-1. Subchapter on Health Professions Education. General Provisions. Generally applicable provisions.)

- "(e) Peer review regarding certain programs; (3) Administration; This subsection shall be carried out by the Secretary acting through the Administrator of the Health Resources and Services Administration."

  (42 U.S.C. § 296e. Subchapter on Nursing Workforce Development. General Provisions. Generally applicable provisions.)

- "(a) Authorization of grant program; From amounts appropriated under subsection (j) of this section, *the Secretary, acting through the Administrator of the Health Resources and Services Admini-*

stration (referred to in this section as the 'Administrator') and in consultation with the Advisory Committee on Heritable Disorders in Newborns and Children (referred to in this section as the 'Advisory Committee'), shall award grants to eligible entities to enable such entities—[to carry out various activities to enhance, improve or expand the ability of State and local public health agencies to provide screening, counseling, or health care services to newborns and children having or at risk for heritable disorders]."

(42 U.S.C. § 300b-8. Subchapter on Genetic Diseases, Hemophilia Programs, and Sudden Infant Death Syndrome. Genetic Diseases. Improved newborn and child screening for heritable disorders.)

- "(a) In general; *The Secretary, acting through the Administrator of the Health Resources and Services Administration (referred to in this part as the 'Administrator'), in consultation with the Director of the Centers for Disease Control and Prevention and the Director of the National Institutes of Health, shall establish and maintain a central clearinghouse* of current educational and family support and services information, materials, resources, research, and data on newborn screening. . . ."

  (42 U.S.C. § 300b-11. Subchapter on Genetic Diseases, Hemophilia Programs, and Sudden Infant Death Syndrome. Genetic Diseases. Clearinghouse of newborn screening information.)

- "(a) In general; *The Secretary, acting through the Administrator of the Health Resources and Services Administration (referred to in this section as the 'Administrator'), shall make grants* to protection and advocacy systems for the purpose of enabling such systems to provide services to individuals with traumatic brain injury."

  (42 U.S.C. § 300d-53. Subchapter on Trauma Care. Miscellaneous Programs. State grants for protection and advocacy services.)

- "(a) Eligible areas; *The Secretary, acting through the Administrator of the Health Resources and Services Administration, shall, subject to subsections (b) through (c) of this section, make grants* in accordance with section 300ff-13 of this title for the purpose of assisting in the provision of the services specified in section 300ff-14 of this title in any metropolitan area for which there has been reported to and confirmed by the Director of the Centers for Disease Control and Prevention a cumulative total of more than 2,000 cases of AIDS during the most recent period of 5 calendar years for which such data are available."

(42 U.S.C. § 300ff-11. Subchapter on HIV Health Care Services Program. Emergency Relief for Areas with Substantial Need for Services. General Grant Provisions. Establishment of program of grants.)

- "(a) In general; *The Secretary, acting through the Administrator of the Health Resources and Services Administration, shall make grants* for the purpose of providing services described in section 300ff-14 of this title in transitional areas, subject to the same provisions regarding the allocation of grant funds as apply under subsection (c) of such section."

  (42 U.S.C. § 300ff-19. Subchapter on HIV Health Care Services Program. Emergency Relief for Areas with Substantial Need for Services. Traditional Grants. Establishment of program.)

- "(a) In general; *The Secretary, acting through the Administrator of the Health Resources and Services Administration, shall award grants to public and nonprofit private entities* (including a health facility operated by or pursuant to a contract with the Indian Health Service) for the purpose of providing family-centered care involving outpatient or ambulatory care (directly or through contracts) for women, infants, children, and youth with HIV/AIDS."

  (42 U.S.C. § 300ff-71. Subchapter on HIV Health Care Services Program. Women, Infants, Children, and Youth. Grants for coordinated services and access to research for women, infants, children, and youth.)

I

Committee and Staff Biographies

Leonard D. Schaeffer, *Chair*, is currently chairman of the board of Surgical Care Affiliates, LLC, and a senior adviser for Texas Pacific Group, a private equity firm. Mr. Schaeffer is the founding chairman of the Board of Directors of WellPoint Inc., the largest health benefits company in the United States. From 1992 through 2004, he was chairman and chief executive officer (CEO) of WellPoint Health Networks Inc. Mr. Schaeffer was the administrator of the U.S. Health Care Financing Administration from 1978 to 1980 and has served in a variety of positions in state and federal government. He is the Judge Robert Maclay Widney Chair and Professor at the University of Southern California, is a member of the Institute of Medicine (IOM), and is on the board of the Brookings Institution and several public and private corporations.

David W. Beier, J.D., is senior vice president of global government and corporate affairs for Amgen. In this role, he is responsible for shaping Amgen's policy on global health care issues; driving health economics and outcomes research; overseeing corporate communications and philanthropy; and managing relationships with U.S. federal and state agencies and legislatures, as well as international governmental entities and organizations. Mr. Beier joined Amgen from the international law firm of Hogan & Hartson where, as a partner, he utilized his extensive background in business and government to represent trade associations and biotechnology, pharmaceutical, and health care companies. Mr. Beier previously served as chief domestic policy adviser to Vice President Al Gore. Before his White House service, Mr. Beier served as vice president of government affairs and public policy for Genentech and staff counsel in the U.S. House of Representatives. He received a B.A. from Colgate University and his J.D. from Albany Law School.

Kathleen Buto, M.P.A., is vice president for health policy, government affairs, at Johnson & Johnson (J&J). She has responsibility for providing policy analysis and developing positions on a wide range of issues, including the Medicare drug benefit, government reimbursement, coverage of new technologies, and regulatory requirements. In addition to reviewing how federal, state, and international government policies affect J&J products and customers, she is responsible for helping to identify areas of opportunity for J&J to take leadership in shaping health care policy. Prior to joining J&J, Kathy was a senior health adviser at the Congressional Budget Office, helping to develop the cost models for the Medicare drug benefit. Before that, she spent more than 18 years in senior positions at the Health Care Financing Administration, including deputy director, Center for Health Plans and Providers, and associate administrator for policy. In these positions, she headed the policy, reimbursement, and coverage functions for the agency, as well as managing Medicare's fee-for-service and managed care operations. Ms. Buto received her bachelor of arts from Douglass College and her master's in public administration from Harvard University.

Molly Joel Coye, M.D., is founder and CEO of the Health Technology Center (HealthTech), a nonprofit education and research organization established in 2000 to advance the use of beneficial technologies in promoting healthier people and communities. Dr. Coye is vice chair of the Board of Directors of the Program for Appropriate Technology in Health, one of the largest and most innovative nonprofit organizations working in international health; a member of the Board of Directors of Aetna, Inc.; and a member of the Advisory Council for the Health Evolution Partners Innovation Network and the Institute of Medicine. Dr. Coye has served as commissioner of health for the State of New Jersey and director of the California Department of Health Services; head of the Division of Public Health at the Johns Hopkins School of Hygiene and Public Health; executive vice president for HealthDesk Corp. and the Good Samaritan Health System in San Jose, California; and director of the Lewin Group West Coast office. She has served on the Board of Trustees of the American Hospital Association and the American Public Health Association, the Board of Directors of the California Endowment, and the China Medical Board, and as a member of the National Academy of Public Administration.

Robert Graham, M.D., is professor of family medicine, and the Robert and Myfanwy Smith Chair in the Department of Family Medicine at the University of Cincinnati, School of Medicine, a position he has held since March of 2005. Dr. Graham has previously been associated with the discipline of family medicine as the executive vice president-CEO of the American Academy of Family Physicians (1985–2000), the head of the Academy's Foundation (1988–1997), and the administrative officer of the Society of Teachers of Family Medicine (1973–1975). In addition to his activities in family medicine, Dr. Graham has held a number of leadership responsibilities in the federal health sector, including the position of administrator of the Health Resources and Services Administration (HRSA) (1981–1985), during which time he held the rank of rear admiral in the Commissioned Corps of the U.S. Public Health Service and served as an assistant surgeon general. He also served in senior positions at the Agency for Healthcare Research and Quality (2001–2004), HRSA (1976–1979), and the Health Services and Mental Health Administration (1970–1973). From 1979–1980, he served as a professional staff member of the U.S. Senate Subcommittee on Health.

Mark B. McClellan, M.D., Ph.D., is the director of the Engelberg Center for Health Care Reform at the Brookings Institution. McClellan is also the Leonard D. Schaeffer Chair in Health Policy. Dr. McClellan has a highly distinguished record in public service and in academic research. He is the former administrator for the Centers for Medicare and Medicaid Services (2004–2006) and the former commissioner of the Food and Drug Administration (2002–2004). He also served as a member of the President's Council of Economic Advisers and senior director for health care policy at the White House (2001–2002). In the Clinton administration, Dr. McClellan was deputy assistant secretary of the treasury for economic policy from 1998–1999, supervising economic analysis and policy development on a range of domestic policy issues. Dr. McClellan was also an associate professor of economics and associate professor of medicine (with tenure) at Stanford University, from which he was on leave during his government service. He directed Stanford's Program on Health Outcomes Research and was also associate editor of the *Journal of Health Economics*, and coprincipal investigator of the Health and Retirement Study, a longitudinal study of the health and economic status of older Americans. A graduate of the University of Texas at Austin, Dr. McClellan earned his M.P.A. from Harvard's Kennedy School of Government in 1991, his M.D. from the Harvard-Massachusetts Institute of Technology (MIT) Division of Health Sciences and Technology in 1992, and his Ph.D. in economics from MIT in 1993. He completed his residency training in internal medicine at Brigham and Women's Hospital, Boston. Dr. McClellan has been board certified in internal medicine and has been a practicing internist during his academic career.

Stanley B. Prusiner, M.D., is the director of the Institute for Neurodegenerative Diseases at the University of California, San Francisco (UCSF). Dr. Prusiner discovered prions, a class of infectious self-reproducing pathogens primarily or solely composed of protein. For his prion research he received the Albert Lasker Award for Basic Medical Research in 1994 and the Nobel Prize in physiology or medicine in 1997. He received a bachelor of science degree in chemistry from the University of Pennsylvania and later received his M.D. from the University of Pennsylvania School of Medicine. He then completed an internship in medicine at UCSF. Later he moved to the National Institutes of Health (NIH), where he studied glutaminases in *Escherichia coli* in the laboratory of Earl Stadtman. After three years at NIH, Dr. Prusiner returned to UCSF to complete a residency in neurology. Upon completion of the residency in 1974, he joined the faculty of the UCSF Neurology Department. Since that time, he has held various faculty and visiting faculty positions at both UCSF and UC Berkeley. Dr. Prusiner won the Nobel Prize in physiology or medicine in 1997 for his discovery of prions—a new biological principle of infection. He coined the term *prion*, which comes from "proteinaceous infectious particle" to refer to a previously undescribed form of infection due to protein misfolding. He was elected to the National Academy of Sciences in 1992 and to its governing council in 2007. He is also an elected member of the American Academy of Arts and Sciences (1993), the Royal Society (1996), the American Philosophical Society (1998), the Serbian Academy of Sciences and Arts (2003), and the Institute of Medicine.

Donna E. Shalala, Ph.D., became professor of political science and president of the University of Miami on June 1, 2001. President Shalala has more than 25 years of experience as an accomplished scholar, teacher, and administrator. Born in Cleveland, Ohio, President Shalala received her A.B. in history from Western College for Women and her

Ph.D. from the Maxwell School of Citizenship and Public Affairs at Syracuse University. A leading scholar on the political economy of state and local governments, she has also held tenured professorships at Columbia University, the City University of New York (CUNY), and the University of Wisconsin–Madison. She served as president of Hunter College of CUNY from 1980 to 1987 and as chancellor of the University of Wisconsin–Madison from 1987 to 1993. In 1993, President Clinton appointed her secretary of the Department of Health and Human Services (HHS), where she served for eight years, becoming the longest-serving HHS secretary in U.S. history.

Stephen M. Shortell, Ph.D., M.P.H., is the Blue Cross of California Distinguished Professor of Health Policy and Management and professor of organization behavior at the University of California, Berkeley, and is dean of the School of Public Health. Dr. Shortell is known as a leading academic voice advocating reform of the nation's health system. His research has helped establish determinants of health outcomes and quality of care for health care organizations. As the Blue Cross of California Distinguished Professor of Health Policy and Management, Shortell holds a joint appointment at University of California (UC) Berkeley's School of Public Health and the Haas School of Business. He also is affiliated with UC Berkeley's Department of Sociology and UC San Francisco's Institute for Health Policy Studies. Dr. Shortell has received the Baxter-Allegiance Prize, considered the highest honor worldwide in the field of health services research. He also has received the Distinguished Investigator Award from the Association for Health Services Research and the Gold Medal from the American College of Healthcare Executives for his contributions to the field. Dr. Shortell received his bachelor's degree from the University of Notre Dame, his master's degree in public health from the University of California at Los Angeles, and his Ph.D. in behavioral science from the University of Chicago. Before coming to UC Berkeley in 1998, Dr. Shortell held teaching and research positions at Northwestern University, the University of Washington, and the University of Chicago.

Susanne A. Stoiber, M.P.A., M.S., is currently consulting with the Commonwealth Fund High Performance Health Care System project. Previously, she has served in a series of senior positions in the National Academies and the U.S. Department of Health and Human Services from 1975 through 2007. She was named executive director (chief operating officer) of the Institute of Medicine in 1998. Her responsibilities included management of IOM program operations and support of the Institute's governance and membership functions. In the Department of Health and Human Services, Ms. Stoiber held a number of senior positions in the Office of the Secretary and at the National Institutes of Health. She was three times appointed as a deputy assistant secretary for health—planning and evaluation (1979 and 1995); health promotion and disease prevention (1996); and deputy assistant secretary for planning and evaluation, program systems (1997). Her accomplishments included coordination of *Healthy People 2010*—the nation's prevention agenda, and oversight of the department's evaluation program and Government Performance and Results Act–related strategic planning. She received her bachelor of arts and master of public administration degrees from the University of Colorado, and a master of science degree from the London School of Economics.

Louis W. Sullivan, M.D., is the founding dean and first president of the Morehouse School of Medicine (MSM). With the exception of his tenure as secretary of the U.S. Department of Health and Human Services from 1989 to 1993, he was president of MSM for more than two decades. On July 1, 2002, he left the presidency, but continues to assist in national fundraising activities on behalf of the school. A native of Atlanta, Georgia, Dr. Sullivan graduated magna cum laude from Morehouse College in 1954 and earned his medical degree cum laude from Boston University School of Medicine in 1958. He is certified in internal medicine and hematology. In 1975, Dr. Sullivan became the founding dean and director of the medical education program at Morehouse College. In 1989, he accepted an appointment by President George H. W. Bush to head HHS. In this post, Sullivan managed the federal agency responsible for the major health, welfare, food and drug safety, medical research, and income security programs serving the American people. In January 1993, he returned to MSM and resumed the office of president. A member of numerous medical organizations, including the American Medical Association and the National Medical Association, Dr. Sullivan was the founding president of the Association of Minority Health Professions Schools. He is a former member of the Joint Committee on Health Policy of the Association of American Universities and the national Association of Land Grant Colleges and Universities. He was a member of the Sullivan Commission on the Future of Higher Education (2007) and chairman of the Sullivan Commission on Diversity in the Healthcare Workforce

(2003–2004). He is chairman of the Sullivan Alliance to Transform the Health Professions and is chairman of the National Health Museum.

David N. Sundwall, M.D., is a primary care physician who has more than two decades of experience in public policy and service. After 23 years of working in various government and private-sector health positions in Washington, DC, he has returned home to lead the Utah Department of Health. He currently serves as president of the Association of State and Territorial Health Officers. Dr. Sundwall earned his medical degree at the University of Utah College of Medicine and completed further training at the Harvard Family Medicine Residency Program. He remains on the faculty of the University of Utah School of Medicine as associate professor in the Department of Family and Preventive Medicine. In a distinguished career of academic appointments, public service, and policy development, Dr. Sundwall has been widely recognized for his professional achievements and contributions to health care policy and advocacy. He holds three medical school faculty appointments, including clinical associate professor, Department of Community and Family Medicine, Georgetown University College of Medicine, Washington, DC. He has held numerous positions in the public health sector: From 1994 to 2004, he was president of the American Clinical Laboratory Association; from 1988 to 1994, he was vice president and medical director of American Healthcare Systems, an alliance of not-for-profit multihospital systems. Prior to that appointment, he was an administrator in the Health Resources and Services Administration. Dr. Sundwall has served as an adviser, task force member, and chairman of numerous committees involved with public health policy and quality, including those connected with the Centers for Disease Control and Prevention and the Food and Drug Administration. In addition, his federal experience included serving as the assistant surgeon general in the Commissioned Corps of the U.S. Public Health Service. During this period, he had adjunct responsibilities at the Department of Health and Human Services (HHS), including co-chairman of the HHS secretary's Task Force on Medical Liability and Malpractice, and was the HHS secretary's designee to the National Commission to Prevent Infant Mortality.

Gail L. Warden, serves as president emeritus of the Detroit-based Henry Ford Health System and served as its president and CEO from April 1988 to 2003. Prior to this role, Mr. Warden served as president and CEO of Group Health Cooperative of Puget Sound as well as executive vice president of the American Hospital Association. He serves as a director of Picker Institute Inc. He has been a director of National Research Corp. since January 2005. He served as a director of Comerica Inc. from July 2000 to December 31, 2006. Mr. Warden serves in numerous leadership positions as chairman of several national health care committees and as board member for many other health care–related committees and institutions. In addition, he is a professor of health management and policy for the University of Michigan School of Public Health. He serves the Detroit, Michigan, community through memberships on various local governing committees and groups. Mr. Warden received an honorary doctorate in public administration from Central Michigan University and an honorary doctorate of humane letters from Rosalind Franklin University of Medicine and Science; a master of hospital administration from the University of Michigan; and a bachelor of arts from Dartmouth College.

Myrl Weinberg, M.A., is president of the National Health Council, the only organization of its kind that brings together all segments of the health care community to provide a united voice for 100 million people with chronic diseases and disabilities and their family caregivers. Made up of 120 national health-related organizations, its core membership includes 50 of the nation's leading patient advocacy groups. Ms. Weinberg has served on the health sciences policy board of the Institute of Medicine, the board of the AcademyHealth Coalition for Health Services Research, as a founding member of the Association for the Accreditation of Human Research Protection Programs, and is chair of the governing board of the International Alliance of Patients' Organizations. She also served on the congressionally mandated IOM committee created to assess how research priorities are established at the National Institutes of Health (NIH) and was a member of the National Research Council-Institute of Medicine committee on the organizational structure of NIH. Ms. Weinberg earned a bachelor's degree in psychology at the University of Arkansas and a master's degree in special education at George Peabody College.

Catherine E. Woteki, Ph.D., is global director of scientific affairs for Mars, Inc., a multinational food, confectionery, and pet care company. She joined Mars, Inc., in August 2005 and, in this role, manages the company's scientific and regulatory positions on matters of health, nutrition, and food safety. Prior to joining Mars, Inc., Dr. Woteki held positions in academia and government. From 2002 to 2005, she was dean of agriculture and professor of human nutrition at Iowa State University. From 1997 to 2001, she served as the first undersecretary for food safety at the U.S. Department of Agriculture (USDA), overseeing the Food Safety and Inspection Service and the U.S. government's Office for the Codex Alimentarius Commission, and coordinating U.S. government food safety policy development and USDA's continuity of operations planning. She also worked for two years in the White House Office of Science and Technology Policy, where she coauthored the Clinton administration's science policy statement "Science in the Public Interest," and served as the deputy undersecretary for research in USDA. Dr. Woteki is a nutritional epidemiologist, and her research interests include nutrition and food safety policy, risk assessment, and health survey design and analysis.

Staff Biographies

Judith A. Salerno, M.D., M.S., is executive officer of the Institute of Medicine of the National Academies. Dr. Salerno served as deputy director of the National Institute on Aging (NIA) at the National Institutes of Health from 2001 to 2007, where she had oversight of more than $1 billion in aging research conducted and supported annually by the NIA, including research on Alzheimer's and other neurodegenerative diseases; frailty and function in late life; and the social, behavioral, and demographic aspects of aging. A geriatrician, Dr. Salerno is vitally interested in improving the health and well-being of older persons, and has designed public-private initiatives to address aging stereotypes, novel approaches to support training of new investigators in aging, and award-winning programs to communicate health and research advances to the public. Before joining the NIA in 2001, Dr. Salerno directed the continuum of geriatrics and extended care programs across the country for the U.S. Department of Veterans Affairs (VA), Washington, DC. While at the VA, she launched widely recognized national initiatives for pain management and improving end-of-life care and directed a national program of geriatric and long-term care services of more than $3 billion annually. Dr. Salerno earned her M.D. degree from Harvard Medical School in 1985 and a master of science degree in health policy from the Harvard School of Public Health in 1976. She also holds a certificate of added qualifications in geriatric medicine and was associate clinical professor of health care sciences and of medicine at the George Washington University until 2001.

Andrea M. Schultz, M.P.H., is an associate program officer in the Executive Office of the Institute of Medicine. Ms. Schultz joined the IOM Board on Health Sciences Policy in 2004 where she worked on a number of reports, including *Genes, Behavior, and the Social Environment: Moving Beyond the Nature/Nurture Debate*; *Reusability of Facemasks During an Influenza Pandemic: Facing the Flu*; *Organ Donation: Opportunities for Action*; and *Cord Blood: Establishing a National Hematopoietic Stem Cell Bank Program*. In 2006 she moved to the IOM's Executive Office and Office of Reports and Communications where she provided health policy research support on a variety of issues for the IOM president and executive officer, coordinated an effort to collect and catalog impact data on IOM reports, and helped lead the IOM's Quality Improvement effort. Currently Ms. Schultz is working with the IOM's Committee on Improving the Organization of the U.S. Department of Health and Human Services to Advance the Health of Our Population. She received her M.P.H. in health policy with honors in August 2007 from George Washington University. Her capstone project analyzed key state-level health care reform initiatives. Ms. Schultz received her B.S. in cellular molecular biology from the University of Michigan in 2004.

Katharine Bothner is a research associate in the Institute of Medicine's Executive Office. She began working with the IOM in October 2006 as a senior program assistant with the Roundtable on Evidence-Based Medicine. She received a B.S. in chemistry with high distinction from the University of Virginia in 2004. With a focus in biochemistry, she conducted her thesis research on a cytostatic cancer therapy involving calcium channels. After completing her undergraduate studies, Ms. Bothner taught high school science for two years in Baltimore, Maryland, with Teach for America. More than 70 percent of her biology students passed the Maryland High School Assessment test, a figure nearly twice the city average.

Amy Packman is the administrative assistant for the Board on Health Sciences Policy. She previously served as a senior project assistant for the Clinical Research Roundtable. Prior to joining the IOM, she worked as a project manager for a medical education and publishing firm in

Washington, DC. She graduated from Whitman College in Walla Walla, Washington, with a B.A. in biology.

Judith L. Estep is a program associate with the Board on Health Sciences Policy. She has worked at the National Academies-Institute of Medicine since 1986 and has provided administrative support for more than 56 published reports. Her interests outside the Institute of Medicine include family (13 grandchildren), reading, needlework, 4-wheeling, and working her draft horses for competition.